Random Acts of Badness

RANDOM ACTS OF
BADNESS

My Story

Danny
Bonaduce

HYPERION
New York

An excerpt from "Living in My High School Daze" was first published in *Esquire* magazine, August 1991. Reprinted courtesy of *Esquire* and the Hearst Corporation.

Original hardcover design by Casey Hampton

MASS MARKET ISBN: 0-7868-9047-9

Hyperion books are available for special promotions and premiums. For details contact Hyperion Special Markets, 77 West 66th Street, 11th floor, New York, New York, 10023, or call 212-456-0100.

FIRST MASS MARKET EDITION

10 9 8 7 6 5 4 3 2 1

For Gretchen:
I am nothing without you.

Contents

Prologue

GOD, I'M OLD . . .

I recently figured it out. Between 1974 (the year they canceled *The Partridge Family*) and 1988 (the year I got into radio) there are 728 weeks. I worked approximately twenty of them. That's right—twenty weeks' work, spread out over fourteen years. It may not sound like a great deal of employment, but it's probably better than most members of the Screen Actors Guild.

There's an old joke that goes something like this. There are two old actors sitting on a bench. One actor says to the other, "How long has it been since you had a job?" The other actor says, "Thirty-two years—how about you?" The first actor says, "That's nothing. I haven't had a job in forty years." The other says, "One of these days we've got to get out of this business!" Somewhere in a joke always lies the truth. So, as you can see, twenty weeks' work is really not a bad career. Unless, of course, you want to eat. Two of those

weeks were spent on the set of a movie of the week titled
Murder on Flight 502. It was an "airplane disaster movie"
with an all-star cast. It was soon after *The Partridge Family*
was canceled. That meant I could be in it—and it would
still be considered an all-star cast.

The movie starred Robert Stack, Theodore Bikel, Polly
Bergen, Farrah Fawcett, George Maharis, Ralph Bellamy,
Hugh O'Brian, and Sonny Bono. There was a group of
other stars whose names escape me right now, and my
mother is not answering her phone to help remind me.
Now that I think about it, it was kind of like *The Love Boat*
with wings. On this set would be the first time I would ever
see "real movie star treatment." To keep the stars happy, we
had an entire sound stage turned into a recreation area.
There were video games, which, back then, meant Pong!
There were massage tables and masseuses, cards, and the
best food I ever had—which was there for the taking. (By
the way, my mother and I did every night.) There was also
this weird contraption that looked something like the table
that is used to administer lethal injections. This one was
leaning at a 45-degree angle. It turned out this "thing" was
used by movie stars as a place to rest—without messing up
their hair or wardrobe. Everyone was also assigned an assistant and their own personal hair and makeup person. That
way no one "individual" would be made—or forced—to
wait until someone else was finished in the chair. This
"wait" would most certainly imply that the person who was

"waiting" was not as big of a star as the person in the chair.

I learned a lot on the set of *Flight 502*. A couple of important lessons came from the late Sonny Bono. Sonny and I had been playing poker, and I lost a lot—of what I thought was "imaginary money." After all, I was only a fourteen-year-old kid! He actually made me pay up! Sonny was also kind enough to teach me something else. I was sitting at a large table (on which I had spent a good part of the day setting up domino rows). It was an elaborate set-up. It had jumps and ramps and spelled my name at the end. I had my assistant stand guard over the table anytime I was needed on the set. This thing took forever to build. When I was just about to knock over that first domino that would start it all, Sonny walked up to the table. He was holding his daughter Chastity. "Oh, the domino theory," he said. Then he asked if I had ever heard of the "suck theory." When I said no, Sonny shook the whole table and all the dominos fell at once. I could not believe it. Sonny looked down at me and said, "There, that's the suck theory. . . . Sometimes things just don't go the way you expect them to." After a few minutes, I wasn't mad at him anymore. I could tell by the look on his face he actually *thought* he was doing me a favor. Things were not going that well in Sonny's career, and I think he was trying to prepare me for what lay ahead.

The producers on that set went to extreme lengths *not* to play favorites with anyone. More appropriately, they played everyone was a favorite. Actors can really be a shitty group of people. That's why I was amazed to see all these "movie star folk" get up and applaud when this *really* old guy walked in. There he was, whoever he was—an old guy, and I do mean old. He was getting a standing ovation from people who had been trying to one-up each other all day. These people actually had some respect for this man. I asked my mother who the old guy was—and she said in a respectful hushed voice, "Honey, that's Walter Pidgeon. He's a great actor." Walter Pidgeon? He meant nothing to me—but as long as everyone else was standing, what the hell? I stood up.

Then, almost twenty-five years later, I get a call from the people at Fox. They would like me to do a guest star spot on their new television show—*That '70s Show*. I thought I had already done the quintessential '70s show. We called it *The Partridge Family*. Some people think *The Brady Bunch* was the quintessential '70s show. Well, they're just wrong—aren't they?

I agreed to do the show, even though I didn't need the money and it was a huge hassle. I didn't need the money because (by this time) I was doing morning radio in New York. It was a huge hassle because *That '70s Show* tapes in L.A. This meant, for me to be able to do my morning show from California, I would have to be in the L.A. satellite studio from 2 A.M. until 7 A.M. This would have me on the air live in New York from 5 A.M. to 10 A.M. Because of the traffic in L.A., I would also have to go straight to the TV studio—where we would work well into the night. I lived on "No-Dōz" and Coke—this time I mean the cola!

Even though it was difficult, I do like to be on TV. Being recognizable is the only thing that separates me from most of the other disc jockeys. Well, that—and the fact I have an opposable thumb.

In deference to my ridiculous hours, the producers agreed to call me on-set only when they needed me. When I arrived on the set of *That '70s Show*, the entire cast, the director, the producers, and a group of other important-looking people were in the middle of a table read. A "table read" is where everybody sits at a table and the actors read their lines and the director reads the stage directions. This way they all can tell what's funny and what's not. The problem with this? No one wants to be the one who's not laughing, so everybody laughs at everything—thereby defeating the purpose. I will say, the episode I did—and many of the other episodes of *That '70s Show* in general—are very funny. I mention that for two reasons.

1. It's true . . . and
2. The people who bring you *That '70s Show* are very powerful and could really hurt my television career—if I ever happen to get one.

When I walked into the room, everybody stopped what they were doing. They turned and stared up at me. Then they all stood up and started to applaud. At first this made perfect sense. I am that '70s guy. I basked in their adulation and started to bow. Then I noticed the kids who make up the main cast of *That '70s Show*. They were somewhere between fifteen and twenty-four years old. They had no idea who Danny Bonaduce was, but they stood, clapping like crazy. I couldn't believe it. I was only thirty-eight years old, and somehow I had become Walter "fuckin'" Pidgeon.

Chapter 1

SOME MEN ARE DISCOVERED; OTHERS ARE FOUND OUT

People tend to ask me questions. I guess I'm just that kind of guy. I've been asked at least a million questions by thousands of people over the years and that doesn't even include the TV talk circuit. I've had so many talk show hosts questioning me, if you put them all together, they would populate a small yet very annoying country.

Still, after all that, there are some questions that give me pause.

1. Did the Partridge Family play their own instruments?
2. Did you know the hooker you picked up in Phoenix was really a man?
3. Are you *ever* going to write a book?

The answer to all three has always been an emphatic NO! Well, at least *one* of those answers is about to change.

Thank God, I am not a mystery writer, and thanks to *The Enquirer*, many parts of my life are no mystery either. So, let's take all those facts into consideration and we'll read-dress those questions one at a time.

Did the Partridge Family really play? NO! Yet a poll in the early '70s put me on a list of the best-known bass play-ers—just behind Paul McCartney and above Stanley Clarke. The only ones who actually sang were Shirley and David. As for the rest of us?—NO! As you may have sur-mised by now, *The Partridge Family* was the original Milli Vanilli. If this tidbit of information is news to you, please tell the person who is reading this to you to put the book down, as the rest of the information will only cause you further pain and embarrassment.

Did I know the hooker was really a man? The answer to that is also NO, but we'll get into the whole story of that magical moment of my life later on in this book.

Book—did I just say book? Well, there goes my stock answer to question #3! With prodding, I took to the com-puter and here we are. The next step was for me to figure out how and where do I start.

There are two people whose counsel I actively seek: my wife and my agent. They both agree the dark and depraved and, in *my* opinion, downright funny stories that will fol-low need to be buffered with a couple of "cutesie" insider *Partridge Family* stories. In over ten years of marriage, I have never known my wife to be wrong—and if my agent's mistaken, she doesn't get paid! So, with a preponderance of evidence like that, who am I to argue? Don't get me wrong. There are tons of funny little *Partridge Family* stories to tell, although you would never know it or hear it from Susan Dey. Come to think of it, you would never hear anything concerning *The Partridge Family* from Susan!

As for David Cassidy? He didn't seem to have much of a better time either. I, on the other hand, loved being Danny Partridge and I still love it. Believe it or not, at forty-one years of age, being Danny Partridge can still get me a table at Spago, albeit not a very good one. Having enjoyed my *Partridge Family* experience so much, one might question my hesitation about writing about it. The fact of that matter is . . . it's been done! I was "just a child" on the set of *The Partridge Family*. Therefore, all my memories are that of a child. I always assumed David's book would be much more interesting. I was mistaken. David entitled his book *C'mon, Get Happy* . . . He didn't! Then there was Barry Williams's book, *Growing Up Brady*. He seemed to have a good time growing up rich and famous, but then there's the rest of his life. I had a far more interesting life last Tuesday . . . *and* I'm a relatively decent person now. In addition, writing a book seems like a lot of work for potentially little money. Unfortunately, when I really needed the money, I couldn't walk a straight line— let alone write one.

So, I thought, what if I combined both books? The sex, drugs, and rock and roll of David's tempered with the oh-so-fond memories of Barry's? The difference? I would tell my story with absolute truth and a good sense of humor like—well—neither of them.

Before I can regale you with my version of a coming-of-age saga on television, we must first take a trip even farther back.

Chapter 2

KILLER MULES AND OTHER THINGS

August 13, 1959. Eisenhower was president, cars looked great with their huge fins, kids still used words like "nifty" and "swift"—and the only person who was called a "Ho" was Don, who turned twenty-nine. Sometime during the morning hours, I entered the world. After that things are a little foggy for the next four years or so. After the age of four, I figure my memories are as good as anyone's—that is, right up until the '80s, when, frankly, things start to get a little foggy again. Not to worry! I have plenty of friends, who, quite unintentionally, have staggered days and nights of sobriety. They, at least, can give you (and me) an anecdotal accounting of some of my whereabouts during disco.

The good news is, they tell me I had a marvelous time. The bad news is, after much painstaking investigation, including the details in her own book, I am apparently the only straight man in America who did *not* have sex with

Cybill Shepherd. Digging up old friends from that era also makes me a little nervous. Unfortunately, many of them are dead! I really would have to dig them up, so the results would therefore be fruitless. Those who survived are a rather motley crew—come to think of it, some actually are Mötley Crüe.

I do not want to get ahead of myself, but before I go on, I must investigate my credentials for writing this book. After all, I am just a low-level celebrity who went to jail a lot. If you ask my wife, this book is a story of redemption. It's the story of a lost and bad man who turned into a good husband and father. To some, it will be an uplifting tale of inspiration. To others? It's a rags, to riches, to rags, to riches story. That's all very nice, but trust me on this. When I go to a party, the thing that breaks the ice is "Hey, you're the guy from *The Partridge Family* who went to jail a lot." It turns out I can't help it. It's in my genes!

So let me take you back to the late '80s—the 1880s, that is. On my mother's side, my grandfather, Jack Steck, makes his first public appearance. My grandfather Jack grew up and would generally be credited with starting radio—then television—in Philadelphia. He was a vaudeville performer, singer, dancer, etc. You name it and Pop could do it. He was a real trouper. He went on to host TV and radio shows and even gave Ed McMahon and Dick Clark their starts, a fact that neither of them will ever forget. On my grandfather's ninetieth birthday, he fell terribly ill. Both Dick and Ed flew in to be at what they were sure

would be Pop's last birthday. They both made very emotional speeches, vowing that they would always be there for
Jack, just as he had been there for them. I am only guessing
that when they made this vow they had no idea he would
recuperate. Much to their credit, they continued to fly in
for his birthday for the next seven years. For this I will
always have a soft spot in my heart for these two men.

That covers the celebrity side of my gene pool; now for
the criminal element.

About the same time Grandpa Steck was making plans
to tread the boards, Great-Grandpa Bonaduce was whack-
ing a guy with one. The two-by-four incident (as it has
become known in my family) was only one of several run-
ins with the law for my Great-Grandpa Constantino. If
brevity is the soul of wit, let me be clever. We'll skip all
misdemeanors and just go straight to the felonies.

One night, while driving his mule team into the little
Italian village where he lived, in the darkness, he ran over a
woman. He killed her deader than Caesar. Luckily for
Constantino, he was able to convince the authorities that
not only was it an accident, but he didn't even know he hit
anything—and that's why he didn't stop. I know that this
seems like a flimsy excuse, but over a hundred years later, it
still worked for Halle Berry. You've got to admire good old
Constantino. The sheer mechanics of a fatal hit and run
involving a *mule* just boggle the mind.

Pleading "it was an accident" would not work the second time for Great-Grandpa. The next time it happened, it

was again on a mule trail in the mountains of his native Italy. Going up the mountain, Constantino ran into another mule team coming down. The other man had the right of way, but Great-Grandpa refused to budge. Angry words were exchanged (imagine that) and all in Italian. You know it had to be done with lots of colorful hand gestures. This did not avail either man. So Constantino decided to explain things the old-fashioned way, with a two-by-four. He then proceeded to "accidentally" beat the man about the head and shoulders some fifty-seven times. I have been accused of doing many things, but actually killing a guy? That takes a level of commitment that has thus far eluded me. Now, Great-Grandpa had killed two people, and interestingly enough, both deaths involved mules! The mathematical probabilities of this must be astronomical.

On the lam from the law, Constantino grabbed his wife and jumped on the next ship bound for the New World. He must have dreamed of the land of opportunity, where the streets were paved with gold, and best of all, no friggin' mules. He was processed through Ellis Island and began his journey to Pennsylvania, where he had relatives. Once there, his wife gave birth to their first son. Believing they would never return to Italy, they gave him a very American name—John. A few years later amnesty was granted to all expatriated Italian criminals. Constantino, his wife, and son returned to the old country. When John was in his adolescence, he and his father stopped getting along and John rebelled. The result of that battle? He left his family for good. For some in my family, this has become a time-honored Bonaduce tradition.

John returned to Pennsylvania. In a small town called Jessep, he found work in the coal mines. He would stay in those coal mines for the next fifty years. If someone asks me about my showmanship, I credit Jack Steck. When things appear to be too difficult to continue, I think of my grandfather John—and I press on. John eventually married my grandmother, who soon gave birth to my father, Joseph, and his brother, Rudolph. These Bonaduce boys would be the first to speak English and go on to college. My father, Joe, eventually married Jack Steck's daughter, Elizabeth.

My parents first became acquainted at Temple University in Pennsylvania. My mother was visiting her sister, Jacqueline Steck, who was then the head of the Journalism Department at Temple. As my mother was walking to her office, she passed by my father and two of his friends in the common area. Back then my father was a strikingly handsome man. He looked a lot like a short Clark Gable, a resemblance that he would cultivate for all the right reasons.

A week or so later, my mother asked Aunt Jacqueline to invite him over for a party they were hosting for the campus newspaper. My mom brought a date; so did my father. At the end of the party they were together, and remained together for the next twenty-two years. My parents decided to make it official about a year after they met. At that time, my mother was hosting her own show on WFIL, Channel 6, the ABC affiliate in Philadelphia. It was called *Features for Women* and was cohosted by a guy named LeRoy Miller. My mom recently told me she was kind of the "Kevin Costner" of her show as she wrote, produced, and starred in it. I give my mom a lot more credit than that. My mom would never have made *The Postman*.

My father was working for the housing authority as a structural photographer. The date of the wedding was set for September 16, 1950. They married at Saint Anthony's Church in Drexel Hill. They walked to the ceremony, as it was so close to the house that they would call home. It was Pop's home, actually. After the ceremony, the reception was held at Drexel Brook Country Club. My grandfather was a great entertainer, but obviously was not versed in the art of the deal. Pop could sing, dance, produce, direct, and do magic. I can do none of these things—but I do know how to bargain. Here is a short list of some of the things for which I have traded my minimal skills.

$80,000 V10 Dodge Viper	22 minutes' work
$60,000 trip to Bali	24 minutes' work
$30,000 Harley Road King	24 minutes' work

These are deals even Danny Partridge would have been proud of. Of course, he would probably have taken the money. I like *very* nice toys.

Pop was able to pay for the reception by trading his skill as a performer, doing shows for the club in exchange for the reception and party. As a gift, the WFIL Orchestra played at the reception—which was a sit-down dinner for 250.

It didn't take long for the West to call on them. My dad was also a writer. Late in 1963, my dad decided to pack the wife and their four kids into a VW bus and move to Woodland Hills, California. He had some sort of showbiz gig. I am not sure exactly what that gig was, but I am sure I could find out with a simple phone call to my mom or my eldest brother, John. I just don't feel like making that call. I have my own memories of my childhood, and I have come to the conclusion that my having to research my own life is ludicrous.

My life is the way I remember it, *not necessarily the way it actually happened.* When we arrived in California, my dad's job, whatever it was, had evaporated. Unfortunately, we did not get this news *before* we moved into our $50,000 home. Back then $50,000 was a great deal of money for a house. We were now "big-time showbiz people" with no job, no future, and even fewer prospects. Aside from the four years of *The Partridge Family*, I would live my life under the umbrella of this dichotomy for the next twenty-five years.

As I recall, we spent the next few months huddled around the fireplace in the dark, not having enough money for heat or electricity. Just when we were about to pack it in and go back to Philly, with our proverbial tails between our legs, my dad did something amazing. He sold an episode of

The Dick Van Dyke Show he wrote while he was holed up in the bathroom. We were off. To this day, there are those who believe Joe Bonaduce is one of the best television comedy writers who ever lived. I count myself among them.

After Dad sold a show to Dick, he was on a roll. He went on to write for everyone who was a who's who on 1960s and '70s and '80s sitcom TV. This included *Mayberry R.F.D.*, *The Ghost and Mrs. Muir*, even *F Troop*. Dad really came into his own some twenty-odd years later when Norman Lear discovered his particular genius. Norm loved my dad, and over the years hired him for several shows, including *Good Times, One Day at a Time*, and *The Jeffersons*. Unfortunately, even the great Norman Lear could not protect my father from himself. In today's climate of celebrity writers, I think my father's eccentricities would have been tolerated with advanced electronics. With e-mail and faxes, he would not have had to physically interact with "television people," whom he considered to be beneath contempt.

Not only did my father hate everything showbiz, but he had a special disdain for actors.

On the set of *One Day at a Time*, Bonnie Franklin, who played the lead, wanted to change a line in one of my dad's shows. From what I understand, it was a fairly inconsequential line—but not to Joe. To him there were no inconsequential lines, just inconsequential actors. When my father heard of this proposed treason, he immediately went into action. He cornered Ms. Franklin. In his trademark teeth-clenched growl he told her, in no uncertain terms, how he felt about her proposed "improvements." He told her to "consider my dialogue as she would the Ten Commandments . . . carved in stone." Joe then added, "The only difference? My dialogue is written better." Dad obviously took his comedy writing seriously, and he was great at it. I firmly believe he had somehow reduced comedy to a mathematical equation. No matter what his mood, which was almost always foul, two plus two always equaled funny.

From what I could tell, the only thing my dad hated more than not working was working. Although great at it, he considered writing for television "beneath him." I always felt this notion to be a bit grandiose, except, of course, when he was writing for *Good Times* and Jimmie "J.J." Walker. The thought of my dad having to write the word DYN-O-MITE makes me want to weep. Today my strong, one-track-minded, brilliant, and tormented dad is in a nursing home and not doing all that well. That also makes me want to weep.

After I got the job on *The Partridge Family*, my fame became a constant reminder that his youngest son had joined the enemy camp. Dad then gave me the only advice he would ever give me on my new vocation. One morning I was on my way out the front door to go to the studio. There were, as always, fans in our front yard. My dad grabbed my arm and stopped me before I could make my escape. I was terrified. My dad usually did not bother with me. My brothers usually suffered far more at his hands than

I ever did. On the few occasions he did take notice of me, violence always seemed to follow. He scowled at me and said, "Remember, acting is one step below pimping." I was ten. When I tell people that Joe said this to a ten-year-old, they look at me with the same horrified expression they might if I told a story of serious physical child abuse. They miss the point. I don't tell people this so they will feel for me, but only to show the high quality and effectiveness of a Joe Bonaduce insult. Even at age ten, any Bonaduce knows a good line when he hears one.

As things would have it, thirty years later, I basically agree with him. I say "basically" because I do not completely get the pimp analogy. I, like all actors, have done things completely abhorrent to my nature and done them in exchange for money. This, if my understanding is correct, would make us actors much more akin to whores.

I do not feel my father had the right to treat actors, or his children, for that matter, as badly as he did, but he did have the right to be proud of his work. As far as I can remember, my dad never made me laugh . . . EVER. Regardless, he wrote some of the funniest scripts I've ever read. It was amazing to watch. He would lock himself in his bathroom, sometimes for days. Often you could hear him screaming, "I was born in the wrong goddamned century." Then you would hear the keys of the typewriter clicking again, and the whole house would exhale.

I do not hold actors in any special disregard. Some of them are brilliant. Basically, I dislike all performers equally.

They have this embarrassing need to be noticed, be the center of attention, and must be the life of the party. You may wonder if I count myself as part of this contemptible crew. Abso-goddamned-lutely. In fact, I am one of the worst offenders. When I find a safe and effective way to spend less time in my own company, I will surely avail myself of it. So, just how *did* I become one of them?

Chapter 3

1964—I AM FOUR, THEREFORE I AM DISCOVERED . . .

Oh yes, I was discovered! It happened at the Copper Penny Restaurant in Burbank. It's my version of the Lana Turner "discovery" at Schwab's Drug Store—only this *really* happened. I was all of four years old and was sitting with my mother, Betty. Mom was complaining about something or other that had happened and I calmly said to her, "As Thoreau once said . . . most men live lives of quiet desperation." Don't get me wrong! I know hearing about a four-year-old spouting Thoreau sounds as if I am trying to come off like some kind of boy genius. The fact is, in my family, you were considered illiterate if you spoke less than three languages. You could not possibly win an argument unless you backed it up with a good quote from the Bible, Shakespeare, or some Greek philosopher. Of course, Socrates or Plato didn't count—Dad considered them way too pedestrian.

I had no idea what I was saying, but the fact that I was saying it at age four was enough to grab the attention of the man seated in the next booth. He leaned over the Plexiglas divider, took one look at me, and said to my mother, "Lady, you have to get that kid to an agent!" Much like the Thoreau quote, this man meant nothing to me. My mother, on the other hand, lit up like a Christmas tree. He turned out to be none other than Richard Chamberlain, "Dr. Kildare" himself! My mother, always one to follow doctor's orders, trusted his diagnosis and filled the prescription. By noon I had an agent and a sudden penchant for medical metaphors.

It didn't take long for my first audition either—and it was frightening. Not the audition itself—just the waiting room. There *they* were, forty-seven kids who looked just like me, redheaded and oh-so Stepford-like. Upon closer inspection, less than half actually had red hair and freckles. The other half had their cuteness factor painted on by using an eyebrow pencil to make freckles and, of course, bad red dye in their hair. And you wonder why stage mothers have such a bad name!

What a collection of humanity! My mother and I, the not-so-redheaded Stepford Kids, and their mothers all huddled in an outer office. All of us are going over our lines and practicing how to be adorable. We could not do our rehearsing too loudly because we quickly discovered—even at age four—an actor (or his mom) would "steal from the blind" if it meant getting the part. I don't remember the particulars of this audition, as I have been on thousands since, but whatever I did, it was enough to get me the job, and it's the job I remember.

It was a Roman Meal bread commercial. It called for two redheaded brothers, one older, one younger—one fat, one skinny. I played the younger, skinny one. The gag of the commercial was the older brother made a "perfect little sandwich." It was the kind "Felix Unger" would make if he happened to be younger, redheaded, and fat. The little skinny brother (me) piled on the lunch meat, tomatoes, and maybe even a little peanut butter. By now the sandwich was over six inches tall. I then crammed as much of it into my mouth as I possibly could. No one bothered to inform me that I did not *actually* have to *eat* the giant bite I was taking. I could have just spit it out when the director called "cut." I don't know if I was really hungry or just too embarrassed to spit it out in front of the entire crew, but I just kept eating. That is, up until take twelve.

I promptly (and may I say, quite colorfully) projectile vomited all over the set. Everyone came running—the producer, the director, the client, the child welfare worker, and, of course, my mother. I have to assume that some percentage actually cared for my welfare. The remaining (and I'm guessing the greater) percentage were thinking, "*Oh, shit!* We have a sick kid and we have to shut down." Then there was the fun task the floor crew had—to clean it all up. I explained to them that I had been feeling sick since take four—and now that I had thrown up, I felt great! So, they

cleaned up the place, got out a bucket for me to spit in—
or, if I needed to again, to puke in.

We finished the spot. People called me a trouper, said
"the show must go on," they cheered and said "I had saw-
dust in my veins." As corny as this may sound, they were
right! Think about it. My first job in television literally
made me puke, yet I've never wanted anything else since.

NOTE TO RICHARD CHAMBERLAIN: Next time, mind
your own business.

Now I was officially a "kid actor"—which is not a rarity
in Southern California. I was just one of ten child actors in
the Woodland Hills Elementary School. Most of them
worked more then I did, but I was still going out on auditions and getting jobs. I did a few more commercials, a
couple of episodes of *Bewitched*, and an episode of *The
Ghost and Mrs. Muir*. I was only seven when I did *Muir*,
and coincidentally, I played a boy genius named "Danny."
Not so coincidentally, that episode was written by my
father, Joe Bonaduce.

Things went on at this pace for quite a while—another
commercial here, another guest spot there—and then it
happened. The phone rang. My mother answered and
when she hung up the receiver, she was beaming again like
that proverbial Christmas tree. I thought it was that Chamberlain guy again! Then she screamed out the magic words:
"Danny, honey, you're up for a series! It's called *The Par-*

tridge Family." I didn't care what it was called. All I knew was, it was a television series, and if I got it? It could only mean one thing—a new minibike.

The audition was set for one-thirty the next day. When we arrived, the gods were already smiling upon us. My mother found a parking space right in front of the building, which is no easy task in the middle of the afternoon on Sunset Boulevard. My mother made no attempt to shield my young eyes from the prostitutes working the corner of Sunset and Gower. For a kid actor, prostitutes in Hollywood were just a part of growing up—like homework or chicken pox. Come to think of it, it's more like homework, since I only had the chicken pox once.

For me, the audition for *The Partridge Family* was much like the hundreds of auditions before it. There was also an obvious and incredible sense of urgency on the part of some of the kids and all of their parents. Everyone there knew what getting this job could mean: "Beverly Hills, that is— swimming pools and movie stars!" Everyone was sitting and waiting for their names to be called by the receptionist. You could tell that she once had aspirations of stardom, but her career must have been cut short, and her skirts cut shorter. Her desk also had no front panel. Needless to say, all the boys that were there for the audition spent a lot of time dropping their pencils. Hey! I dropped mine too, and it was my first real peek at a pair of ladies' panties (other than some intimate moments with the Sears catalog).

Finally she called my name, and—if I might add—she

mispronounced it. Little did I know this was the last time a receptionist in Hollywood would mispronounce my name . . . well . . . at least for the next few years. As I walked in and the door closed behind me, I was immediately terrified. It was a long room with a big conference table in it. Sitting in the chairs were a half-dozen or so network and studio muckety-mucks. At the head of the table was the show's director, Jerry Paris. You might remember him from playing Rob Petrie's next-door neighbor in New Rochelle on *The Dick Van Dyke Show*. Jerry went on to become a top Emmy-winning director and did almost every episode of *Happy Days* until he was struck down by cancer.

I could not have known any of that then; all I knew was he was the director who had thrown me off the set of a movie of the week when I was eight years old. The reason why Jerry had me thrown off the set was innocent enough. He was teaching me how to read a line and I said to him, "You're a very good actor." He told me, in all good humor, that maybe he should play my part and I should direct the movie! In equally good humor, I responded, "That's okay, we are far enough behind schedule already." I had no idea how seriously behind we were, I had just overheard some grown-ups talking about it. With that, Jerry went insane. He ripped out all of the pages on which my character appeared, threw them in my face, and screamed "There, kid! Now we're all caught up and *you're* off the fucking picture." As you can see, I had reasons to be afraid.

Still, I did well on the audition. I knew all my lines and was as charming as a terrified nine-year-old could be. After the reading, Bob Claver, the executive producer, asked me why I wanted the part. The question was answered simply enough: "the money." Claver smiled and said, "That's perfect." Then he went on to explain the "Danny Partridge" character to me. He said Danny was "a forty-year-old midget trapped in a kid's suit" and that Danny was "a financial wizard." He went on to explain how important it was for Danny to come off "precocious, but not greedy." He asked if I knew the difference. "Sure," I said. . . . "Money is not the root of all evil . . . the love of it, that is." I also told him I didn't love money, but I would sure like the new minibike I would get if they gave me this job. There was a long silence.

Once again a good quote had come to my aid. I was in—or so I thought.

NOTE TO READERS: I had the job, but before you can work on a series as a kid actor in Hollywood, there are numerous child welfare rules and requirements you must go through. These requirements included passing a standard psychological test and hearing test. It meant my mother and I would be taking a few trips to the doctor's office. This would, by the way, be my first of many visits to shrinks throughout my life. (This was the first one; one during my drug crisis era in Philly; another when I was "clean" in Philly; and one with a great guy in Detroit.) As always, the testing was almost as interesting as the results. After numerous conversations with this studio-assigned shrink, he came back to my parents and the producers with a startling conclusion:

He certified me as "gifted"—this would come up a lot in the future. Even *USA TODAY* recently reported I had a "genius IQ." Just goes to show you can't believe everything you read!

Chapter 4

BANG, I'M DANNY PARTRIDGE

For months now I have been racking my brain trying to come up with some *Partridge Family* stories that have not yet been told to *death*. This is not as easy as you may think. The reason I am having such difficulty is twofold. There has been a kind of *Partridge Family* resurgence lately. Our music is now being used as background for TV commercials. Nick at Night has run the series again, and David Cassidy and I both produced movies on the subject. *The David Cassidy Story* and my movie, *C'Mon Get Happy* (mine was way better), aired within weeks of each other. Both movies got a great deal of press and because there were two of them, *Access Hollywood* even did a story on what they called the *Partridge Family* feud.

Access Hollywood begot *Entertainment Tonight*—they even did a one-hour special on the making of both movies. *Entertainment Tonight* begot the *E! True Hollywood Story,* which is a behind-the-scandal show. Thank God for Susan's anorexia and my "transvestite moment," or they would not have had the scandal to make a show. The *E! True Hollywood Story* begot *VH-1's Behind the Music*. Thank God for David Cassidy, or they would not have had any real music to get behind. *The Partridge Family* has been on TV this year for more hours than when we first aired on network. All ninety-six episodes come out to a mere forty-eight hours of original show time. So, between *ET*, *AH*, VH-1, Nick at Nite and *E!*, our lovely faces were broadcast for approximately 11,000 hours.

The other problem in finding stories that have not been told is that most of the members are not—for the most part—extraordinary people. Do not get me wrong. They are all very nice and talented individuals. But extraordinary? Impossible.

What are the odds of six random strangers being tossed together and all six of them turning out to be extraordinary? It just seems logical to me that—at the very least—five of us would have to have been ordinary—just so the word "extraordinary" would have meaning. Now, throw in the fact that we have all been telling *Partridge Family* stories for thirty years. Even ordinary people can tell if a story is working if they have thirty years to practice. Then I noticed on some of these shows, little Tracy was stealing some of my best sound bites. I hope now you can see the horns of the dilemma on which I hang. There is no way this book would get published without *Partridge* stories. Yet if you were to read the same old tired stuff you have heard before, you would most certainly feel ripped off.

What to do? What to do?

I was about to take Dante Alighieri's advice and *"abandon all hope."* Then I got lucky. I was flipping through the channels one night—when what did I see? Me! There I was on VH-1 with the rest of the gang. Some of the interviews were new, some were a few years old. I had a great deal of fun watching my weight fluctuate. I was about to change the channel when I saw something. I had seen this show before, so I knew I would not glean pearls from what I heard. This one picture of us reminded me of a great story. I had a stroke of genius. I turned off the sound and watched the whole show in silence. If one picture could spark an untold story, surely there would be more. Just like someone who suddenly goes deaf, all my other senses were suddenly heightened. I watched in amazement as my experiment bore fruit. When it was over, I also knew that deaf people are bored with *The Partridge Family* too.

Luckily, the untold story of which I was reminded also reminded me of *another* story. Not so luckily, both are about me getting the rest of the Partridges in trouble.

The old publicity picture I saw was of me, Shirley, David, Susan, Brian, Suzanne, Dave Madden, Howard Cosell, Dub Taylor, a fake TV reporter, and a killer whale. This strange group was gathered to film an episode. It was one of the shows where *The Partridge Family* takes another one of its many shots at becoming socially relevant. We took up the plight of the killer whale. Some of you may remember our song with whale sounds incorporated. Pretty cool stuff for its time—really! So there we were, in front of this whale tank at Marineland of the Pacific. The now-defunct Marineland could best be described as a poor man's SeaWorld.

Shooting a TV show on film, as opposed to videotape, can be quite a time-consuming experience. Shooting this one particular four-page scene could only be described as an epic struggle. Here's how it worked. Shirley Jones always gets a close-up. Then I would, and so would David. Then the two kids would get a "two-shot" (both of them in the same shot). Howard Cosell got a close-up. Dub the same. Then we had to deal with the guy playing the reporter. Susan would either get a close-up or a two-shot with David or me. Same with "Reuben" (Dave Madden). Let us guess-timate that we did five or so takes to get it all right on a good day. Now you have to throw in the fact that the whale is doing tricks behind us throughout the whole scene. Every time we had to do a different shot—the whale also had to do the exact same trick—at exactly the same time. This way the continuity of the shots would match when it was edited. Don't forget—this was a whale that wasn't trained well enough to get into SeaWorld. We had to have done this scene over 100 times—and in all of the shots, this gigantic whale would leap out of the water at least ten feet in the air. Then, at just the right moment, it would wave its tail at the camera. At the end of the shot, the whale would again leap into the air, only this time? It landed on its side, soaking poor, abused Reuben.

As any self-respecting ten-year-old would do, I became bored and my mind began to wander. After "take ten" or so, I noticed the whale trainer was standing just out of frame and doing the hand gestures that make the whale jump. After a whole day of this, I had apparently committed these commands to memory.

For some reason, the entire cast was staying on the grounds of the park that night. As always I could not sleep, and I decided to go out to the whale tank. Suddenly it occurred to me that I knew how to make the sham Shamu jump. I went over to the edge of the tank and repeated what I had seen. Sure enough, six million pounds of sushi suddenly leapt from the water like a nuclear warhead. What power I had in my little hands! It was amazing.

I made the whale do every behavior I could remember. I made him jump. I made him wave. I made him splash. Stranger things would happen to me in the future, but as of that moment, this was, by far, the weirdest thing I had ever done. This went on for quite a long time. Then the whale stopped playing along. Either he had come to his senses— or since the stadium was empty, he had come to the same conclusion as I did: "Nothing is worth doing if there is nobody to applaud."

Whatever his motivation, he went down and stayed down. After about ten minutes of giving commands to a pool of black water, I got bored again and went back to bed. The next day filming resumed. *Still* the same god-damned scene. The park was still open for business, so we had to stop filming in order to let the whale do his scheduled shows.

With this particular show, it started out like all the others. People crowded into the stands. The trainers would say some corny patter peppered with socially relevant and sanctimonious crap about whales. Then, when the audience felt sufficiently guilty for being part of orca's exploitation, the beast would jump out of the water and take a fish from the trainer's mouth. Everything else was moving along "swimmingly." Now it was time for the finale—the death-defying riding of the whale. Just as in every other show, the whale swam up to the stage and the trainer jumped on his back. Just as always, the whale swam to the middle of the tank as the parasite on his back waved to the adoring crowd. Then came trouble. Instead of the whale circling the tank, he swam straight to the middle and then straight to the bottom.

If you did not know any better, you might just think this scene was all a part of the regular show, possibly even funny. The trainer went down and disappeared for about thirty seconds. Then he popped up in the middle and swam frantically for the dock on the edge of the pool. The crowd loved it. When the trainer finally reached the dock (and started to climb out), the whale would emerge from the deep then bash him off the dock with his nose. Again the crowd voiced its approval at this trainer-buddy-orca show. They must have thought they were watching the *Dean and Jerry* of the aquatic kingdom.

The powers that be were obviously not amused. When the huge mammal was friendly, everybody was responsible! If one of them eats one lousy trainer, you'll quickly see who your friends really are. Showbiz—it's the same all over.

As the scene in the tank grew more violent, there was no missing the fact that something had gone awry. The whale was now taking to beating the trainer with that tremendous tail. The man in the tank was about to be seriously injured—or worse. In the movies, when a group of people come to the realization that a man is going to be killed right before their eyes, there usually is pandemonium. They run from the stands screaming. They cover the eyes of their terrified children. In the chaos that follows, usually an old couple is trampled to death as people rush to save themselves from seeing this terrible sight. In real life? They just sat there. They weren't exactly motionless—as they had the presence of mind to whip out their cameras. If the pool turned red, they were going to have a killer Kodak moment. There was no covering the eyes of impressionable children. In fact, some kids in the audience yelled words of encouragement—to the whale! No doubt these kids grew up to make the WWF what it is today.

Backstage, important-looking men suddenly started to discuss the merits of a tranquilizing gun. I'm not sure if it was for the whale—or themselves. Eventually the trembling trainer was able to save himself and get out of the water. Showing himself to be a true showman, the second he was on terra firma he waved to the crowd, took a bow, and ran off the stage. The whale show was canceled until further notice, and we shot all the scenes that did not include the whale. *The Partridge Family* was not part of this mess, so that night we went to bed as if nothing had happened. In our little world, nothing had happened. Once again I could not sleep, so I went out to play with my pal. He came through like a trouper. Jumping, dancing, diving. Before he could get bored with me, a large group of people suddenly came running toward me. They had been watching the tank like little wet ninjas. When they saw me, all their questions were answered.

You got it—I was the one who had *caused* this terrible attack! It turns out that this particular mammal, like every performer I have ever known, did not perform for the love of his art. He did it for money—or in this case, fish. Because I had asked this magnificent mammal to perform without remuneration, he staged a coup. When it was discovered my playing had nearly cost a man his life, the brass on both the park side and the Partridge side were understandably concerned. There was a big meeting—and it was agreed by all. If I could not refrain from aiding in the killing of people, the entire *Partridge Family* would be *banned* from the park, show be damned.

The next year I would put us all in a similar situation.

Again, we were surrounded by water and threatened with eviction. The next time was on a cruise ship. When situation comedies start to run out of ideas (usually around year four), they do one of two things. They either go to exotic locations or they add a "cute" kid. *The Brady Bunch* did both. They went to Hawaii and they added a cousin, Oliver.

The Partridge Family was no different. We added "Little Ricky" and we also took a cruise. By the time we started to use such devices, some of the Partridges were starting to be hard to handle. David was letting his displeasure with the show be known, and somehow I had become a total asshole. David's bad behavior was understandable. He was, by now, an international superstar making $50,000 a night for a two-hour concert. Yet he also worked on *The Partridge Family* for about seventy hours a week—and made just over $600 per show for his efforts. To make matters worse? The writers and producers started to make him into a buffoon. The fact that he had now become the straight man for a ten-year-old must have been bad enough, but when they started to call Keith "stupid" in the scripts, he could stand no more.

A prime example of this stands out in my mind. It was in an episode with guest star Arte Johnson—the "verrrry interesting" guy from *Laugh-In*. Arte played a criminal who somehow ended up hiding from the law in the Partridge garage. Shirley, not knowing he was there, walks in. Arte jumps out, says he has a gun, and demands to know "Who else is in the house?" Shirley swears she is alone. Then Chris and Tracy walk in. Arte is understandably upset and once again wants to know who is in the house. Once again Shirley says, "That's all." Next Laurie and I saunter in. Now Arte is mad as hell and yells, "I thought you said we were alone—and now I've got Snow White and the six Dwarfs! All we need now is Dopey." You guess it—bang!! In walks Cassidy. Add that kind of treatment to the fact that by doing the Partridge show, it was *costing* him money. I am sure you can understand why David had become one unpleasant Partridge. David got a little demanding. One of his demands? He would not—under any circumstances—play backup guitar for the new adorable neighbor kid, played by little Ricky Segall.

Little Ricky was supposed to be the answer to our sagging ratings. He played the adorable little next-door neighbor who would come over to our house and sing for no apparent reason. With David refusing to play backup for the kid, I was left holding the guitar, literally. I couldn't fake the bass and make it look realistic—and that only had four strings! You can just guess what I did with six. Looking back, I don't think I could have gotten away with refusing to accompany Ricky. That would have left Tracy to add the background sound. I was certainly no impresario—but this girl could not even fake the triangle.

By the time we got to the cruise ship, David was asking for everything under the sun. He was also getting it! David even wanted some friends to go on the boat—and the studio gladly obliged. One night I was walking around the ship unattended (big mistake) and I found myself outside David's cabin. I wanted to go in, but it's not like we were pals. People always ask me, "What was David Cassidy really like?" I have no idea. It's not that he was unfriendly, it's just he was a twenty-year-old sex symbol and I was a twelve-year-old redheaded fat kid. Had David wanted to spend quality time with me, there would have been something wrong with him! Nowadays, they have laws against such relationships.

I stood outside his door trying to work up the courage to knock. I don't know if David ever knew this but he was my absolute hero. All I wanted was to be let into his inner sanctum. Finally I took my shot and banged on the door. It opened slowly and the now-familiar scent of marijuana came pouring out. David was not to be found. His pals let me in. They didn't know that David and I had no relationship to speak of, and I'm guessing theirs was tenuous at best. They did not want to piss off "Keith's" little brother. This was it! I was in David's world—and it was just as I had hoped. *"GROOVY!"* I do not know how many of these guys came with David and how many he met on the boat, but his cabin was standing-room only. There were cool-looking guys with long hair and even cooler-looking girls. I could barely tell them apart; that was a problem that would come back to haunt me.

There were guitars on the floor and Hendrix blasting from the stereo. Eventually someone turned to me and said,

"Here, want a hit?" I looked and he was about to hand me a joint. I think he was kidding me. I don't believe they even thought I knew what a joint was. (The fact of the matter was I had been smoking pot for over a year.) I picked up the gauntlet. I grabbed the reefer from his hand and was about to take a power hit that would put David's hippie friends in their places—when Cassidy came in. There he was, my hero, as big as all outdoors—at least to me. It turns out Cassidy is tiny, but I wouldn't realize that until I was thirty. Think about it—50,000,000 Americans would have killed just to kiss the hem of his bell bottoms, but he and I were about to share a felony. Now that's what I call bonding!

I beamed at my new buddy, and, unlike former President Clinton, I was definitely prepared to inhale when David stormed right at me. It was somewhat of a mad rush and it kind of frightened me. He made it across the room and grabbed my wrist right as the reefer was about to hit home. He pulled it away from me and turned to the people in the room and went crazy. He was screaming at the top of his lungs. "Are you guys out of your minds? He's a little fucking kid." David went on to give quite a strong speech (in very colorful language) about right and wrong. Then, in an obvious reference to my dysfunctional family, he said, "If no one is going to watch out for you, I will!" Part of me was thrilled that David had taken up for me—no matter how embarrassed I was. David had also broken my heart. He called me a little kid. I was crushed.

After being unceremoniously thrown out of David's

cabin, I was left to wander the halls of the ship alone. I had been in a bad mood since we boarded the ship, mostly because the producers of *The Partridge Family* did not get me my own cabin. Of course, the two little kids would be expected to stay with their moms—but I was damn-near a teenager! This would not do. Not only was I too old to sleep in a room with my mother, but in my incredibly over-inflated opinion, I was way too important. The show had begun to revolve around *my* character by the end of the first season. If they were going to work me like an adult, they could sure as shootin' treat me like one. There was a run-ning gag (in the show) in which I would do something very unchildlike. Someone, usually Reuben, would call me a "forty-year-old midget trapped in a kid's suit." A forty-year-old man is not expected to sleep with his mother, midget or not. After Cassidy had reaffirmed my stature with his "little kid" comment, I was out for blood. I stole a pack of cigarettes from Dave Madden and was out on the deck smoking. A waitress came up to me and started to give me the You-are-too-young speech that I had heard so many times before. Normally, when an adult called me on this, I would become embarrassed, act as cute as possible, and say I was sorry. Not this time! This waitress had picked the wrong midget. I snapped, "These are international waters and I can do anything I goddamn please. If you don't like it, maybe you should call Interpol." I don't know if she bought the "international waters" thing or if I had just terrified the poor girl. Whatever it was, she ran like Secretariat and reported me to the captain.

The captain had already been made aware of my presence on his ship and already had reason to be concerned. It was now 1 A.M. I was still refusing to go to my mother's room. I had already told anyone who would listen, "If I cannot have my own cabin, I will sleep on deck." I meant it. If my mother was trying to show me "tough love" by not coming to look for me, she was the only one. The rest of the cast and a good portion of the crew were already in hot pursuit. I should not have been all that hard to find. All they had to do was look in the last place a kid should be. That would be the bar.

There are many bars on a cruise ship. Some put on glitzy Vegas-style shows and also serve food, so kids are allowed. Others are your everyday seafaring-type saloons where men in country club attire hit on ladies with blue hair. I went for the "blue hair" bar. I was playing one of my favorite games. I had learned this trick at Dave Madden's house. With my many problems at home (my dad, by now, had a habit of getting physically violent with me, and Madden had noticed), I often stayed weekends with him. In turn, he often had cocktail parties. I now think he probably had them just as a diversion from me.

When the party was in full swing, I would walk around and talk to all the grown-ups. When they would get distracted or have to go to the rest room, I would chug their drinks. When they came back, I would watch in amusement as they held up their glasses. They would study the empty with the same I-don't-remember-drinking-this look on their faces. I noticed this look on almost all intoxicated adults. I am fairly sure that Dave knew of my little charade, but he said nothing. Dave was—and is still—one of my favorite people, but don't ever let him baby-sit.

Having noticed that people not in complete control of their faculties were such easy marks, I really am surprised that I became so chemically inclined later on in life. On this occasion, I did not bother to engage the "blue hairs" in conversation. I was far too upset. This time I just sat back in the darkness. I was also planning my move—ones like those crazed women of the Roller Derby. Here I was, waiting to swoop down on the unsuspecting revelers. The moment they would get up to dance or relieve themselves, I would dash in like a nautical ninja and relieve them of their 80-proof refreshments.

Soon I became brazen—and very bombed. I moved in from the shadows to the table directly behind my next intended victim. All they had to do was turn their heads and I would soon be seeing the world through the bottom of their glasses. To this day, I am still amazed how often this would work. They would turn their head for a split second—and when they went to take their next sip? They would be astonished to see "they" had finished their drink. Some of them even assumed they had had too much to drink and would act accordingly. Of course, I became over-confident—and got caught. To my amazement (and great relief), they didn't seem to care all that much. They would turn around and find a strange twelve-year-old helping himself to their libation. They would act concerned, but when I would run? They would never give chase.

If someone had stopped me, everything might have been okay, but no one did. Soon I was stone-cold drunk. I have seen in movies where young people get drunk and it is often quite adorable. Unfortunately, it had been quite some time since anything about me was adorable. As soon as I moved out to the dance floor and started to fall, something had to be done. The bartender came over and tried his best to control me, but his efforts were fruitless. I am fairly sure that I also gave him my "international waters" speech and he went for it.

The captain was called. Soon the cast and crew who were looking for me on the outside, and the new group looking for me on the inside, got together. They did their damnedest to try to contain me. This was nothing new for me. Often studio security would try to hunt me down when I disappeared on set. It didn't matter if I had just tried to kill Jeremy Gelbwaks, the first "Chris Partridge," or had stolen the studio chief's golf cart. Trying to catch me had become kind of a game. The big difference here? The boat people weren't playing. As soon as I realized I was under their surveillance, I dashed. It was like a bad Keystone Cops short (assuming there is such a thing as a bad Keystone Cops short). The cast and crew went one way and the crew (all dressed in white) went another. I finally gave them the slip by diving into a lifeboat. Their efforts were fun to watch.

As I peered out from under the boat cover, it made me laugh to see they had now taken to calling me as if I were a dog. "Here Danny, here, Danny! Come on, boy." I swear to God, they would even whistle for me—much like a come-here-boy command. Did they really think I was Lassie? I fooled them. Just as I had promised, I would not go to my mother's cabin. I went to sleep. Little did I know what losing a drunk kid on a moving cruise ship would do. It was in the middle of the night and we were hundreds of miles out to sea. Trust me, it's a *very* big deal. Add to that the kid himself was a big-deal actor and you really do have pandemonium in high gear. The cruise line had to be thinking "losing Danny Partridge at sea is bad for business." The cast and crew of the show must have thought the same thing. Others, I am sure, were quite pleased to think they had lost me to Poseidon.

The next day I awoke in my lifeboat. Cassidy may have liked Hendrix's music, but I was covered in my own vomit. In that regard, I *was* Hendrix. I may have been hungover, but I was a trouper. I showed up on time and knew my lines. Unfortunately, there was no work to be done. The captain had called off the shoot. It was first assumed I was lost at sea. Now it was worse. I had been found.

Captains can marry you, throw you in the brig, or have you buried at sea. They also take their jobs very seriously. This captain, like every other captain I ever met, would not be made a fool of, especially by a punk kid. We were on a cruise to Acapulco and the skipper made it clear he had no qualms about putting the entire show, cast, and crew, off the boat in Mazatlán "if I could not be controlled." The truth of the matter was, by this time I could not be controlled—but I could be reasoned with. I suddenly got my own cabin. It used to belong to one of our crew. Lord knows where that poor bastard slept the rest of the trip.

NOTE TO READERS: Allow me to change the pace a bit here. See this as a warning—a "footnote" in the middle of the page. In the upcoming pages, I will go on to many disgraceful and unbecoming things for which I feel great shame and remorse. The feeling of shame that has lasted the longest, and is the most enduring, is for the way I treated adults. These were the adults who were forced to take this kind of abuse from an ill-mannered and ungrateful child in order to feed their families. For this, and many other transgressions, I will never fully forgive myself.

As my dear old dad used to say, "Sharper than a serpent's tooth to have a thankless child."

If, by chance, you are one of the many people whom I treated badly, I can only ask that you remember youth is wasted on the young and let me, in all sincerity, beg your indulgence and forgiveness. Trust me, keep reading and you will see I get my well-deserved come-uppance.

Chapter 5

MORE TALES FROM THE PARTRIDGE SIDE

Not all Partridge stories end with me drunk and in trouble. Just the good ones. Some Partridge stories are fun, light, and even downright wholesome. The time we filmed at the amusement park Kings Island in Ohio is a good example. Ohio had always been a hotbed of Partridge popularity.

The first time we went to that state, we caused quite a stir. It happened in Cleveland. We were new to television and were fairly insulated from our fame. It was our first major appearance since the show aired, and David, Susan, and I were very excited to be the grand marshals of their annual parade. I have absolutely no idea in whose or what's honor this parade was being thrown—and it didn't matter. All I knew was, I was the center of attention. I liked it.

In years past, I had been told, the Cleveland parade had been hosted by many a major celebrity. The most people to ever show up for it was about 25,000. When the Partridge Family showed up? Over 100,000 of our closest friends and fans lined the streets. David, Susan, and I were riding on top of a big red fire truck. As with all parades (I have been in hundreds), the floats start around a corner—and when they hit the main strip, the parade begins.

The Cleveland parade was no different, at least at first. David, Susan, and I got on the float. We had seen parades before and knew what was expected. The standard "wave and smile." Having done so many parades, you might think I would be able to convey how ridiculous you feel riding on the back of a giant snail, as I did in the Macy's Thanksgiving Day parade. I can't. I don't think anyone ever gets used to the weirdness. Now, as back then, I have absolutely no reason or right to be famous. The difference between most performers and me is that I know it. I had no such trepidations that day in Cleveland. I got on the fire truck as if I belonged there. We turned the corner—and I don't just mean the corner on that street in Cleveland.

There we were, the Partridge Family. There were also thousands more people than the police could possibly handle. We didn't make it five feet out before we were swarmed. The driver of the truck had two choices. He could run over thousands of screaming teenagers or stop. Depending on who you ask, the driver made the wrong choice and stopped. It was a riot. We knew what to do. Everyone knew what to do. We have seen it all before. For example: Jerry Springer gets a lot of crap for telling his guests to fight. This is not true. Nobody has to be told what to do. They (we) instinctively know. To paraphrase Shakespeare, "The world is just a stage, and we are merely people willing to beat the shit out of each other for $490 and a free trip to Chicago."

We were no different. We had seen *Beatlemania* and the Monkees and the lessons from both were clear. RUN. The reference to *Beatlemania* may seem like overkill, but it is not. At the height of his career, David Cassidy had a bigger fan club than the Beatles and Elvis combined. The whole scene seemed like a movie at first. Young girls screaming for their faves look exactly the same—whether they are screaming for the Beatles or 'N Sync. The only difference here is the 'N Sync girls will feel foolish about it soon. I am sure these young ladies won't believe me—so they should just ask the New Kids on the Block girls, some of whom may very well be their mothers.

Having seen *A Hard Day's Night* and *Help!* didn't help. Everywhere we turned to run, we ran into a solid wall of humanity. Soon a good portion of Susan's clothes were ripped off and David had huge chunks of hair ripped straight out of his head. It wasn't like the movies at all. I don't believe that Susan ever got over her fear. David also lost a fair amount of his flesh (along with his hair) and was bleeding profusely. Once we made it to our hotel, the realization of what had just happened finally sank in. Susan broke down and wept and David went into some kind of funk. I don't believe he came out of it until recently! My problem with crowds would be they would get smaller and smaller every day, while David's only got worse. Over the next few years, two young girls tragically died at David Cassidy concerts. To his credit, David has never forgotten either of them. All you have to do is watch an in-depth interview with David. He always mentions them.

The parade, or at least our part of it, was over. David, Susan, and I were now different people. I won't go into any details about the change in us. I have never had anything but contempt for people who try to tell me "how hard it is to be rich and famous." Sure it's hard, but so is working in the West Virginia coal mines or pulling a double at a Denny's in Fresno. So, it was no surprise that when we returned to Ohio to film an episode, throngs of people turned out for the event. The show had a simple premise. The Partridge Family was the musical act at the park. Just like at the parade—there must have been 100,000 people there to watch us "sing." The subplot was Keith and I fall in love with the same woman. The woman was played by Miss America beauty queen Mary Ann Mobley. She was a fine woman and a good actress—not to mention the fact that she was outstandingly beautiful. At this point, I would nominally tell you about the impure adolescent thoughts I was having about her, but it turns out, not only is she a fine Christian woman, but her daughter Clancy is now a showbiz TV development bigwig and might someday give me a real job.

Keith and I would vie for Mary Ann's attention throughout the entire show, and much comedy ensues. Keith, who by now had become a total bumbling idiot in the show, tries to win her over by doing a fancy dive into the hotel pool. Of course he hurts himself—and I am left to save him. David may have been embarrassed to once again play the fool—but I will never forget the shot of me diving into the pool. By this time I was fat and my entire school got to see what I looked like without a shirt. I was thirteen. I had breasts. We shot a lot of the scenes at Kings Island on the rides. Much like the whale show, we had to shoot the shots over and over again. That meant I had to ride the rides over and over again. At thirteen, I spent the entire week, dizzy, stumbling around, and throwing up. A precursor to how I would spend most of the '80s. At the end of the show, Mary Ann teaches Keith and me both a lesson by falling for little Chris. To my amazement, art was about to imitate life. I was quite accustomed to the fact that David Cassidy was the sex god of the show. It never bothered me. After all, I had started the show as a prepubescent, whipped right into puberty, and ended the show as an adolescent. As a prepubescent, I obviously didn't care that David had all the girls. That would be like Karen Carpenter being mad because her brother Richard had all the cookies. Once puberty reared its ugly head, I had indeed developed a sizable ego and a lot of things about the way David was treated had started to bother me. Not the girls. David had so many girls clamoring for his attention that he could not possibly service them all, no matter how hard he tried. I would often get his overflow.

> **NOTE TO READERS:** Writing a book is a strange experience. It seems like just a few pages ago that I told you I couldn't think of any new Partridge stories to tell you. Now I can't decide when to stop. Should I go with "I was the least loved Partridge" or "I was the pleasantly plump Partridge" or "Carnal knowledge of a Cassidy castoff"? Six months ago I didn't think I had enough stuff to write the Cliffs Notes of a good book. Now I'm afraid it may well be bigger than the *Encyclopaedia Britannica*.
>
> Please also take note. By my saying bigger than the encyclopedia, I mean by sheer poundage, not substance. I'm sure someone, somewhere will end up burning it in disgust! Wait a second. I just thought of something. Before anyone can burn a copy of my book, they first have to go out and buy a copy. I take it back. HEY! This book is more controversial than Salman Rushdie's *Satanic Verses*. It has more sex and drug-use scenes than Sidney Sheldon or Jackie Collins combined! Hemingway could not imagine these adventures.

Okay, enough literary blasphemy—back to the stories! I will take them in order.

I WAS THE LEAST LOVED PARTRIDGE

As I stated, I was quite comfortable with David getting all the groupies. It was a different story when it came to hot ladies liking little Chris Partridge more than me. By "little Chris Partridge" I, of course, mean the second Chris— Brian Forster, not the "first" Chris. The first Chris was played by Jeremy Gelbwaks and nobody liked him . . . he bit people. That's another story. Will this never end?

When we shot the show at Kings Island, I met the most beautiful girl I had ever seen. She was very tall and had bright red hair. We spent a great deal of time together. She was the first girl I shared a real-live grown-up kiss with and I loved her. You may think that I mean that I *thought* I loved her, but I was thirteen and it's almost thirty years later—and I still think of her fondly. We fooled around a *lot* and I went as far with her as I had gone with any girl— up to that point. One day I went to meet my "true love" under the roller coaster or wherever it is that young lovers usually go to meet at an amusement park.

There she was. A goddess. The sun shining off her red hair made it appear as if she had a halo. I couldn't help myself. I marched right over to her, looked up at her, and virtually shouted, "I LOVE YOU." She looked down at me and said the magic words. "I love you too, Danny, but only as a friend." I wasn't sure what to do. I had never been given the I-like-you-just-as-a-friend speech (of which many women seem to be so fond).

Soon it became as clear as crystal. Brian Forster came out of the shadows where he had been lurking. He walked right up to the woman I loved, stood next to her, and then, GASP! he reached out and was holding her hand. There I stood, rejected. My first thought to remedy this situation was to kick his ass. I thought better of it. Not that he didn't deserve it (the little bastard), it's just that I had spent the first year of *The Partridge Family* killing the first Chris— and they fired him. This time it might be my turn. So, I bit the bullet. How could this be possible? Brian was a freak. I need to make myself clear on the "freak" statement.

When I refer to Brian as a freak, I mean in his personality, not his physical deformities—of which he has two. Unbeknownst to most people, Brian had a short leg and a club foot. To dress him, the wardrobe people had to get two matching pairs of shoes in two sizes, one adult and one children's. I don't think the viewers ever noticed and it most certainly never held him back. He was a totally normal kid as far as running and playing were concerned. Today Brian is a well-respected race car driver and lives up in California's Wine Country.

By freak, I mean his total lack of "childlike" qualities. He could run and play like any other kid, but he rarely did. His mother was sure that he would fall and break his leg. Brian had the epitome of "an overly protective mother"—

and she had a right to be afraid. If Brian ever did fall and break his leg, because of his condition, it might never heal properly. Brian's "real" handicap may have been his mother. She was a nice lady, but she rightly or wrongly oversheltered him. I was thirteen, I knew all about these things!

A perfect example of this was after he "stole" my girl-friend. He came up to me and asked for *me* to explain *to him* "the facts of life." I couldn't believe it. How come his mom hadn't taught him? It wasn't just the fact he didn't know what every eight-year-old knew, but that he had the audacity to ask *me*. I knew that he would use this informa-tion to deflower my one true love. I took pity. I sat him down like the big brother that he obviously thought me to be and summoned all the sexual expertise a thirteen-year-old virgin had to offer. I wanted to do it right. Even though I was quite embarrassed, I did the right thing. I got all mature and prepared. It was going to be just like the movies we would see in sex ed classes. I looked in his eyes and told him in all earnestness "a man takes his penis and puts it into a woman's vagina."

He stopped me abruptly. I thought, at first, I might have the facts wrong (having never done the deed myself), or, more appropriately—I had only done the deed *by* myself. It wasn't that I knew what I was saying. It was the *way* I was saying it that Brian took great exception to. He looked at me and said, "I know all that, I want you to use the dirty words." I did. The next day I was sure he had done it with my girl and I was heartbroken. Twenty years later, my fears were laid to rest. In 1995 I did a *Partridge Family* reunion (of sorts) for my daytime TV talk show. After the show, I invited Brian up to my WLUP Chicago radio show, which was a wild affair. During the broadcast, I decided to do an impromptu bar appearance after the show. By then the station was charging $1,000 an hour—just so some bar would have the privilege of having me get drunk in their club. Stranger still, they were getting it.

That night I decided to trade my services in exchange for drinks. I said the name of the club on the air, and when we arrived, it was mayhem. It seems everyone wanted to see Danny and Chris together again, which, of course, implied we had been together in the first place. If the bar held 300 people, there were at least 1,000 in attendance. Brian was not accustomed to drinking—let alone the way we had perfected it in Chicago. Soon he was telling me things only an innocent could—and I was listening as only a drunk would. I then told Brian that I was still smarting over the "Ohio girl." Not only did he remember her name, but he knew her new number, date of birth, and—if I'm not mistaken—her horoscope for that day.

Then he said something that astounded me. "I am still a virgin," he said with a rather downtrodden expression. "Holy shit . . . You're thirty," I thought, "and still a virgin?" Albeit, I am sure I said something more sympathetic, like "Are you fuckin' kidding?" Brian had obviously failed to take full advantage of the *Partridge Family* connection, save the fact that his overprotective mother had made sure that he had boatloads of money. Even though I was taken aback by this turn of events, I was relieved to know he had not known the fruits of my redheaded memory.

There was an uncomfortable silence. I didn't know what to say or do; he was once again looking at me as if I were his big brother. He had only said that he was still a virgin, but his face also said that I should do something to rectify this injustice. My burden was soon lifted. One of my listeners, who came to all my appearances, walked up to the table. Her name was Doresse. She was a tall black girl and was one of the few latter-day *Partridge Family* fans who was not a psychopath. We had become good friends over the last couple of years. It was hard to hear her over the enthusiastic crowd, but it was obvious that she really wanted to meet Brian. I introduced them. I had to shout over the loudness of the crowded bar. *"Brian, this is Doresse. Doresse, this is Brian. Brian is still a virgin!"* Doresse gave me an evil smile, then she took Brian out to my limo. There, just like the lyrics from the song "Lola," she said, *"Little boy, I'm gonna make you a man"* . . . and she did. I can only assume that, to this day, Brian still loves me. Or he is going to kill me for telling this story.

The "Ohio girl" was not the last time a girl would like Brian best. The next time it happened we were back on our home turf. It was Stage 30 of the Columbia ranch in Burbank, California. I remember this episode quite clearly—

because it was about one of my favorite subjects! Me. The title of the show was "Danny Gets a Girl Friend."

The episode opened in my classroom. I smiled at a little girl and she smiled back. It was done in a way only sitcom kids can, especially if they need to establish that they "like" each other within the first thirty seconds. The teacher then says, "All the students who will be taking the day off in observance of the Jewish holiday, please raise their hands." The girl does. In an attempt to have something in common with the girl, I sheepishly raise mine as well. The rest of the show comedy revolves around me (and my understanding family) trying to get away with "acting Jewish."

A young actress named Lark Gibe played the girl, and once again she was a beauty. Once again I loved her, and once again she loved Brian. The girl in Ohio loving Brian (instead of me) made some sense. After all, I was an ass. Brian was a nice boy and she was a really nice girl. The same could not be said for Lark. She was an actress. Brian was still a nice boy, but my assholyness should have been far outweighed by the fact that I was a "star." Showbiz 101 clearly states that an actress is supposed to like the guy with the bigger part. That's right, in show business, even at age thirteen size *does* matter.

There were other women who were guests on *The Partridge Family* who also paid little to no attention to me. The original "Angels" from TV—Farrah Fawcett and Kate Jackson and even Farrah's replacement, Cheryl Ladd, were on the show. They were grown-ups so I understood being ignored, although I think Farrah's first network acting job was with us, and all I did—on camera—was stare at her butt.

Alas! There was another little girl on the show whom I personally had a crush on, and she wouldn't give me the time of day. It was the episode with a guest star named Jodie Foster. I was a kid actor. Jodie was a *real* actor. I had a good grasp of the English language, but hers was far superior. We were two tiny titans of TV, and we should have had a lot in common. We didn't. There was absolutely no communication between us. It was as if we were speaking different languages. In fact, we were. At the ripe old age of seven, Jodie spoke only French when she wasn't busy filming. She didn't have a special tutor, so she had to make do with ours. Our tutor knew enough to know she didn't know enough. She wisely left Jodie alone, which seemed to me the way Jodie liked it. Jodie now has an Academy Award®, I have a rap sheet!

I had always been the "boy wonder" on the set of *The Partridge Family*. When any guest star of merit, young or old, came on the set, I did whatever it took to regain my rightful stature of wunderkind. Not so with Jodie. Why bother? Competing with Jodie would only have shined a light on a dark secret I always tried so hard to hide! I was just a kid. Under any other circumstances, I would have done my best to undermine her. I couldn't. I, like everyone else, was burdened with a fierce admiration of her. Unlike everyone else, my admiration had turned to love. The feeling was not mutual. I guess redheaded kid actors aren't Jodie's cup of tea.

I WAS THE PLEASANTLY PLUMP PARTRIDGE

Somewhere in between seasons two and three, I got fat and I had not really noticed it. As overweight kids already know, other kids can be cruel, especially to a fat kid. This did not happen to me. They also say being a child star is hard on a kid. Not true. Being a child star is a party. Being an ex–child star is what really sucks. In Southern California, kids learn—at an early age—never to hassle the kid with the cash for the "candy." In my youth, this actually meant candy. In showbiz, candy can mean anything from limos to cocaine or almost anything Charlie Sheen spent his money on. Being a celebrity also protected me from the evil that children do. Unfortunately, it also exposed me to producers. Anything that could be made into a show was.

Kids may have uncharacteristically ignored my weight gain, but the writers were not so kind. The episode in question was titled "Danny Goes on a Diet." The show's main theme was that I had become "so fat" that I was ashamed to go to my girlfriend's pool party. As you can imagine, this came as quite a shock to me. I already said I didn't even know I was fat. I was devastated. There was a bright side to all this. The subplot of the show was that I would have a contest with Reuben Kincade. I would try to lose weight and he would try to quit smoking. The reason this was a bright spot for me was that out of all the *Partridge* shows, the ones that revolved around the relationship between Reuben Kincade and me were always funny. It was unfortunate when someone tried to "improve" the show by attempting to make this type of relationship happen between David and me. Not only didn't it work, but it actually came off looking mean when David became my straight man.

During the filming, I had a massive meltdown. The producers (and my mother) tried to placate me with the fact that at the end of the show, I lose so much weight, I win the "best body contest" at the pool party. This, of course, was to no avail. Because of the show, I started to weigh myself—and not only did I not lose any weight, I gained ten pounds. For the last twenty-five years I have been on a diet. I even went so far as to have liposuction a few years back. Nothing has had any lasting effect—except the celebrity-endorsed cocaine diet I went on. On that I lost a ton. Sure, I got thin, but it cost me $11,000 a pound and my self-respect, not to mention my stereo.

CARNAL KNOWLEDGE OF A CASSIDY CASTOFF

To get to the Burbank Studios from my house was about a thirty-minute affair. To travel the 100 feet from the sidewalk to the guard gate could easily take the same amount of time—or more. Every morning, upon arrival, my mom and I had to wade through a sea of women. The moment we would arrive in the morning, hundreds, sometimes thousands, of women would scream with desire. The second they realized it was me, their disappointment became palpable and audible. They would throw themselves against my car and yell, *"We love you."* Then they would see it was just me, turn their backs, and shout to their friends, *"Never mind, it's only Danny."* Then they would repeat the process with the next car. I am quite confident that a number of grips got laid this way.

There was also a slight rivalry on the set of *The Partridge Family* between David and me, although to be honest, I am not sure that David even knew that one existed. The competition in my head played out like this: I truly believed that I was the *star* of the show. As preposterous as that sounds now, there was some evidence to back up my hypothesis. I always had the most lines. I know this because my mom and I counted. The shows were—more often than not—about me. I know this because on a recent episode of *VH-1's Behind the Music,* Paul Whit, the producer on the show, said that he was getting uncomfortable relying on me for all the laughs. My name was, as often as not, in the title of the show: i.e., "Danny Goes on a Diet," "Danny Runs Away," or "Danny Gets a Girl Friend." My name was even in the original theme song until year two when somebody thought to change it.

So why, if I was the star of the show (as I was in my demented little mind), was David treated as if *he* were the star? Well, of course, there was the fact that he actually *was* the star. That fact escaped me. All I knew was I was working harder and he was treated better. Often I would be summoned to the set from my classroom only to find David wasn't there yet. When this indignation would occur, I would storm off the set and shout, "I'll be in my dressing room. Wake me when Cassidy shows up." I told you I was an asshole.

I called off this covert competition on the day I realized there were certain perks to being the sexual second banana. On this particular day, much like every other day, there were throngs of women at the gate waiting and hoping to meet David. There also was a bunch of young women milling around the set as well as David's dressing room. No one was ever quite sure how these women got there. Did David open up his car door upon his arrival and just load up? Did he send someone out to pick out the pretty ones and have them escorted to him? Or, as most of us suspected, did these girls sneak onto the lot and David would merely do his "teen idol" duty? Whatever the case, there were always a lot of women around. This only helped to further fuel my resentment of David. "Why should he get all the girls?" That was the obvious question. (At least it was for me.) Now, when I look back on the old shows, the answer is obvious. David was absolutely gorgeous. I was a fat, freckled kid and had a mane of red hair that made me look like one of those popular troll dolls of the day. You remember them—the ones with arms open wide that stated

"I LOVE YOU THIS MUCH." Troll or not, I was about to get my turn at bat.

Once there was this "girl." The poor thing was lost, just roaming around the lot looking for David. Apparently "Hotel David" had the no-occupancy sign turned on—and this girl was dejected and rejected. I took pity. She was somewhere between the ages of eighteen and twenty-two. As I remember, she was gorgeous. I walked straight up to her. In the sexiest voice a thirteen-year-old could muster, I said, "Hi, I'm Danny!" I could tell she was mulling over her options, which were far and few. She made her decision. It seemed her motto was about to become "Any Partridge in a storm." She didn't travel all this way to *not* have a story to tell her friends. With the same attitude one might have if one were helping an old lady across the street, she took me by the hand and led me toward my dressing room. She started to kiss me as if I were a man, but it became incredibly clear that I was not. It was just too embarrassing for her (I guess). She cut out all the preliminaries and went right to the main event.

There must be something instinctual about sex that is passed down to us genetically. I guess it's imprinted on our DNA in the same way it is with wild animals. I may not have known exactly what to do, but the moment she crossed her hands over her chest and pulled her T-shirt over her head, I knew that this was going to be the greatest thing that had ever happened. She then started to take off the rest of her clothes. My father was not the type to subscribe to *Playboy* magazine, and I did not have a lot of time for the standard teenage fare of periodicals. In other words, I had never even seen pictures of a naked woman.

I had not moved an inch since this process started—and she didn't wait. She reached behind her back and unhooked her bra and slid it down her arms. What dexterity. It was like ballet. Finally she noticed my sheer amazement and started to laugh. This was good—or this lady wasn't going to have any fun at all. With a roll of her eyes and a slight chuckle, she took my hand and placed it on her breast. I knew what to do. I wanted to squeeze them and hug them and kiss them and love them.

I did none of these things. I squished them like they were the bike horn on my Schwinn. I half expected her to honk. She didn't, but she did laugh some more. Today I can't think of anything more horrifying than a woman laughing at my sexual advances. That day I was glad. All tension was gone, and she was having a good time as my "tutor." Then her pants came off. In 1973, fashion and its designers had not yet discovered the market of creating overpriced underwear. There she stood. She was now naked—except for her big white cotton panties. That is a look that still drives me wild (by the way). I was mesmerized. I wore the same expression that one might wear if they had just seen a weeping Madonna (the deity) or Elvis walking through a minimart.

My total shock and amazement only encouraged her. She started to dance around in her underwear. She was laughing out loud. The spell was then broken for a moment. I started to wonder where the hell my mother might be and—more important—when would she be back? Thinking of one's mother at a time like this is just wrong! No matter what Freud and Oedipus say about this, I was happy—and that thought soon left me. Without a moment's hesitation, she took off her underwear. It was awkward. While pulling her panties over one foot she was forced to stand on the other. There was a great deal of wobbling. Not to say she was high or anything—it's just I have yet to meet a woman who is graceful at this and if I ever did meet one, I would be highly suspicious. She was now (as they say) full-on naked.

If fashion had yet to reach the underwear world, in 1973 grooming was still most certainly ignored in the pubic region. A thousand years from now, if future cultures look back at us, they will have to assume that women were born with pubic hair in the exact same dimensions as Hitler's mustache. This was not the case in 1973. This woman looked as if she were smuggling a Chia pet in her pants. She told me to take off my pants. I obliged. I was sitting on the couch and she sat on me. Pretense returned. She must have felt obliged to act as if we were actually having sex. She rolled her eyes, but this time it was different. She started to moan. Which was kind of the lady. It was over. To this day, I like to think I gave that woman the best thirty seconds of her life. Not exactly Romeo and Juliet.

Today that woman must be about fifty. If you are reading this, please don't feel ridiculous, as I have always loved you and, obviously, will never forget you. Thank you!

Chapter 6

BANG! I'M NOT DANNY PARTRIDGE ANYMORE
DID SOMEONE SAY "CANCELED"?

Sometime in 1974, *The Partridge Family* finally came to an end. Not with the proverbial bang, but with a cliché whimper. In my humblest of opinions, this is how TV shows, especially sitcoms, should meet their demise. The "good-bye" episode is a recent phenomenon, and it is totally inappropriate. If a sitcom has been on TV long enough, been good enough, and somehow become important enough to pop culture to command a farewell episode, that means the show has spent several years ignoring our presence. Stars of sitcoms don't break the fourth wall and then, when the end is near, feel the need to personally bid us adieu. The other obvious problem with the grand finale is expectations are far too high. And the show? No matter how good it is, it's bound to fall short. All it will do is leave loyal viewers with a bad taste in their mouths. Just ask anyone who rearranged their day so they could say good-bye to *Seinfeld*. I rest my case!

As you can see, I do not mind that *The Partridge Family* ended without any fanfare, but somebody on the staff might have told me. My mother and I pulled up to work just as we had every day for the past four years. Unlike every other day, the guard did not smile, wave, and open the gate. On this morning he stopped us. He looked at us as if we were crazy and asked, "What are you doing here?" Before we could answer, he said some very cold words: "Go home, *The Partridge Family* doesn't live here anymore." I was fourteen, I was canceled! He only let us in long enough to make a U-turn. Cosmically speaking, it was a huge U-turn. We were about to head back to our normal lives. Somewhere on the Ventura Freeway, on or about the same moment, my mother and I realized: We did not have normal lives to return to.

I would now like to tell you a story that I believe will give you a little glimpse inside the house in which I grew up. Before I can tell this tale, I must do something loathsome to me. I have to give away the ending. In essence, I have to tell you the punch line before the joke. Any journalism student or stand-up comic would tell you what a big mistake this is. If I do not tell it in this peculiar sequence, I am quite confident you may not be able to enjoy the story with the same relish everyone in my family gets every time we get to tell it. I am sure my brothers and sister are going to be mad at me for writing this down, but every one of them has told this story with a big smile on their face.

THE PUNCH LINES: *My dad smashes my brother Anthony over the head with a chair.*
My brother Anthony mauls my dad.

Okay, enough buildup. I feel you are now sufficiently prepared to enjoy.

I was sixteen. My parents were divorced at this time. For some ungodly reason, I went to my dad's house. (I think it was because he had cable.) I was watching TV with my friend Dave when my father and my brother came home. They were arguing. Soon the arguing turned into my dad pushing my brother and slapping him in the face. I could tell that Dave thought this was a bit odd. Odd? Not only was my dad hitting my brother in front of a stranger, but it was the sheer stupidity of the sight. You see, my dad is five foot two and weighs 125 pounds. My brother, on the other hand, is six feet tall and weighs 250 pounds. I don't think my dad ever forgave Anthony for having so little respect for his father as to grow as large as he did.

Anthony was just standing there, taking this assault. After all, this really was nothing new to him—but I was getting embarrassed with all this happening in front of my new pal, Dave. Trying to put Dave at ease, I said, "Don't worry about this, it happens all the time." With that remark, my dad stopped hitting my brother and turned his gaze upon me. After what seemed like an eternity, Joe bellowed, "Are *you* apologizing for your father? How dare you!" With that, my father walked over to where I was seated and grabbed me by the throat. I don't remember much after that, but Dave tells me afterward I fell to the floor and my face started to change into some pretty cool colors.

It is a tough way to start a friendship—when the nicest thing you can think about doing for a guy is to club his dad. Finally Dave was rescued from his indecision. Anthony pulled my dad off me and sent him flying. I don't know if Anthony meant to use as much force as he did. Even at 250, Anthony is much stronger than he should be. I regained my senses and got to my feet just about the same time my dad did. My dad lunged for one of us. I am not sure who—but I would certainly have been the prudent choice. It didn't matter. Anthony caught him in midair, plucking him straight from the sky. Anthony held Dad at bay and calmly told Dave and me to leave. He would "handle things." I was terrified. Even though I was bigger than my dad, if he escaped Anthony's grasp, I was doomed. Another reason to be afraid? The rules had just changed. I was used to violence, as it was a part of growing up in my house, but in pulling my father off me, Anthony had done something no one else in my family ever had: He had fought back. It had always been the Bonaduce way to just stand there and let Joe rain his version of justice down upon us. I was smart; I listened to Anthony, and ran.

Dad continued to attack Anthony. Out of frustration, he was growing ever more angry because he could not inflict any real damage. When his fists failed him, he turned to his best weapon, words. I won't burden you with all the nasty things he said, as that might take some of the fun out of the story. Suffice it to say, he called Anthony a coward, told him he was "to honor thy father," and he dared him to fight back. Then Joe went too far. He spit. *POW!* Dad got what he wanted. Anthony hit him. Once again, Joe goes flying—but this time, the catalyst was a fist the size of a Buick hitting him in the sternum. Dad did not hit the ground for at least six feet—then fell down a small flight of stairs. When my dad hit the floor, he didn't move, but he did moan. Anthony assumed Dad was still alive, so he casually went up to his room and gathered his belongings. Anthony does not like to be hurried.

When Anthony came down to make his exit, he turned a corner and there was Joe. He had a large wood dining room chair over his head. As Anthony turned away, my dad yelled, "Sharper than a serpent's tooth to have a thankless child." As Joe delivered one of his favorite quotes, he simultaneously brought the chair down and smashed it into bits over his thankless child. Apparently this annoyed my brother, and he gave my dad what can only be described as a dog-with-a-rag-doll type of beating. I don't know if it was just the years of this sort of treatment that made Anthony mangle our dad so badly. It also could have been the fact that the rag doll would not stop egging him on. Dad continued to fight. He kicked and spit and bit. Joe comes from a long line of biters. Their difference in dimensions being what they were, Anthony was able to literally lift up my dad and bang him against the ceiling! The ceiling was the natural choice since he already had banged him off the walls and off the floor. Joe not only would not stop but he kept saying things like "Is that all you've got?" Finally Anthony could not take it anymore. He hit Dad so hard, the neighbors felt it. Joe fought no more.

Anthony grabbed his knapsack and headed out the door. He was troubled by what had just transpired, but he also left with a feeling of righteousness. Anthony jumped in his yellow Firebird, started it up, and was almost on his way. Then what did he see out of the corner of his eye? Joe Bonaduce making his way from the doorway. My brother put the car in drive and tried to make his getaway, but it was too late. Joe had somehow or another dragged himself in front of the car. Anthony had a choice to make. He chose badly—and stopped the car. There was Joe. His injured leg was trailing behind him. His hands were gnarled—either broken or bruised from fruitlessly beating my brother. Dad looked through the windshield at my brother (who did not have a mark on him). Then he asked, "Have you had enough?" All Anthony could bring himself to do was to say "Yes." Anthony indeed had had enough. There now, wasn't that fun?

Chapter 7

LIVING IN MY
HIGH SCHOOL DAZE

Yup, school daze. (Pardon the obvious pun, but that's what it was!) A lot of people mistakenly believe that being a child actor is what led me to a life of crime. Not so for me! I started life out as a cute little criminal—you just didn't hear about it until later on. If you asked any one of my teachers, from kindergarten on up, they would have told you that I would come to no good.

I take great solace that Einstein failed math. I failed math. I also failed English and home economics. Einstein was an underachiever.

It all started at Woodland Hills Elementary School. This is the first "institution" of learning to label me as a gifted child. I am not exactly sure what that "gift" was, as my only distinction there was that I held the record for the most swats from the principal, Dr. Arnet. Swats were a

quaint colloquialism for beatings with a wooden paddle. I
didn't mind the swats. In fact, they gave me a certain feeling of power. I could always take more than Arnet could
give. Don't get me wrong—it's not as if it didn't hurt! It
sure did! It just didn't hurt enough. I was the one on the
receiving end of the paddle. In the end (no pun intended),
it would be Dr. Arnet who had the pained expression. I
could always force Dr. Arnet to give in. He would hit with
what (in those days) was a reasonable amount of force to
reprimand a child. When he was done, I would ask him, "Is
that it?" He would hit some more, and I would smile some
more. Eventually, Dr. Arnet (being a fine and good man)
would cave to the rules of convention and stop hitting. I
could see by the look on his face that he felt ashamed for
losing control. That was the price I would make him pay.

When my father would beat us, his rage was so intense,
it was easy to believe he might actually or eventually kill
one of us. Dr. Arnet's only weakness was I knew he would
not and could not kill me with his paddle. I also knew
Voltaire was right when he said, "What doesn't kill me,
makes me stronger." Even at seven, I knew if Dr. Arnet
wasn't willing to kill me, therefore logic dictated I was
stronger. This kind of fucked-up reasoning would cause me
nothing but grief in years to come.

Apart from the most swats, I also had the distinction of
being the youngest person to be thrown out of Woodland
Hills Elementary. I was eight. I don't remember any particular incident that resulted in my expulsion, so I am sure it

was a cumulative reason. After being asked to leave Woodland Hills, I went to Calabash Elementary School. They also asked me to evacuate the premises. Having nowhere else to go, poor Dr. Arnet reconsidered and let me back into Woodland Hills. It was while I was attending Woodland Hills that I landed the job on *The Partridge Family*. The fifth grade was the last time I would attend a real school.

The description of my "real" high school is a little misleading. It wasn't real—but everyone seemed high! My high school was called Cal Prep. The name was 50 percent misnomer. It was, in fact, located in California, but it didn't prepare you for anything except a life in the pharmaceutical trade. I can talk this way because its long closed now. By the time I enrolled at Cal Prep, my mother and father had divorced and, unlike any other California divorce I have ever heard of, my mother ended up with nothing. When we pulled into the school parking lot the first day, it looked like a Ferrari showroom. As we drove, we noticed what wasn't an expensive sports car was a Rolls-Royce or a Bentley. My mother and I had a 1968 VW bug. To make matters worse, Mom had taken tacky wallpaper and cut out some giant psychedelic flowers and tacked them to the doors and the hood of the car. Ten years earlier or ten years later, the flower power bug would have been cool, but in 1974—we were losers and everybody knew it. My poor yet patient mother spent the next year dropping me off around the corner.

The very next year, my Love Bug dilemma was allevi-
ated. It was now 1975 and I was sixteen, so I simply moved
out. At that age many teenagers rebel and run away from
home. I was no different, except when I ran, I didn't run
away to a friend's house or some tree fort. I ran away to a
two-bedroom apartment in Encino, never to return. My
mother did not want me to go until the night the police
came by (at two in the morning) and told her that I had
just robbed a 7-Eleven store. She could take no more of me
or my father and moved back to Philadelphia alone. I
should have gone with her, but I still had delusions of
grandeur and believed I still had a career in show business.
So I stayed.

It was at Cal Prep that I first noticed I was different
from other people. Sure, I had been thrown out of the
fourth and fifth grades, but that was for stuff other kids
were doing. I just did it better. A fourth grader might tell a
teacher he or she was a dumb-dumb. I would remind them
of the old saying "Those who can, do. Those who can't,
teach." Sometimes, if I was upset with the physical education coach, I would also add, "And those who cannot teach,
teach gym." The turn of a phrase could also mean the turn
of the screws. With words, my father had done more damage to his kids (and other people in his life) than he had
with violence. Trust me—he excelled at both, and I wanted
to be just like him.

They say (whoever they are) that high school is a micro-
cosm of American society. Not mine. My high school was a

who's who of the extraordinarily fucked up. Let me put it this way. Cal Prep, nestled away in L.A.'s "valley," had only eighty students—and that was from the seventh to twelfth grades. My graduating class included Christian Brando, Michael Jackson, and me. I find it very amusing that even now, after four felony arrests, I seem to be the only one with his reputation intact. It was very difficult to make friends with Michael because he was so quiet and reserved, and I was so loud and crazy. And, if I remember right, Michael was still Black back then.

Chris Brando and I, on the other hand, became fast friends. On the first of my many trips to Chris's house in the hills of Beverly, I remember passing through security— then stepping over a group of drunk Native Americans passed out in the driveway. When Brando turned down the *Godfather* Oscar in '72, he sent Sasheen Littlefeather to the Academy podium instead. It was his protest against the way Native Americans had been depicted in movies. After looking at the driveway scene, I immediately got the feeling he backed the wrong horse. I know this may not seem very PC—but if these were representative of your standard Native Americans, we did them a huge favor when we stole their country. If Marlon's tribe was any indication, they were just gonna wreck the place.

After I passed through that scene, I went inside. There was Marlon. He was sitting at a big table that was completely covered in food. I don't mean just food—I mean it was like a *Henry VIII* banquet scene. He even had some type of roasted leg in his hand that could easily have doubled for a cricket bat. It was awesome—it was Brando—but what a sight! Here was one of the biggest movie stars in the world (literally) with absolutely no concern for his physical appearance. He was my hero, and I was bummed!

Then I heard him speak on the phone. He had to look for it, as it was buried somewhere in the mountain of food. It was located somewhere in between the huge turkey and the mac and cheese. When he finally found it, he picked up the receiver and said, "Hello." Those were the last of the great man's words that I could understand. I was incensed. The greatest actor in the world was incomprehensible. Mostly he mumbled. What I could understand was a person trying to sound so *difficult* that no one would want to work with him. This was an obvious coverup for a man who either no longer wanted to or could no longer do his job.

I was so heartbroken, I could only think of one thing to do. I went to Chris's room to take lots and lots of drugs. At this point, Quaaludes and cocaine were very popular. I didn't particularly like cocaine—yet—but I loved 'ludes. Chris, on the other hand, loved angel dust. For those of you who do not know about "dust," the main ingredients are elephant tranquilizer and rat poison. If someone is "dusted" (on dust), it's easy to mess with his brain—and it can be fun. So I decided to have a little fun at Chris's expense. I walked over to the TV and grabbed the remote control.

I pointed it at Chris and said, "When I push the button, I'm going to change your mind." He went for it. I would push the button and he was sure his opinion had changed. This might sound cruel to the uninitiated, but it was fun to watch. Every time I pointed the remote at Chris and pushed the button, no matter what he was saying, he would lose his train of thought and blame me. I had a good time for a while, but if you've heard one thought from Chris Brando, you may have heard them all. It was about ten years later that Chris would be convicted of shooting Dag Drollet—his half sister Cheyenne's husband. I felt really bad for all of them. When the police arrived at the scene, they found Chris holding a gun and Dag holding the remote. Dag was dead, but the remote in his hand was still changing channels. I guess Dag didn't have the time to change Chris's mind. Sadly, and not too long after, Cheyenne would commit suicide over the entire episode. Marlon would do a few flop films to help pay for Chris's defense, and, ironically, one of Chris's brothers would become a bodyguard for Michael Jackson.

Cal Prep, as you can tell by now, was what it was. We were "the rich and the famous." The teachers failed to change our minds because we were "the chosen few" and we knew it. Their daddy's money, or in my case, mine when I turned eighteen, would never run out. We would live out our lives like the little princes we were born to be. Of course, over the next ten years, we found out that we were wrong. Even rich kids need to know how to do something. By then it was too late. There were many other moments, great examples of sheer delight that seemed cool at the time, so indulge me.

EXAMPLE ONE: THE CAL PREP "RACING TEAM"

With only eighty students in the entire school, the basketball team was bound to suffer. Although bad, we did have a surprise ringer. It was Jermaine Jackson. On the court, he was The Jackson 5 all by himself. Not only could he shoot hoops like Shaq, but he was truly adept at a skill most of the other rich kids lacked: Jermaine could also fight. The fact of the matter was, we didn't give a rat's ass about losing or winning the game. The outcome had little significance to us. We would do other things to entertain ourselves—things that the other school couldn't possibly do.

We would often race. Racing the Cal Prep team was a demoralizing task. First of all, we had the most amazing cars. The truth is, Ferraris are not that fast—especially in a straight-line drag race against a street rod—and other kids had street rods. The thing that would always make us win? Most of the kids I went to school with didn't care all that much about dying.

Often, after a game or a race, we would invite the other team out for drinks. I know what you're thinking: "Don't you mean ice cream or pizza?" No! I mean cocktails. Every member of the Cal Prep racing team had at least one portable bar in his car—or a joint in his pocket. If we got some poor sucker from some prissy school in one of our cars, we would do the line-up. The line-up worked like this. Mike (not Jackson), in his Dino Ferrari, would take the far-left lane on the 101 freeway. Chuck, in his Ferrari, would pull right next to him. Then came Kit in his custom Trans Am. By far, that Trans Am was faster than the imports. Then there was me. I was in a 1968 custom Pontiac Firebird 400, with 300 thirsty horses under the hood. Then there was Dennis in his Rolls. Did you know that Rolls-Royces can be very fast?

Once we had control of all five lanes, we would speed up. Once the driver in the first car felt we had reached sufficient speed, he would light a joint. Then, at 120 miles an hour or so, he would give the joint to his passenger. The passenger would take a hit, lean out the window and pass it to the guy in the next car, and so on, and so on. Ahhhh, school! Truth is, I was quickly running out of money, but I had a fast car—and my own apartment—so I was still cool. Although I think (at the time) if they knew I was almost out of money, I would also have been out of favor. By the time they reach high school, Southern California kids know that failure is a highly contagious disease. So, to keep up with appearances? My Encino apartment turned into a den of iniquity. If you wanted to take drugs or have sex? You always had a place to go.

EXAMPLE TWO: DEAD AND DISSED ON THE SAME DAY

Leaving my mother's home when I did might have been the safest thing to do, but it wreaked havoc on my high school attendance record. Then one day I was driving to school on the 405, minding my own business and listening to one of my favorite songs on the radio. All of a sudden, the song stopped. The announcer broke in with that annoying sound effect that indicates a special report. Before I could change the station, the bulletin caught my attention. Apparently I was dead. This was news to me—but I was proud to think that it actually was considered to be news to someone else.

The disc jockey, in an emotional state, said, "The world of show business has been delivered a devastating blow. Danny Bonaduce, a.k.a. Danny Partridge, has been found dead in his car. At this time, details are sketchy—but it appears to be drug related." This was fairly amusing. I could not get a job in show business, yet my death could deliver it a devastating blow. Then things got very weird. The radio started playing old interviews of me. Then they played Partridge Family songs. I started to wonder: "What if I really was dead? Was this my life flashing before my eyes? Was Heaven (or more likely, Hell) for me having to drive the 405 forever?"

I quickly came to my senses. Much like Mark Twain, the reports of my death were greatly exaggerated. Even though I felt fine, I couldn't think of a better reason to cut class than to be pronounced dead by a reputable journalist. I went home. Once I got there? My day got weirder. I had not thought of this, but other people could also have heard the newscast. I had to spend a great deal of time answering the phone and assuring my family and people I owed money to that I was not dead. I would pay them all soon, and, yes, I would make it for Thanksgiving dinner. Eventually my resurrection was complete. The phone stopped ringing. Everyone who cared knew that I was alive—except, of course, my agent.

It was now time to get back to my favorite pastime. Watching TV. That weekend, as I was flipping through the channels, I came across *Soul Train*. Under normal circumstances, in those days I would not give *Soul Train* a second look, but there was Don Cornelius talking to my classmate Michael Jackson. I didn't know Michael very well. As a matter of fact, I can only remember one real conversation with him. There's actually a photograph somewhere of the two of us together dating back to my Partridge days. Now, I had been in class with him for over a year—and I had yet to hear him speak. So, one day I walked up to him and said, "Hey, man, why don't you talk?" He looked at me, then looked down at the Bible he was always carrying, and said, "Because I am in constant remembrance of God." "Cool!" I said. "But what about chicks?" That was the last time we spoke.

Anyway, Michael finished his *Soul Train* song. Now it was time for the obligatory chat with Don. Don wanted to know about Michael's school—and did he go to school with any other young stars? Michael said, "Yes . . . Tony DeFranco and Danny Bonaduce." "Really!" Don then asked, "What is Danny Bonaduce like?" Michael, ever the polite young man, said, "Oh, he's nice." I thought that was sweet and I made a mental note to thank Michael the next time I saw him. Unfortunately, the interview wasn't over. Don looked at Michael and said, "That's not what you said about Danny backstage." Suddenly I was all ears. Poor Michael looked nervous as he looked straight into the camera and said, "Well? Danny is a little crazy. The teachers don't like him, and he gets in fights all the time."

That was it! I couldn't decide which made me angrier— being called crazy, or being compared to Tony DeFranco. You remember him? The song "Heartbeat, It's a Love Beat"? Either way, I was pissed. I may have been home with a nasty case of death, but this was more than I could bear. First thing Monday, I jumped in my car and drove to the school.

I pulled into the parking lot, ran into the auditorium, and screamed at the top of my lungs: "Jackson, get your skinny ass out here, 'cause I'm gonna kick your butt." I had just made one gigantic error. I forgot I went to school with all the Jacksons. Jacksons started pouring out of doors. The Jackson 5 is a misnomer, because—I swear to God—it seemed like there were hundreds of them. Now they were all going to kick my ass—with choreography! Right then and there, an age-old question was settled—conclusively. The Jackson 5 can, most definitely, beat up the Partridge Family. I went back home.

EXAMPLE THREE: EDUCATIONAL EXCELLENCE, THE CAL PREP WAY

The faculty at Cal Prep was an understanding group. I had missed sixty-eight days of school and they were starting to worry about their accreditation. Then again, nobody wants to fail a gifted student. They told me if I missed one more day, I would not be allowed to graduate. Literally, one more day *would* put me below the minimum attendance requirements I would need to graduate.

I didn't care about graduating "for my sake"—but if I didn't graduate, my dad would think he was right. He always called me "an asshole who got a lucky break that would eventually amount to nothing." I could not have that. It became paramount for me to graduate. I tried everything I could think of to get up on time. I had friends call. I placed alarm clocks all around the house. I even asked my neighbors to bang on my door. Nothing worked. Eventually I came up with an idea that I believed to be foolproof. I would sleep at school. This did not work either. Kids passed out in their cars—at Cal Prep—was not a rare sight. People walked right past me! I still thought this plan had some merit. It just needed some refinement.

The next night I grabbed some blankets from my house. I pulled into the school parking lot and soon was tying my blankets on the outdoor basketball courts—cleverly stringing them between a fence post and the hoop backboard pole—to make a simple hammock. The hammock slung for about seven feet in length, and every morning, one of my teachers would wake me, by poking me with a stick. This plan actually worked for a while, but eventually the people in charge of poking children with sticks thought this way of ensuring attendance put the school in a bad light. The gods were conspiring against my academic achievement.

This time the school came up with a plan. The theory was, if I was too irresponsible to get myself to school, maybe I would try harder if I had to get someone else there. It worked. They assigned to me a kid named Scott Dahlgren. A fine young man with perfect attendance. I don't know why it was so important for me to get this kid to school on time—but it was almost a mission! Maybe it was the fact that he was our star athlete. Of course, at Cal Prep, if you could walk a straight line you could become our star athlete. Kids who could open their doors before the limo driver could get back there were considered joggers. When the book *Less Than Zero* came out, all my classmates were pissed. Not because it was an exact portrayal of our school—but because we failed to get any royalties.

EXAMPLE FOUR: PASSING TIME, PASSING OUT, AND PASSING GRADES

A case in point. The owner of Cal Prep (yes—owner!), Dr. Yardam, called an assembly. Apparently someone close to her family had died of a drug overdose—and she was going to tell us how we were killing ourselves with this "poison." Dr. Yardam took to the podium and started her heartfelt speech. She wasn't up there five minutes when a girl named Debbie fell from her chair to the floor, unconscious. Too many 'ludes. Debbie was taken away and Dr. Yardam continued to speak. Bodies continued to fall. By the end of her speech on the dangers of drugs, the floor of the auditorium looked like the battlefield at Gettysburg. After seeing the lack of effect her talk had made on our useless little lives, she ended the speech with "The hell with you people."

Getting my new friend Scott to school paid off—and it put an end to my attendance problem. It looked like I could graduate. Then the teachers started getting pushy. They wanted to see some work. It took them only two months before graduation day to realize that I had not turned in a single assignment in two years. This time, if I did not meet the minimum educational requirements, they could not let me graduate. Parts of this dilemma were easy to remedy. Mike de Martini, our history teacher, was a reasonable man. He had no desire to fail a student who actually had a grasp on events past. History has always been my strong suit, and Mike was kind enough to give me an oral exam. I passed with flying colors. My television and communications class wasn't any different. How, in all good conscience, do you fail a kid in a class on TV who was a star on a hit TV show? Once again, an oral—once again, I passed.

Believe it or not, I also had a class called Marriage and Family. It worked like this. We were assigned spouses and jobs. We were also given a specific income and a set of bills to pay. My job was a plumber, and my wife was supposed to be a nurse. In real life? I was a stoner and my wife was worse. To pass this class I was going to need a ton of paperwork. Even if the teacher would let me take an oral exam, I would have failed. To this day, I have no grasp of money—but I am also a shitty plumber. Why should I have to know how taxes and stocks work? I had an accountant!

Then it dawned on me. "Hey—I *do* have an accountant." I took my fake job and fake bills to my very real accountant.

Within two days, I was in possession of a detailed report that went so far as to make adjustments for our first child and start a retirement plan. The teacher knew I had not done this kind of financial wizardry on my own, but what could she do? I passed.

Once again I was just sliding by. Two problems remained. One was PE. It seemed preposterous that anyone at Cal Prep could fail PE. The fact that on most days I could actually walk under my own power made me more athletic than at least a third of my school. I had also won every fight I was in. The "P" in "PE" stands for Physical, so I thought my excellence at violence should have stood for something. I was mistaken. This "lady"—my PE teacher—hated me, and said so. As a matter of fact, it was my propensity for fighting that might have been responsible for this woman's animosity toward me. Miss Dickhead, or whatever her name was, was not only the PE teacher but she also taught that lame-ass marriage and family class. It was in this class that a fight broke out between Neil Shapiro and myself. Neil was, by far, the toughest kid in our school. Sometimes, after we would lose a basketball game to another school (which was often), Neil would beat up the entire opposing team. There was *no way* I was going to win this fight. That's why it made perfect sense (at the time) to pick up my desk and throw it at his head. Smashing Neil in the head with a desk would in no way stop him, but I thought it would at least give me time to get away. It was a good plan—except for one thing. Desks are really heavy. By the time I lifted the desk into a throwing position, Neil had all the time in the world to duck. The desk caught on my thumb, causing a gash, and the lid broke off. Einstein's theory took effect and force vs. reaction had the lid fly right into my teacher's head. It hit with a force I would not see again until Round Ten of the George Foreman/Oliver McCall fight, some twenty years later. She was also just as unconscious. There was one bright spot. Neil was so impressed by the knocked-out teacher, he completely forgot to kick my ass.

When the teacher came back to school a few days later, "forgiveness" was not exactly in her heart. I tried to apologize—but she would have none of that. She really should not have been so angry with me. It was poor physics, not malice, that caused her injuries. She was unmoved. Finally I broke out something that usually worked for me in the past: a good quotation. "Remember," I said, "to err is human, to forgive, divine." Not to be outdone, she quoted me something I had heard all my life: "Fuck you, you little prick!" Hey, she was the gym teacher! What did I expect from her, Shakespeare?

Even with the PE fail, I could still pull off graduating— if I could get by my last obstacle, "Creative Writing." This teacher was a reasonable woman, but she had a "set criteria" from which she would *not* waver. I don't remember exactly what it was that she wanted, but I do remember there was no way I could get it done in time, even if I wanted to.

She wanted something like ten short stories, eight book reports, five poems, and so on. This was physical paperwork—and she wanted it in her hand. There was no way to fake this one. I had to come up with a plan. I did. Her name was Celia, my cute and charming little sister. Celia was (and is) one of the finest writers I know. Luckily for me, she needed money. We worked out a payment plan— and the work started to pour in. At first, I actually bothered to take the time to read it. As expected, it was brilliant. Soon I stopped reading her work. There were two reasons for this.

1. It was insulting to imply that I could somehow improve her work; and
2. I was lazy.

At first, this arrangement went along rather swimmingly. Then something strange started happening to me at school.

Teachers, the principal, even the owner of the school, all started to be nice to me—I mean, surprisingly nice to me. I was starting to become concerned. I was quite accustomed to being the object of their dismay. Most kids think their teachers hate them, but this is just an excuse. Poor artisans blame their tools. Poor students blame their teachers. The fact that a good percentage of my teachers really did hate me gave me solace. After all, remember I was gifted, or so they kept telling me. So, my academic failures must be a reflection on them.

So, why—all of a sudden—did everyone seem to care so much about my welfare? Things were getting "curiouser and curiouser." Finally, a teacher did something that raised my curiosity even more than I could bear. My creative writing teacher pulled me out of class. She told me with a straight face that "I had friends and that I could count on her as one of them." Never bullshit a bullshitter. These guys hated me—and that was just the way I liked it. Something was up. It turned out to be my goddamned sister! I had stopped reading her work over a month or so before. That is, apparently, just around the time when her boyfriend dumped her. When I finally did read the work I had been turning in as my own, it was a bunch of teenage suicidal crap. Worse, it was suicidal crap about losing a boyfriend. I don't remember much of her work, but what I do recall went something like this:

A POEM: GOD DOESN'T LIVE ON WEDDINGTON ST.

You guessed it. *I* lived on Weddington St. There were lines like: "If I blow my brains out, he still won't love me" and "I won't get my security deposit back."

The teachers not only thought I was a major screw-up, but now they were convinced I was also a suicidal homosexual screw-up, to boot. I was about to proclaim my heterosexuality, when I thought better of it. Half the kids at school were gay—and nobody bothered them. I also had the bonus of the staff thinking they failed me. That might just be enough to "send me over the edge."

I went for the "I, Homo" thing. It started with me writing my own poetry. It wasn't as good as my sister's but it was a lot spookier. Her pain was real, and that was no fun. So I started writing about my failed relationship. I poured it on about how "one more failure would surely cause me to fall on my sword." I hoped the reference to Marc Antony (not the singer, Cleopatra's lover) would not be wasted on them. Except for Mr. de Martini, they weren't exactly a bright group of people.

The suicidal homosexual thing not only worked out for

me, but it was great fun to see how far I could take it. Then, as now, gay teens tragically have an extremely high suicide rate—and I think my teachers knew that. Sometimes I would just burst into tears in the middle of class and run out of the room. The teacher would follow, console me, and tell me to take all the time I needed to recover. Then I would go get high with Christian Brando, who thought this was the funniest thing in the world.

When it came time to graduate, my future was still not assured. We were told that, "to save any student from embarrassment, we would all get diplomas." For those of us who did not make the grade? The diplomas would just be blank pieces of paper. Some people bought into this. I, on the other hand, did not. The blank-paper thing was purely to save face for a school that had a graduating class of twelve—but only six would make it.

We were told if we received a blank sheet, we should shake hands with the principal and take our seats. This would "save ourselves from any further embarrassment." BULLSHIT! If they handed me, a kid with an alleged high IQ, a blank sheet of paper, the world was going to know. As the night wore on, I started to stew. Who the hell were these people to hold me back? I had read Dante, Shakespeare, and Homer. How dare they? I was working on a speech so full of venom, it would make the bite of a king cobra pale in comparison. For a brief moment, the prom band distracted me. It consisted of Stevie Wonder and Michael Jackson along with Wendy and Lisa Melvoin. The

Melvoins were the children of musician/producer Michael Melvoin, and Wendy went on to fame performing with Prince. Our prom rocked, but alas, even Stevie Wonder, three Quaaludes, and my dad showing up could not dissuade me from my planned revenge. I knew then and there when they called my name and gave me a blank sheet of paper, I was going to let the world know and they would hear me screaming, "This school is a disgrace and the papers most of us are holding are blank. It isn't to save us from embarrassment but to hide the fact that this so-called bastion of education is nothing more than a sham. . . ."

The moment came, my moment. The teacher I had hit in the head with the desk called out my name. Jimmy Stewart's filibuster in *Mr. Smith Goes to Washington* would be like Jay Leno's opening monologue compared to the speech I had set and ready to go. When I reached the podium, I accepted the parchment. The administration told us not to open them—again to save face for those unfortunate few who had failed to graduate. I opened mine and was fully prepared to expose the charade. When I looked down, there it was—a DIPLOMA!

NOTE TO MY CREATIVE WRITING TEACHER: This book was written without any help from my sister or friends. Please don't contact me unless you think it's worth extra credit.

Chapter 8

DEATH BY TATTOO!

I have tattoos—to be precise, twelve of them. They are what some would call prissy little tattoos. You would never be intimidated by me, or confuse me with a rock star or a gang member because of them. In fact, you cannot see any of them if I am wearing a T-shirt and jeans. In other words, I was trying to look "tough" yet not become a fashion "don't." They are now a collection of memories, good and bad, that are permanently attached.

Out of the twelve tattoos, seven of them are people's names. The rest include a bird (no, not a partridge), a heart with musical notes through it, a shooting star, and a radio station logo. Of the seven names scattered around my body (located as if they were blasted from a shotgun), you will not find my wife Gretchen's name among them. To paraphrase the great Groucho Marx, she would never belong to a club that would have her as a member. When I walked around the house without a shirt, the only name that could be seen was "Debbie." It was on my left shoulder. The reason I use the past tense about this tattoo? For my wife's birthday or our anniversary or some such thing, I had it covered with another tattoo—that of a rose. Gretchen had never mentioned it, but I was sure it hurt her feelings when she would see it first thing every morning. I thought it was the "gallant" thing to do. She was pissed. She wanted a coat.

The cover-up job was done by an artist named Stinky, who was not only a reasonably good tattoo artist but an excellent sideshow freak. He took great delight in hammering a six-inch spike up his nose every time a potential customer came through the door. Tattoos are always a dangerous proposition no matter who does them—or how big they are. The tattoo that almost killed me was a small tattoo, all in white, the Tattoo on the old TV show *Fantasy Island.*

One of the few TV jobs I got after high school was an episode of *Fantasy Island.* To show you just how low on the acting totem poll I had sunk, it wasn't even my fantasy. It was the fantasy of actor/comedian Paul Sand. He played a middle-aged man going through a midlife crisis. It was his fantasy to go back to the days of street rods and drag races, when he was "King of the Strip." When he gets back to the days of his youth, I had replaced him as King of the Strip. As you may have surmised by now, the episode was titled "King of the Strip." The climax of the show was the big race. We are dead even, then Paul pulls out and is a little ahead. We come to a tunnel or an overpass or some situation where there is only enough room for one of us to make it; the other one would surely die. Even though Paul is clearly ahead, he slows down and lets me win. He learns what is really important in life. Pretty heavy stuff for a show that was essentially *Gilligan's Island* with magic.

To be truthful, I loved the show and was proud to be on it. Also, one week on *Fantasy Island* would make me eligible for six more months of unemployment. By age nineteen, that was what I was living on. I really wanted to impress the studio or writers or whoever might be able to get me another job. So, unlike *The Partridge Family*, I was *never* in my dressing room. As a matter of fact, I never left the set. If the director needed me, I was already there. This sounds better than it actually was. I was mostly in the way. When I failed to ingratiate myself with Ricardo Montalban, I went for the next best thing, Herve Villechaize—better known as "Tattoo." He was a little stand-offish. I remembered something my grandfather Jack used to say when dealing with people like that. Always open with a joke. Herve was standing next to his dressing room, which was a full-size Winnebago. I casually walked up to Herve and told him that if he split the trailer into two levels, he could give the top floor to his stunt double.

Not only did I think this was a funny line, but it really was a dreadful waste of space. Herve did not see the humor. All of show business is surreal in a very real way. Real to me because that's how I pay my rent. Surreal because anything can happen, but what happened next was the weirdest thing I have ever seen without the benefit of hallucinogens. Herve reached down into his boot and pulled out a dagger. The technical term for this particular type of weapon is a punch dagger, and it is very dangerous. The way it works is simple. Your fist wraps around the handle and the blade sticks out between your middle fingers. Then you just "punch" your victim with it. Under any other circumstances, I would have been scared to death. Now, imagine a three-foot-tall man in a white suit, holding a dagger, and screaming (in a bad accent), "I vill keil you for zat." It only made me laugh.

The truth is, from where we were standing, unless he had a gun, I could have drop-kicked him to the Lido Deck of *The Love Boat.* I continued to laugh. Sure enough, the little bastard *did* have a gun. He reached behind his little white coat and pulled out what appeared to be a full-size, nickel-plated, pearl-handled .38 revolver. There he was— three feet tall, with a gun in one hand and a knife in the other. Now I knew he wasn't kidding—and I got scared. I apologized profusely. He put his weapons away and dismissed me.

Years later, when I heard he shot himself, I really felt bad for the guy. How tough his life must have been. If memory serves me, he shot himself in the chest with a .357 Magnum. A .357 can drop a horse at fifty feet—but three-foot Herve had (somehow) missed his heart and lived for quite a while in terrible pain. This guy could not buy a break.

Chapter 9

DO I REMEMBER THE '80S? NO!

Although my family had a long business and personal relationship with Dick Clark, my business relationship with Dick was mostly a figment of my imagination. That is about to change. Six days from the time of this writing, with a resilience I thought reserved only for John Travolta, I will shoot the pilot for my fourth TV show, a daytime talk show. It's called *Guys*, and it will be hosted by, you guessed it, Dick Clark and Danny Bonaduce! Doctors may think they are God, but I firmly believe God thinks He is a comic.

The show is a lot like *The View*, only it's hosted by men and with Dick Clark in the Barbara Walters seat. When you read this, one of three things will have happened.

1. The show will be on the air.
2. The show will have been on the air and already been canceled.

3. The pilot will have sucked and the show will never have seen the light of day.

I am rooting for option #1.

This will not be the first time I worked for Mr. Clark. In the very early 1980s, Dick came up with the idea of the now–ever-popular *Where Are They Now?* show, and he wanted me in it. That was my first one. I have done dozens since.

At first, it was an honor to be on the *Where Are They Now?* tour, but soon they would start to irritate me. After doing ten of these shows in as many months, I started to get a little bitter. I mean, if all these people wanted to know where I was, how did I get to be so goddamned hard to find? Unfortunately the answer to "where am I now?" was in a hovel of a home I owned in Reseda, California. I had yet to become the poster boy for failed ex–child stars, but I was on my way. I was also not ready to admit I was a failure, even though it was true. I still had a couple of things going for me—absolutely no respect for the truth and a very rich friend. Both would soon come into play.

I called my friend Scott Dahlgren, from my Cal Prep days, and I told him of my dilemma—and my "plan." Scott, being the buddy he is, went for it. I called the people from Dick's office and gave the address. It wasn't my place in Reseda, it was Scott's father's mansion. I quickly filled my car with props and dashed over to Scott's. We ran around Scott's house pulling down pictures of his family and putting up pictures of mine. When the crew arrived, I was glad to see that Dick was not with them. Not that my long association with him would have prevented me from attempting the charade, but I think he would have known immediately. You don't get to be Dick Clark by being an idiot.

The director wanted me to give him a tour of the house. This was a problem. We only redecorated the living room! What was worse, I was sure of the location of only two things: Scott's room and where his dad hid the liquor. We ended up doing the interview by the pool with Scott's mom and dad staring at me in disbelief that I could look right into the camera and lie. They were appalled. Fortunately, the director mistook their stares for that of adoration for their loving son. I was a hit.

In between the time I sold my nice home, lived in the hovel I didn't want seen on camera, and before surrendering myself to life on the streets of Los Angeles, I decided to live a life of adventure. I tried working straight jobs and immediately realized I had no knack for it. Furthermore, it didn't seem like anyone particularly wanted me to! There were the times when I tried to be a waiter at Sushi on Sunset or a Sizzler-like chain restaurant called Black Angus. Calls of "Hey, Partridge, my soup is cold!" or "You're not a movie star anymore, move it!" were common.

A few nights of depression (and even more nights of fisticuffs) and I was out of the restaurant business. I also tried my hand at other real jobs. At one point I ended up as a security guard in Marina Del Rey, and occasionally I bartended at a restaurant in the marina. As a security guard, it was my duty to make sure that homeless people did not use million-dollar yachts as crash pads. I did my duty with due diligence. I would scour the marina looking for unlocked boats, and the minute I found one—I would immediately enter, drink the bar dry, and pass out cold. And my days as a bartender? Well, it's easy to guess what I did as a bartender. One time, after I was arrested, a tabloid television show decided to interview some of my old bosses. The owner of the bar said, "I cannot believe I put that guy in charge of the liquor." The owner of the security company said, "I cannot believe I gave that guy a gun." They were right to be concerned. Something good did come out of my short but tumultuous stay in the marina. I met a wonderful group of people, kind of a marina subculture called the live-aboards. The live-aboards are like seafaring gypsies. They have no money and usually no jobs. They were often seen on the decks of multimillion-dollar yachts, hobnobbing with major movie stars or having cocktails at the private yacht club. All this VIP access was received in exchange for them telling their stories of life on the high seas to the rich boat owners whose vessels never left their slips.

I had the great good fortune of getting to know some of the live-aboards as well as anyone could. You just had to be prepared for the fact that one day they would just be gone. It took almost nothing to sustain them. All they needed were their skills, a fishing pole, and an abundance of liquor.

Then one day they would return, sometimes months or even years later. They would be back with more money than they had left with, deeper tans, and more wonderful stories.

I decided right then and there that this was the life for me. No more would people, right or wrong, punish me for squandering my life and money. I liked living the Life of Reilly. (Trust me, being a recognizable celebrity and your bus boy is a shitty combination, even under the most favorable of conditions.) I decided I would set sail. I would no longer be a has-been and the butt of jokes. I would be Danny Bonaduce, "Redhead, the Pirate." As you can imagine, almost immediately I ran into some problems. What I lacked in seamanship made up for the simple fact that I did not own a boat. The fact I had almost no money and even fewer nautical skills made remedying the boat thing seem like a daunting task. I did, however, have a couple of things going for me: three hundred in cash and a 1971 VW camper bus. Not exactly the swashbuckling life of a buccaneer, but it would do. I was off to Mexico.

I headed south on the 405. With any luck at all, no one would ever see me again. As darkness fell on the first night of my journey, I started to get a little nervous. My dreams of sleeping by the light of the moon on the pristine beaches of Mexico were thwarted. Very little is pristine once you go twenty miles south of TJ (Tijuana). Also, I was certain every odd sound I would hear would be bandits coming to abscond with my VW land yacht.

I decided to play it safe. I would sleep in the parking lot of the local police station. I soon learned my first lesson of life on the road. Sleeping in the parking lot of a Mexican police station does *not* necessarily make you safe. It just means the Federales don't have to travel all that far to extort you.

I am sure that I am looking back on my poorer days in Mexico through rose-colored glasses. From my house in the hills, I can now see more than just a great view of Los Angeles. I am surrounded by a family who loves and respects me (sometimes it's even my own), and I am working at one of the best jobs in America. It would simply be just bad form to *miss* my poverty. The reality? Mexico was fun! I lived on twenty-five-cent tacos, ten-cent barbecued pig intestines (on a stick), and a brand of hard liquor known as Tic-Tac that went for fifty cents a bottle. After a few nights I heard some alarming news. The Mexican government was blaming Tic-Tac for an epidemic of blindness that was afflicting the indigenous Indians. Faced with being broke, blind, or, worse, sober, I quickly came up with a plan. I took one of the books I had brought for the ride and set it up in the sink of my van. I would then back away from the book until I could barely make out the letters, measure the distance, then I would repeat this process every morning. You see? If I woke up and could not read the book from the prescribed distance, I would either stop drinking or move up to a better poison. Was this great logic, or what? I know what you are thinking: "What a good plan!" Believe it or not, it had *some* flaws. The main problem with this theory was that I would go to bed almost every night pretty buzzed.

I would wake up around ten the next morning, in a closed car, and in 100-degree heat. I was covered in sweat and had enough film in my mouth to shoot *Apocalypse Now*. I often could not make out my hand in front of my face! Imagine what it was like trying to decipher what the hell Tolstoy was rambling on about. I immediately came up with another plan. Have a couple of drinks and reconfigure at noon. After many thorough and highly scientific tests, I concluded, not only did Tic-Tac not cause blindness—but often it actually restored my vision.

I had bounced around TJ and Ensenada for about a month, and it was getting near the time to move on. I decided to go to Rio de Janeiro. My plan, if I actually had one, was to drive there—or die trying. I do not actually mean I wanted to die, but I did start thinking "Wouldn't it be great to be kidnapped and held hostage by guerrillas in Honduras, Nicaragua, or El Salvador?" I knew full well there would be no one with the money or inclination to pay the ransom. The advantage was I would be on the eleven o'clock news every night—and that was good enough for me. During the Iran hostage crisis, I would watch the footage of those poor tortured hostages. I would think, "What if I were one of them!" If I had been—and I ever made it home—I would definitely get a miniseries or maybe even my own show. Yes, I was actually jealous of the Tehran hostages!

> NOTE TO READERS: I know my overwhelming desire to recapture the glories of my youth may seem a bit shallow. If you have read this far, by now you must surely know that "depth" is not one of my stronger assets. Now, of course, the things I have done (or at least thought of doing) to again be rich and famous embarrass me. Now, at forty, I have yet to learn a grown-up vocation. If I had to do it all over, I surely would. Eventually I would make a small "comeback," but this only spurred me on to try to make it bigger. My goal in life then, as it is now, was to one day be bigger than Carson. Not the noblest of pursuits to be sure, but it is all I know—and I would have done anything to achieve it.

Back on the road. . . .

I had no idea how to get to Rio, but how hard could it be? All I had to do was drive to Brazil, then ask directions. I knew Brazil was in South America. So, I started in America and drove south. Unfortunately, one of the things that kept me from my original plan of sailing the high seas was my total lack of navigational skills. That deficiency would also plague me on dry land. Did you know, if you do not turn left at the border, you cannot get to Rio? Funny, I didn't either!

I found all this out when I got to Cabo San Lucas. The world ended. Faced with this rather egregious error, I decided to head for home. My dreams were dashed on the tourist-infested shores. Before I left, I would spend some money drinking at a civilized bar—a hot local club called Cabo Wabo. The bar was owned by some of the members of the group Van Halen. In keeping with the theme of my entire trip, there was a problem—a long line and a red velvet rope. Believe it or not, if you count poverty, drugs, and degradation, the red velvet rope may be the number-one enemy of the has-been. Red velvet ropes that guard the entrances to private clubs and VIP rooms exist to part the yes-people from the no-people. It's like what Moses did to the Red Sea. In those days, when doormen would see me coming, they would slam down those ropes as if they were the iron gates at a border crossing.

If you ever decide to open a bar and no one comes calling? Just put up a red velvet rope, a huge bouncer, and a sign that reads "VIPs only" and the world will beat a path to your door. Customers with righteous indignation will swear to your doorman they were supposed to meet Leonardo DiCaprio inside an hour ago. I, on the other hand, did not mind waiting in line. It's not as if I was busy! It's just that waiting in line begets embarrassing questions from other patrons. Questions like "Hey, why are you in line?" Or "Don't they know you are here?" My favorite? "Why are you in line—don't you know somebody?"

Eventually, all pretense would drop and my fellow wrong-side-of-the-ropes people would get down to the nitty-gritty. "Hey—weren't you Danny Partridge?" Or "How did you get to be such a loser?" The truth of the matter? I was, in fact, a loser, but there is *no* reason to cop to it—if you are clever. So, I got clever! The idea came to me as if by divine intervention. (Interventions, divine or otherwise, would become quite commonplace with me in the next few years.) I pulled the bus up to a phone booth and tried to get the number for Cabo Wabo. That is no easy task in Mexico. I then called the bar and asked for the manager. Luckily for me, he was an American. I told the manager my name was Steve Sutcliff and I was the vice president of Dick Clark Productions. I went on to explain that we were in Cabo filming a special called *Twenty-five Years in Rock and Roll History* and two of our major stars wanted to come in for a drink. Taking the bait like an albacore, the manager asked me for the names of the "guests." I told him, "You can expect Mick Jagger of the Rolling Stones and Danny Bonaduce of the great rock group the Partridge Family." When I said Mick, he was hooked. "Yes, sir" was his reply. "I'll have everything ready."

When the time was right, I left the van parked around the corner and I walked up to the red velvet ropes. I asked for the manager. When he arrived, I said "Hi, I'm Danny. Is Mick here yet?" The poor guy was so excited. "No, sir,

Mr. Bonaduce, not yet—but your table is ready." I was whisked inside, passing by all the "other folks" who were still in line. Again I was a star. Not only did I drink free of charge all night, but the manager would stop by every fifteen minutes or so just to see if everything was satisfactory. I would apologize for Mick's shameful breach of etiquette. Not only did I drink to an elegant sufficiency, but the whole bar was abuzz and girls were everywhere. Unfortunately, even I could not explain (with a straight face) to some hot babe that I was staying in a VW "just for the charm of it." So, I got drunk but didn't get laid!

I started my drive home to Los Angeles the next afternoon, hung over and nearly broke.

HOW TO GET CAUGHT IN A VELVET ROPE

I used the "Is Mick here yet?" ploy for the next ten years, and it worked every time. I was privy to the secret bastion of celebrity all over the country. Years later, on a fateful night, my game worked too well. I wanted to go to the Roxbury, a famous club (they sort of made a movie about it—*A Night at the Roxbury*) on the Sunset Strip. I had heard a great deal about it. Shannen Doherty started fights there! Madonna kissed chicks there! This was my kind of place.

This time, when I called the manager, I claimed to be the executive producer of *The Tonight Show*. I told him two of our guests would like to be let in that night. After ten years of success, I had become quite ballsy—and told him what Mick and I would like to drink so they could have it ready. When I pulled up in front of the Roxbury, I of course immediately asked for the manager. He scampered down at a full run. "Is Mick here?" I asked (with total confidence). This time the manager said something I had not expected. "Yes, sir, Mr. Bonaduce, he's right inside." *Shit!* I was then escorted in by the manager (and two obligatory bouncers) and seated right next to Mick "goddamn" Jagger.

The manager was so pleased with himself, he would not leave. I did what I had always done when I didn't know what to do, I started talking. "Hey, Mick! What's new? How's Jerri?" Mick just stared at me mystified. Mercifully, the manager finally left and I decided to confess all. What the hell? Mick might even find it funny! I told him how I had been drinking on his coattails free for over ten years and I thanked him for "some of the best nights of my life." Mick chuckled slightly, called me a "cheeky bastard," and then dismissed me with a wave of his hand. I felt like such a whore! Luckily, that's a feeling I have become quite comfortable with over the years.

A HELPFUL FOOTNOTE TO READERS: You too can pull off the "Is Mick here yet?" act. All you have to do is say you are the percussionist for any '70s band. Really! Think about it! What doorman could identify, by sight, the drummer for Three Dog Night?

Chapter 10

DANNY AND THE CHINESE COCAINE COWBOYS

My radio career basically starts off like so many of my stories—with me in jail. Before I sat down to write this book, I thought of my little stories as charming and myself as a colorful character. When I look at my life, now condensed down to a few hundred pages, it turns out I was nothing more than a piece of shit. A piece of shit of operatic proportions, but nonetheless, a piece of shit. Believe me, I am as *surprised* about this as you are!

When I get busted, it's usually for the same old thing: *drugs.* The now-legendary transvestite incident is one notable exception. On September 13, 1985, it was drugs. Under normal circumstances, I would not bore you with another celebrity drug bust story. If you've heard one, you've heard them all. I don't mind if some of you are thinking that I'm crazy, but I couldn't take it if you thought me redundant. This particular bust does deserve some background information, so ride along with me for a little bit here.

One night in July, I was in a club in West Hollywood. I had been to this club a couple of times and didn't really care for it. However, it had one thing going for it. Unlike every other hot spot in L.A., they had neglected to remove my name from their guest list.

On this particular evening I noticed a little doorway I had never seen before. The doorway led to a long hallway, the end of which I could not see. I decided to investigate. At the end of this hallway was a very cool, private room. Always trying to prove I was still a VIP, that is where I had to be. The room was filled with twenty or so Asians dressed to the nines. Not out of any personal ethnic or national preference, I sort of hoped they were Japanese. I speak Japanese, having studied it for years—and actually learned more than the basics. I thought by using that, I might make some new friends. This was not to be. Not only were they Chinese, they were also pissed. Of course, I did not know this when I sat down. At this point, it certainly would not have made a difference. I had the common sense to not start speaking Japanese to people just because they were Asian. I had learned the hard way that Koreans just *hate* that.

Just as my ass hit the leather of the chair, the head Chinese guy walked over to have a chat with me. You could tell who was in charge of these guys just by the amount of gold jewelry he wore. I instinctively knew this guy was the boss, just by the fact that he looked like an Asian version of Mr. T. *"This room for Chinese only,"* he screamed. This statement made me mad. I always considered myself quite patriotic—even somewhat nationalistic. In what other country could unskilled labor (such as myself) grow up to be rich and famous—even if I wasn't anymore? I informed him, quite calmly, "This room is for Americans only—but it is okay with me if you stay." There was much yelling in Chinese, but I sat there, unmovable and stoic. After about a minute, two or three of the men in the room opened their custom-tailored sport coats to show me they were carrying guns.

"Mr. T" then asked me a question: "What you do now, tough guy?" He obviously learned English from Edward G. Robinson movies. "Fuck you! You don't have the balls to shoot me in here." This was my extraordinarily stupid answer. I was not being brave. In 1985, people shooting people over a bar argument was still a rarity in L.A. Besides, I meant what I was saying. I really didn't think they would shoot me in there. I thought they would at least wait for me to go outside before they would shoot me. In reality, I was afraid to leave. Mistaking my statement for bravado, "Mr. T" turned to his friends and again started to speak whatever it was—Cantonese or Mandarin.

This time, however, there was much laughter and, to my great joy, no further display of their weaponry. Finally

"Mr. T" patted me on the head and said, "You okay, tough guy!" Again there was much rejoicing—this time, most of it was being done by me!

Eventually, I would end up doing business with these guys. They would front me thousands of dollars. There was one Chinese American in the group who spoke both languages perfectly. He was the only one of the group to tell me his name, so I will obviously leave it out. Actually, all names have been changed here—to protect my ass! These guys were dangerous.

I don't know what happened to these guys over the last fifteen years and I really don't care to find out. Unlike the so-called gangsters I have met in New York, Chicago, and Philadelphia (who were nothing more than street thugs), these guys were the real deal. In case they have learned to read English, I want to make sure not to offend any of them.

The American, whom I will call "Steve," recognized me and started to tell "Mr. T" who I was. Even in Cantonese I could tell what "Steve" was saying. In Cantonese, *Partridge Family* is pronounced *Partlidge Famiry*, and me, being the master linguist, was able to break their code. As things would have it, *The Partridge Family* was a huge hit in Hong Kong, and these guys had no idea of what a has-been is. To them I was as big a star as a Seinfeld would be. I turned into their pet celebrity—or, more accurately, their "monkey boy." We sat around drinking ridiculously expensive cognac, which was awful. The taste was not helped by the prodigious amounts of cocaine they would pour into each glass. To this day, I cannot figure out how they did it. They sat with their snifters in this cool little warmer thing and every now and again took a sip like nothing was happening.

I, on the other hand, was totally unaccustomed to drinking flame heated "coca-cognac." By my second or third sip, my mouth was so numb, the elixir poured out the sides of my mouth and onto my lap. Once again, much laughter ensued. I didn't know what was so funny. The stuff they were drinking was $60 a glass, and that was before they dumped in a mountain of blow!

After the night's festivities had concluded, I was invited to join them again the next day. I gave them my address. It was a thirty-two-foot motor boat (with no motor) foundering in the east basin of Marina Del Rey. The next night a limo driver knocked on my door—or, more appropriately, my hatch. I was whisked off to meet the boys in Korea Town at something called a hostess bar. On this night we were drinking scotch, again with copious amounts of cocaine dumped in. We also snorted cocaine, in full view of the other patrons. We were doing it off individual mirrors with little designs carved in them. These mirrors were quite ingenious. The boys would just pour a pile of cocaine on the top right-hand corner. When they wanted a hit they would just drag the whole pile across the mirror to the bottom left. Just the right amount of coke would fall into the design. This maneuver would prevent them from having to do anything as tacky as cut lines. If they wanted more, they would reverse the process. Several of the guys handed me their mirrors that night. I noticed the design on each mirror was different. Some had dragons, others had simple initials, and another had the Mercedes-Benz emblem.

Trying to make small talk, I asked "Mr. T" if the designs had anything to do with their heritage or their standing in their organization. He patted me on the head and told me I was "very observant." Later on, "Steve" told me this question had caused much nervousness—and I was never to ask any questions again, EVER! "No sweat," I responded, "just bring on the blow." And they did!

I did not really get the appeal of the hostess bar. Even though we snorted enough coke to kill David Crosby, it remained a fairly dull place—high or not. The boys and I just sat there, for the most part, being quiet. On the other hand, the hostesses were *completely* silent. All these girls did was constantly pour a lot of expensive scotch. We probably had no more than two or three bottles, yet the bill? It was more than $2,000. The crowd I would normally be hanging with around this time, I can assure you, would spend $2,000 differently and more wisely. It would have bought us 100 bottles of tequila and 37 blow jobs, and not necessarily in that order!

My new friends not only *didn't* know how to have a good time, but their economic strategies confounded the hell out of me. Things improved a bit as time went on. I went out with them again a few days later. We went somewhere in Chinatown. "Mr. T" told me—quite matter-offactly—that I should dress more "appropriately." I asked "Steve" to explain something to him. I looked at him right in the eye. I then said, "Because of the limited space on my boat, I do not own anything more appropriate." I did not bother to tell him the truth. The fact is, I didn't own anything at all. "Steve" then told him this, and nothing else was said. The very next day, a tailor showed up at my boat and took my measurements. Within hours he returned with five new suits. Except for my distinct lack of gold and my bright red hair, I looked just like them in my shiny new suits.

I really thought I was going to become a Chinese gangster, and I liked the idea. These guys moved around in a shady underworld I had never seen. It was exciting. Contrary to popular belief, before this time in my life, I had *not* done a great deal of hard drugs. I am also certain my idea and *your* idea of what a great deal is differs dramatically. This cocaine was still new to me, and I was quickly becoming an addict.

That's when things changed. No more were bottles of Dom Perignon and piles of coke put so freely in front of me. Now, if I wanted a drink or a line, I had to ask—and the response time was getting longer. That's when it happened. One night "Mr. T" pulled me aside. He spoke a lot more English than he initially let on. This was the deal. Why didn't I buy an ounce of coke from him for $1,500? There are twenty-eight grams in an ounce. At $100 a gram, I could sell it—and make $1,300—or snort thirteen grams myself and still break even. And that's before I "stepped on it" (cut the pure coke with an additive to stretch out the amount of coke). Guess which road I took? It did not matter that I didn't have the money, as "Mr. T" would front it to me, and I could pay him later.

This made sound fiscal sense to me, and I went for it. Alas, the best-laid plans! A few days later I woke up with some crazy-looking girl, no blow, and a very bloody nose. To make matters worse, I was now $1,500 in debt to a real live Asian gangster. I got rid of the girl, which was fairly easy to do. When she discovered the blow was gone, so was she. I cleaned myself up—and that night I went to the club. I found the boys in their little hideaway, and I sat down as if nothing had happened. Drinks were being passed around, and so was some coke—but not to me. By now I was already craving it, if only to stop the pain in my nose. "Mr. T," the consummate host, never broached the subject of money. I couldn't take it any more. I told him that I had sold all the coke, but I fronted it out to people I trusted. I was, of course, lying on all avenues. Not only had I not sold any of the blow, but also I knew very few people, none of whom I trusted. I went on to explain that I wanted him to front another ounce to me while I waited for the money to come in from the last batch.

Without a moment's hesitation, "Mr. T" reached into his jacket pocket and pulled out a tightly rolled plastic bag of coke. He handed it to me as if it were a congratulatory cigar! I was back in business. At the time I thought I had

"T" snowed, but looking back on it, he must have known what was happening and I bet my being in indentured servitude was his eventual goal. I didn't care—I had a plan. The plan was to cut the ounce of coke with two grams of Manitol. Manitol, an Italian baby laxative, is considered the standard additive for cutting. The deception would give me thirty grams, which I would sell for $3,000, pay "T" off, and end the relationship.

That night, as I sat in my boat making this cocaine concoction, I decided to do a few lines—for "research and medicinal proposes." Even after I put in the cut, there was no discernible difference in the taste or high of the coke. I must have been some kind of genius alchemist. I could step on this stuff all day—and no one would be the wiser. Unfortunately, it did not take long for me to realize it *also* meant I could snort several grams and cut the remaining coke even more. There were several flaws in this plan— the most noteworthy being that cocaine had already stopped being fun and had become a necessity. I now passed the point of *me* doing the drug, now "the drug was doing *me*."

After what seemed like only a few lines, I sat at my galley table with all my chemicals and tools mixing up my witches' brew. I had great wads of toilet paper stuffed up my nose to stop the blood from my ever-present nosebleed. I would take out the tissue long enough to take a snort— and immediately lie upside down. This was to ensure the cocaine would have the desired effect of going up my nose instead of pouring out all over my chest from my now-permanent nosebleed. The only breaks I took were several trips to the bathroom, thanks to the laxative effect of the Manitol. The bathrooms were only a couple of hundred feet from my boat, but the trips were terrifying—thanks to my ever-increasing paranoia. Everyone, tourist or yachtsman, was in my mind an undercover cop—and they *all* knew what I was up to.

My fear level got so bad, I took a small Tupperware container, cut holes in it with a fishing knife, and put a one-pound lead fishing weight inside. These items were a holdover from my more wholesome boating days of just two weeks before. I poured all the cocaine into the now–weighed-down Tupperware, crawled into a two-and-a-half-by-three-foot space, and hung the bowl out the window.

I stayed hunched over in this position for five days. The reason for doing this was perfectly clear to me at the time. You see, when the SWAT team came charging down my companionway, and I was *certain* they would, I would drop the bowl of blow out of the window and into the channel. Even if they sent a diver in after it, and I was *certain* they would, all they would find would be a plastic bowl with a lead weight. The dark saltwater would save me. I waited for the SWAT team to arrive. Every few minutes or so, I would bring my arm in the window, stick a rolled-up dollar bill into the bowl, and take a hit. I was in agony. In *The Bridge on the River Kwai*, the Japanese tortured the British prisoners by having them hold their arms out all day. I did it with my right arm—for a week. After a week, there was nothing left in the bowl except for the coke dust on the lead weight. I immediately licked it clean.

Things went along at this crazy pace for a couple of more weeks. Then I got a lucky break, literally. It was in my right hand. It was August 13, my birthday. I had just seen "T" and given him some money that I had dug up somehow. In return, he gave me a quarter ounce as a birthday present. Instead of going to my boat and snorting it all as usual, I decided to go and get some food. Not that I specifically remember, but more than likely, I had not eaten in a few days. I was sitting in the Jamaica Bay Inn, a hotel and twenty-four-hour coffee shop just a few hundred feet from my boat.

I was just sitting there, minding my own business and contemplating the good pie and my bad life, when I noticed two other customers. One guy was drunk, the other one was just loud. The loud guy was a real bore, badgering the waitresses and cursing at an ever-increasing decibel level. I hated him. I may have been a washed-up, ex–child star drug addict, but I still knew the rules of convention. These gentlemen were certainly breaching them. Still, I sat quietly.

The waitress handed me my bill and, half under her breath, she muttered, "I wish that guy would shut his mouth." That was all I needed. An invitation and an opening! "Hey, buddy, shut the fuck up," I bellowed. (I know . . . I can get fairly glib under pressure.) He reacted immediately by standing up . . . and he kept rising. He was big, really big. Oh, shit—he was GOLIATH!!! I decided to say something "tough." With a piece of pie still on my fork, I looked up at him and said, "It's my birthday and hospitalizing a dick like you is *not* how I had planned to spend it, but, if you insist . . ." He started to walk toward me. Could it be this guy never went to the movies? I had said the cool, tough-guy thing. He was supposed to run off into the night, or at least sit down with his nerves shattered by my amazing display of machismo. Apparently this guy did not get out much. He kept coming.

I was wearing a thick leather jacket at that moment. It was the kind that makes bikers look so tough. Unless you think you are about to be stabbed or your opponent really knows how to work the body, leather jackets are quite restrictive and can be a hindrance in a fight. I took mine off. My foe had no knife and no one ever works the body in a real fight. That's for movie stars and pugilists. A real fight looks exactly as you might remember it from the sixth grade. Somebody smashes somebody in the face, everybody falls down, they wrestle around on the floor for a while, somebody gets somebody in a headlock, and then somebody "gives." Real fights are awkward, clumsy, and never ever impress chicks.

H. G. Wells once said, "The first man to raise his fist in anger is the man who has run out of ideas." This beautiful philosophy proves one thing to me. I absolutely could have beaten the shit out of H. G. Wells. In the real world, the man who raises his fist first usually beats the crap out of the poor bastard who failed to. When he came into range, all my martial arts skills went right out the window. I threw a right hand at him and I swear it came from another area code! Somehow it landed flush on his cheek. I had hit him so hard that I naturally assumed he would hit the floor unconscious—or at least so confused that I could make my exit. My haymaker had a small portion of its desired effect. Goliath fell.

Unfortunately, his butt barely hit the linoleum when he started to get back up. He wasn't dazed or confused. He didn't even look hurt. All I could think was "That prick!" He most certainly wasn't unconscious, and he was far too big to let me let him back to his feet. I jumped on him to begin the "rolling and wrestling" portion of our program. Somehow I got him in the "obligatory headlock" and again assumed victory. He soon reminded me of why it is never *smart* to assume. He did something unprecedented in my limited fistfight experience: He reached his free hand over my head, rammed his fingers in my eyes, and ripped. The pain was intense and immediate—but it took a backseat to the fear.

This was a fistfight! No one was supposed to get seriously injured! This guy was crazy and I no longer wanted any part of him. Anybody who would blind someone over a small altercation was too crazy for me. It was like having the proverbial tiger by the tail. I could not let him go. He kept gouging at my eyes and his fingers were starting to come back bloody. I realized I was fighting for my life. I had given some thought to dying over the last couple of years. Lately, on any given day, I honestly didn't care too much either way. Being beaten to death or blinded at the Jamaica Bay Inn did not meet the "minimum requirements" for my final curtain call. The rules suddenly changed, and as it turned out? There were not going to be any.

I kept one arm around his neck. Then, with my free hand, I grabbed an old-fashioned sugar dispenser off the counter. I smashed it into his head. I must have swung too hard because it immediately shattered and had no effect on my adversary. On the bright side, I also noticed it did not cut my hand. This guy had only one tactic—to go for my eyes. He was a one-trick pony—but it was a great trick. Blood started to stream down my face and I could no longer see out of my right eye. At this point, I began to hyperventilate. I was terrified. I thought I was going to faint, and I am lucky I didn't. It was obvious to me now, if I became unconscious or otherwise incapacitated, he would have continued to beat me until I was dead.

My next move was to grab a glass salt shaker. I wrapped my fist around it like it was a roll of quarters. I repeatedly brought it down on the back of his head. This was a much better weapon. It did not break. Being bashed on the head with a condiment also had little effect on Rambo. He continued to fight, undaunted by the salt shaker—or me. He

clawed at my face a little bit more. I was now bleeding profusely. Somehow I got him on his back, and that sudden
motion turned the tables on him and the fight. I sat on his
chest, my ankles pinning his arms down and my knees
next to his head. I put my thumbs on his eyes and rammed
my fingers in his ears. For a moment he stopped strug-
gling. I then said, "I want to end this now so we can both
go home in one piece." I also let him know if he was not
willing to call it a night, he would leave me no choice but
to "ram my thumbs straight into his brain." He must have
doubted my intestinal fortitude, because he then did something unbelievable. He actually started pushing his face
against my thumbs! It was as if he were *daring* me to do it.
His bet paid off. I couldn't do it. Just the thought of
plunging my thumbs into his ocular cavities was too much
for me. I thought about the sounds it would make—the
texture—not to mention his screams of agony that would
surely follow.

This was a real bad time for me to realize that I totally
lacked true killer instinct. Before I could plan my next
move, he raised his face up enough so that it was buried in
my crotch. As I looked down, he clamped his teeth down
on my penis . . . and I mean *really* hard.

NOTE TO READERS: I realize at this point, many of you
might be saying to yourselves (or out loud, for that
matter), "There is *no way* it really happened like this."

Fortunately, for verification of many of the facts in this book (and unfortunately for my reputation), there are usually police or medical reports to back me up. In this particular case, there are both.

The fight raged on. As you can well imagine, when he bit me, I jumped high enough to make Michael Jordan green with envy. Goliath turned over and pushed himself up by his hands. This time I jumped on his back. I ended up getting him in what is commonly known as a police choke-hold. I had practiced this hold for years in karate class and then again in security school. I also had even seen training tapes of the police rendering a suspect unconscious in less than two seconds. I am happy to report this hold really works. The fight was over—and this time he knew it. I told him again, "We are done, I just want to go home—but if you continue to struggle, I will absolutely kill you." I meant it. I could not go on and my face was now gushing blood. I was also beginning to notice the pain in my right hand; it was seriously injured. Another major concern for me at this point was, I had no idea how badly he might have perforated my penis. So now it was end it or end him. If I did kill him, I was sure the staff of the restaurant would explain to the cops that this madman left me no choice. By now I certainly hoped the cops were on their way.

We negotiated his terms of surrender. This was not exactly the Treaty of Versailles. I would let him up and we would part company. The moment he got to his feet, it became abundantly clear he was not only a raving lunatic but had another nasty habit. He was a big old fibber. He immediately broke our agreement by hurling everything at me that wasn't nailed down. Knives, forks, spoons, plates, and cups were suddenly airborne. It seemed as if half the Williams-Sonoma catalog was whizzing past my head. Fortunately, nothing hit me. This guy may have been incredibly tough, but as a marksman, he was sorely lacking.

Eventually he picked up an ashtray. (Yes, you could still smoke in restaurants back then.) He threw it at me and it quickly reached terminal velocity. Again it missed its mark, but it did manage to take out the glass of the dessert display case. This was more than I could bear! These actions made me realize that the fight was going to start again. I had nothing left in me. I also have to tell you, I have never been so scared, before or since.

I ran with jetlike speed—at least out the back door and down to the beach walk. I had not made it 100 feet when I noticed my body was sending me a signal—major fatigue. I could not take another step. It felt as if I were having a heart attack! I crawled in behind a trash Dumpster to hide and lick my wounds. I was sure this guy was out there somewhere hunting for me. Even though I had *technically* won the fight, I knew I could not do it again. Suddenly I started to hear footsteps. They were getting closer and closer. Eventually I worked up the nerve to peek out from behind my fragrant hiding place. I was saved! It was not him—it was the cops.

I could not make it to my feet, so I crawled out and yelled for help. The full extent of my injuries were now making themselves known to me. The police helped me into their cruiser and drove me the 100 or so feet back to the coffee shop. He was still there. To my surprise, the cops gave us two choices:

1. We could both go to jail.
2. We could not press charges and both go home.

Psycho boy wanted to go home. I, on the other hand, was voting for jail (and I called *him* psycho!). I didn't have to be anywhere else—and, after all, I was the one that had been attacked. Just as I was about to make my case for jail, I remembered my jacket. It was lying in the booth inside the restaurant. In my pocket was a ten-year prison sentence, all rolled up in a Ziploc bag. I quickly agreed and voted for home. I asked the deputy if I could go in and get my coat. I had caused such a disturbance that he insisted on getting it for me. When he (so nicely) helped me put the jacket on, I about wet myself.

I, of course, went back to my boat and snorted all the blow. By the next day, the pain in my hand had become unbearable. It had swollen up to the size of a Buick and was completely useless. I went to the ER and found out I had crushed several bones in my hand with the first and only real punch in the fight. It was going to take major surgery to repair. There also was nothing that could be done for the purple ring of teeth marks on my penis—but the doctor was duly impressed. He told me he could have me out of the hospital in twenty-four hours, but it would be best if I could stay a day or two. I knew I had Screen Actors Guild insurance and I needed the rest—not to mention the painkillers! I told him I could stay as long as he liked. I believe I stayed three days. It was more like a vacation, only better. Breakfast in bed with narcotics. When it was time to check out, I was sad to leave. Not just because I had become quite comfortable in there, but the bill was already over $8,000. My union had neglected to tell me—or more likely, I had failed to notice—that, as an actor, you have to earn a minimum of $3,000 a year to qualify for insurance. I had not made $3,000 as an actor for quite some time. Who knew?

Let us recap the events of those amazing two weeks. Fourteen days earlier, I was a gentleman of leisure. No money to speak of, but I lounged or fished all day on a boat that was two slips down from Sylvester Stallone's. Now, I was a drug addict, $8,000 in debt to a doctor, $3,000 in debt to a Chinese gangster (whom I am sure had a more effective collection method). I now had steel pins in my hand (along with stitches) and I was wearing a cast. The Marina Del Rey Sheriff's Department was watching my every move. I found out I had no insurance and my face looked like I had lost a fight with a bag of cats. Time sure flies when you're an asshole.

The reason I refer to the damage to my hand as "a lucky

break" is because when I got out of the hospital, the pain in my nose was gone and I had no physical craving for cocaine. I was going to get my life back. Once again I found some money to give "Mr. T," and once again he gave me more coke. Like the fool that I am, and the one I had become, I took it. Every time I gave him some cash, he would give me twice the amount of coke. Even if I sold it, it didn't seem likely that I would ever get out of debt. The fact that I was snorting most of it made that impossible.

I was searching for a way out. I thought about running. I had no job and was familiar with Mexico. I also thought about turning the gang in. Neither scenario seemed plausible. One night my answer found me. I was on my way to the club to give "T" some money when I got pulled over. My behavior must have been erratic because the cop decided to search me and rip apart my car. He found eleven individually packaged grams of cocaine and $800 in cash— or was it eight grams and $1,100? No matter—I was busted.

When we arrived at the West Hollywood Sheriff's Station, I thought the deputy was having a little too much fun rolling my broken finger around as he took my fingerprints—and I told him so. Then some very ugly words were passed. I would like to take this time to apologize to the deputy. I believe his name was Johnson. As a matter of fact, I would like to apologize to all the cops who had to deal with me during my drug years. After eleven years now with not so much as a traffic ticket, I would like to thank any cop who treated me well and tell any cop who treated me badly that I realize now, I had it coming!

Having made this act of contrition, I will admit that (while in the police station) I was treated in a way that seemed unfair—if not extraordinarily humorous. As I was sitting in the holding tank, the police were playing the news reports of my arrest over the intercom system. Ten or so other criminals were serenading me with their versions of "I Think I Love You" and "Come on, Get Happy." Unfortunately, the things they were singing that were making them happy were going to be a pain in my butt . . . literally. The news reports continued to play over the loudspeakers, and every fifteen minutes they kept getting worse. The first reports had me busted for *possession*. The next report said I was popped for possession—with intent to sell. Twenty minutes later? The news said I was going down for *possession with intent to sell and felony resisting arrest*. This last report resulted in cheers of respect from my fellow captives. It's nice to be respected by ones' peers, but I don't think it helped my case for freedom. Seems every time Deputy Johnson passed by the cells, he was greeted with taunts like "Ha-ha—Danny Partridge kicked your ass!" The news continued to grow. By the end of the night, things had escalated so much, I thought they would have me dead to rights for the Lindbergh Baby kidnapping.

I was lying down on my concrete slab, slowly digesting my powdered eggs and trying my best to figure out what I was going to do, when the jailer came by. He opened my cage and said a most remarkable thing: "Bonaduce, you can go." How could this be? I hadn't called anyone. The jailer was not done astounding me. He told me the *National Enquirer* was outside and had posted my bail. I looked at him square in the face and said, *"I am not leaving."* There were more hoots from my new friends. I would not become an object of national ridicule for at least another year, and I had some imaginary dignity to protect. I repeated, *"I am not going."* The jailer told me that this was fine with him, but if I didn't go now, I would be shipped by bus to "County" (a real jail) and I would have to stay there until my court date. I was scared. I had never been to a real jail, and the only bus I had ever been on had a nervous mother driving it. I mulled over my options—freedom and humiliation or incarceration and sodomy. I checked out.

On my way out the door, I was met by a small English gentleman. He had a microphone in his hand and he asked me if the charges were true. I, of course, said, "No comment." Then he said something that appealed to my sense of justice and fair play: "We'll give you $200." I talked for hours. I was out of the frying pan and into the fire. Not only did I still owe thousands of dollars, but I also had no cocaine to sell—even if I would have sold it. When I went to the club to explain myself and ask for more time, "T" had heard the news of my arrest. He didn't want to talk to me. He didn't even want to know me. Most of all, he didn't want my money! Who says the cops are never there when you need them?

I waited for what was next.

Chapter 11

FROM BAIL TO BROADCAST

As you can imagine, when the *National Enquirer* article came out a few days later, it was quite embarrassing. Over the years the *National Enquirer* has written some awful, disturbing, and even downright hateful things about me. Every word of it true. The tabloid headline read DANNY PARTRIDGE, DEAD BROKE AND STARVING. Believe me, it was *very* true. There was a silver lining. My phone actually started ringing. The first or at least the most important call came from Jonathon Brandmeier. Jonathon was a morning disc jockey in Chicago. The call came in at 6 A.M. L.A. time! Unlike the lifestyle I had adopted over the past months, I was actually sleeping that fateful morning. Nothing gives you time for "R & R" like being busted! I answered the phone while still half asleep.

My voice is deep and raspy under the best of conditions. I usually sound like Brenda Vaccaro. When startled from my bed that morning, I sounded more like Jack Klugman after his throat surgery. "Hello," I mumbled. The voice on the other end of the line was deep and deliberate. "Danny?" he asked. He was almost singing.

"*Daaaaaaaannnnnnnnyyyyy????*" he repeated. It was my turn to ask the questions. "*Who is this?*" That was the first thing to come to mind. He did not answer. He just kept talking in this annoying wacky disc jockey voice and then he hit me with a barrage of questions:

"Say it's not so . . . *little* Danny Partridge wouldn't take drugs!"

"What would Shirley Jones think?"

"Tell me it's all a lie. . . ."

My first inclination was to hang up on this asshole. I thought better of the situation. Besides, it wasn't as if I had a career left, so, I thought, why not help this guy with his?

I said to him in a heavily exaggerated sleepy voice, "Of course it's not true, I would never take drugs. . . . It's 6 A.M. and I'm tired. . . . Can you hold on for one second?" I then put the phone up to my nose and made the longest snorting sound anyone has ever heard. This was, of course, supposed to sound as if I were snorting a giant line. I put the phone back to my mouth and spoke as fast as I could and still be intelligible. "Hi—how's it going? . . . Nice to talk to you . . . What's new? . . . Can't talk long. . . . Gotta go. . . . Gotta paint the boat. . . . Wash the deck. . . . Scrub the dock. . . . Read *War and Peace*. . . . Nice to talk to you. . . . Bye." I hung up the phone. As I put down the receiver, I could hear him laughing hysterically. I thought to myself, "You still got it, kid." I went back to bed. The next day he called again. This time we did a real live interview. He was very funny.

I hate to admit it, but I thought about this a lot. If this book is going to be honest and as accurate as my flawed memory allows, I have to tell the truth, regardless of how bad it makes me look. I am where I am because of an unexpected door he opened for me. Johnny B. (as he likes to be called), well, he and I are friends and now on competing radio stations. By the way—to this day, I still think *he* is the *funniest* guy on the air.

On his third (or was it the fourth?) call, Johnny B. thought it might be funny to have a food drive for me. All this was in reaction to the *Enquirer* article—where they had me starving to death. I went along with the gag and for some reason or another I told him my favorite food was Spam. This was back in 1985! So, when Gary Coleman went on-line with the "Gary Coleman Telethon," in 1998 after he declared bankruptcy, I was one of the few people who did not look down on him. By the way, *not* looking down on Gary Coleman? It isn't as easy as it sounds.

I didn't talk to Johnny for a few days and had pretty much forgotten him when I got a call from his station manager. Apparently the phony food drive (which I had completely forgotten about) had taken on a life of its own. According to the station manager, thousands of cans of food, including hundreds of pounds of Spam, had been delivered to the station. There was even a statue of me carved completely out of the delicious meat product.

He wanted to know if I would come to Chicago and give it to a homeless shelter. This was my first entry into "involuntary" charity work. There would be a lot of that in the years to come, court appointed or not. The station (WLUP) flew me first class. I know a lot of people complain about airline food, but when you are not eating on a regular basis it can taste like goddamn gourmet cooking!

When I disembarked at O'Hare International, I could not believe my eyes. There were hundreds of people waiting for me! Some were even cheering words of encouragement! Girls were screaming "We love you, Danny!" There was even a guy with a giant poster of a skeleton with bright red hair. . . . It had a slogan that read STOP HUNGER BEFORE IT STOPS DANNY PARTRIDGE! It took airport security over an hour to get me out of there. Who the hell was this Johnny B.? I was whisked into a white stretch limousine, and we headed toward downtown Chicago. Johnny called me in the car. This was the first time I had ever used a cell phone, and I was very impressed. On that call, we did a lot of drug and has-been jokes—all at *my* expense. In fact, I realized I was making most of them! It also turned out that I had quite a knack for ridiculing myself, an ability that came in handy—because soon, I would be making a *living* at it. I knew why I was there and I was determined to earn my keep. Besides, in one fell swoop, I was being supplied with things I had not had in over a decade, things I so desperately craved: attention, fame, and all the VIP trappings. I had first-class plane tickets, limo rides, and, most of all, adoring fans. I still did not know who this Johnny B. guy was, but I knew I loved him.

The moment we got downtown, Johnny called me again. "Where the hell are you?" he asked. "How the hell should I know?" was my honest reply. Johnny told me to pull the car over at the next major intersection and give him my location. I did as I was told. Within seconds of saying my location over the airways, what seemed like thousands of people descended on the car. Cops actually showed up, helicopters buzzed, and local news crews appeared. What the hell was going on here? All these people were coming out to see me on a moment's notice just because some disc jockey said it would be funny? Who was this guy? How was it possible for anybody to be a *star* of this *magnitude* and no one I knew had ever *heard* of him?

I finally reached the radio station. There he was, the great Johnny B.! In truth? He was of average height, average weight, with average hair. Aside from being hysterically funny, there was nothing that you could say was exceptional about him. Needless to say, I was more than a little confused. In my world, stars looked like *stars*, they didn't look like real people. That is exactly what Johnny was— just some guy on the radio, and as it turned out, that is what made him famous.

Johnny B. and I fooled around on the air for the remainder of his show. We took dozens of calls. Remember, some fifteen years later, Dana Plato of *Diff'rent Strokes* would appear on Howard Stern's show under almost identical circumstances. She too was washed up, on drugs, in denial, and out of work. She also took calls that day. Unfortunately, her callers were so vicious that a lot of people believe it may have driven her to take her own life. On the other hand, Johnny B.'s callers could not have been nicer, and that still has an impact on me.

After the show, I was taken, again by limo, to the Ambassador East hotel. I had a suite. This beat the hell out of my boat. My luck continued. The station, or whoever was in charge of this shindig, had failed to put any kind of limit on my room service bill. I called down and ordered two of everything and I think five drinks. When the waiter arrived, I tipped rather generously—just by signing. Then he said the magic words. "If you would like anything else, don't hesitate to call—or if you would prefer to serve yourself, feel free to check out the minibar."

I searched the room like a kid at Christmas time. OK, where the hell did they hide it? Was this guy lying to me? There was no bar, mini or otherwise. How could he be so cruel? Seeing my dejected look, the waiter quickly realized I was really Jed Clampett masquerading as a celebrity. He reached into the envelope I was given at check-in and retrieved a small key I had not noticed. Then he made his move. With one twist of his wrist he opened the gates to paradise. Inside the disguise of an antique brown cabinet was candy and alcohol, caviar and alcohol, fancy cheese and, yup, more alcohol. Once I realized that all this was mine for the taking, and there were dirty movies on cable, I made a decision. I was going to be a DJ!!

Later Johnny called me. He wanted to go out on the town. I had already achieved three of my favorite states: full, drunk, and sedentary. I didn't want to go. Johnny made it clear that I really didn't have a choice in the matter. He would be there at eight. It was such a busy and amazing day, I hadn't noticed it was only noon. I passed out. Next thing I knew, the phone was ringing. Johnny was downstairs waiting for me. Somehow it had become eight o'clock. Time sure flies when your credit is good and your intentions are bad. I jumped in the shower and dressed as fast as I could. When I met Johnny in the lobby, my hair was still wet and slicked back. I could see the disappointment on his face! "You don't look like Danny Partridge at *all* with your hair like that. . . . Go dry it," he demanded.

I explained to him I had neglected to bring a hair dryer. He looked at me in just the same way the waiter did—and Johnny also took pity on me. He explained all I had to do was call the front desk and they would immediately send one up to me. Would wonders never cease? Alcohol and hair-care products delivered! This was really neat! When I finished grooming, we had an amazing dinner at the world-famous Pump Room.

On the wall were pictures of hundreds of movie stars, including David Cassidy and Shirley Jones. The house photographer came up to our table and asked if he could take my picture to place on the wall of fame. He was *serious*. I could not believe it. I had not taken a picture that did not involve numbers across my chest in quite some time. I wasn't a joke here. I wasn't a loser. I was in the Midwest. I was the guy from *The Partridge Family*. I was still famous.

I would have done anything to keep that feeling alive! After dinner, we hit the streets. Division Street, to be precise. On Division, there are forty bars on one block—and we stopped at *all* of them. The reaction to Johnny and I was astounding. They would see nothing like it again until the New Kids on the Block three years later! Even if Johnny and I had made it up to the bar to order, it would not have cost him anything. Johnny's money was no good in Chicago. It was a moot point. The moment our heads appeared at the door, every waitress in the place would come over with entire trays of drinks sent over by fans. I am talking about thirty, forty, drinks at a time! Johnny had been getting up at 2:30 A.M. for years—and he paced himself accordingly. I, on the other hand, consumed all that I could before *these* people came to their senses and took it back!

I drank blue drinks, red drinks, green drinks. I drank shots of tequila, whiskey, and vodka. Johnny did not try to slow me down at all. Half of my appeal was that I might self-destruct—and I knew it.

People also dropped by with drugs. Not one to disappoint my fans, I took them all. Johnny noticed someone handing me a bunch of blue pills. He asked, "What do those do?" I told him, "I have no idea," and immediately swallowed three of them. I am not clear on the rest of the night, but somehow—contrary to my best efforts—I lived. I not only lived, but I flourished. When the knock came on the door I was ready. Day 2 with Johnny B. It was 7 A.M. and I was on the air.

After all my shenanigans of the previous night, the one thing that scared Johnny most was the fact that I felt fine. I was told I had been banned from three bars on Division Street and from the Second City Comedy Club. This was a surprise to me. To this day I have *no recollection* of ever going to the Second City. I apologized for hours for my behavior. I was so naive. The three bars and the comedy club that 86'd me received thousands of dollars in free air time, just for banning me. I would not be so easily duped in the future. I would soon be charging good money to be a fuck-up. We finished his morning show, and once again I headed to my hotel. I stayed in a few nice hotels when I was a kid, so I knew to expect the usual: clean towels, free shampoo, and a freshly made bed.

By 1985, if I had an occasion to stay in a hotel, it usually meant I was in hiding. The only service I would be accustomed to at hotels like that? "They would leave the light on for me!" This minibar thing, on the other hand, was a new invention. I was elated to find out that they refilled these things. I went to work on it. Once again I passed out by noon. I needed to rest up for tonight anyway. Apparently Johnny had a band. I had no mental image of disc jockeys doing "appearances." So, I conjured up an image of a sad little man in a black satin jacket, handing out flop CDs in a 7-Eleven parking lot. Often this is still the case. Johnny was way more than one step up from this.

His band, Johnny and the Leisure Suits, was playing at a hockey rink that night. Hockey rink, roller rink, state fair—they were all the same to me. This was familiar ground. These are the types of places DJs play "on their way up" and TV stars play "on their way down." I know, because I had played them all until it became too sad to have me around. One of the first signs that my career was over was when I failed to outdraw the two-headed lamb fetus at the Bakersfield County Fair.

That night I arrived at the rink. It turns out, Johnny actually meant the Rink. We are talking about the one where the Chicago Black Hawks played! The one with 14,000 seats, and every one of them was filled with screaming fans. The closest I can come to describing it? Imagine a Jimmy Buffett concert—if only his fans liked him more.

I was a nervous wreck. Needless to say, I had *no* act and had no idea what to do. The band was brilliant. This was no garage band. This was a well-polished musical comedy act—complete with a brass section. A couple of days before I flew to Chicago, Johnny had sent me a tape of his band playing one of the Partridge Family's hit songs, "Doesn't Somebody Want to Be Wanted." I actually had to rack my brain! "How *did* that song go?" I had never sung it before—but I had heard it a lot! Too late. Johnny's voice boomed out over the PA system. *"Ladies and Gentlemen . . . Danny Partridge."* I was on! The moment I heard my name, or at least the name I had been called for so many years, I leapt for the stage. I guess it's like riding a bicycle, except there are 14,000 people watching to see if it's true you never forget.

In one sense I was lucky. There was *nothing* for me to forget. I didn't have to do anything before. I had been in front of crowds this large, but that was with the Partridge Family. My entire job description there was to smile, and that had taxed the limits of my talents. These people wanted something from me. I went on stage using (what I like to call) "the game show host entrance." You've seen it. It's the one where the guy in the sweater vest hops onstage while simultaneously waving and smiling with his piano-key teeth. The crowd roared its approval. The band started playing. I had no idea when to start singing! The crowd continued to applaud. Then it dawned on me. I was here because I was a screw-up! The only thing I could do to *hurt* my image with these people was to act professional. Am I the luckiest man in the world—or what?

I looked out at the audience and shrugged as if to say "What the hell am I doing here?" Thunderous applause. The band stopped playing. There was an uncomfortable silence, then more applause. Johnny walked over to me and asked me, "What's the matter? Don't you remember the words?" "Dude, I don't remember yesterday" was my reply. The crowd went wild. The band started playing again. I just stared at the guitarist hoping he would give me a signal as to when I should start singing. He did.

Oh, I wasn't Bob Dylan, but I thought it was pretty good for something off the cuff. When I got to the chorus (as if on cue), 14,000 people started pelting me with ice. I tried to keep going but I couldn't see—and a shower of ice to the face and head can really hurt. Out of sheer self-preservation I turned my back to the crowd. The band had already turned away and stopped playing. I was hurt and embarrassed. They had turned on me. I knew I had been a joke the whole time, but (at least) I thought I was part of the joke. I never got the feeling the joke was on me. I was about to walk off the stage, my head hung in shame, when I noticed something. It wasn't ice they were throwing. It was money . . . coins, in fact. We're talking thousands of them. Within seconds the stage was awash in money. A blanket of coins two inches deep. As soon as I realized I wasn't being booed off the stage, I noticed the cheers. They still loved me. It must have been many hundreds, probably even thousands of dollars. I turned back around toward the audience. If they were going to throw money, I was sure as hell going to earn it! Instead of singing the chorus, I started screaming it! The people there didn't know what to think. It would be quite some time before people heard of Sam Kinesin, but there I was.

The crowd had long ago gone silent. It was a very uncomfortable moment. The band started playing again. God bless them. I continued to rant. Johnny came up behind me and draped a coat over me (just like they do at the end of a James Brown concert) and helped me from the stage. This was a smart move. I was running out of things to yell and I think Johnny thought I had really lost my mind. As we neared the end of the stage I was forced to drop the mike. In response? I continued to scream. With Johnny's arms wrapped around me, we exited the stage. I was still howling. I yelled at the top of my lungs all the way down the halls and into the dressing room. I only stopped when I was positive I could no longer be heard. The rink was silent. Not a sound could be heard. I looked at Johnny and asked, "How did I do?"

The place was as quiet as the proverbial morgue and had much the same ambiance. It seemed like forever, but then it came . . . applause! Applause like you never heard before! Along with that, there was cheering and the thunder of stamping feet. Most important, there was laughter. Johnny grabbed me by the arm, and we ran back to the stage. Fourteen thousand people were now on their feet and cheering.

Thank you Chicago, and good night!

All of a sudden, I had an act. I was the really fucked-up guy and I was naturally good at it. The fucked-up guy is not a new character. Dean Martin did it and comedian Foster Brooks perfected it. The big difference here? I was one up on them. When Foster and Dean did it on Dean Martin's TV show, they were usually stone-cold sober. I, on the other hand, being the Method actor that I am, was usually fucked up . . . for real. Let me assure you, the truly sad overtones of this story do not escape me. Yes, I was playing the fool, but it certainly beat my "real life." In my real life, I was the fool—and nobody was paying me for it!

Over the years I have learned to find the silver lining in everything. I had to in order to survive. This is no exception. Aside from my meeting my wife and the birth of our daughter and son, this chance meeting with Johnny B. gave birth to the best thing that ever happened to me: my radio career. But my road to radioland was still to be paved with white lines.

Chapter 12

BACK STREET BOY

On a regular basis, I used to go to (what many would have called) the worst corner in the world. Nowadays, it is a very nice residential corner in Southern California. Palm trees, sunshine, California bungalows. Back in the '80s, it was certainly the worst and busiest corner in my world. It took what seemed like forever to find that corner, and the pleasure cost me thousands of dollars. Every day that I smoked crack, I promised myself it would be my last. That is why, unlike my friends, I never had a dealer. I always planned to quit.

By the mid-1980s, all my crack-head friends had a "man." It was very convenient to have a "man." With the type of "man" I am talking about, you make one phone call, and your crack was delivered in thirty minutes or less—or you got your life back, free. To me, having a dealer was admitting that I was going to buy more tomorrow. I always went to the streets.

The first time I wandered into this neighborhood was by accident. I was just driving along Venice Boulevard, took a right, and there I was. In the middle of a crack-head war zone. This neighborhood was approximately a two-square-mile area, near the corners of Venice Boulevard and La Brea. The moment I was "in the hood" (as they say), I decided to score.

The first time I decided to score, I was robbed. Usually, when I was robbed during a drug buy, it was "buy trickery" or sleight-of-hand. I have been robbed at gunpoint at least three times (that I can think of). It's probably more, if I really think about it. When buying crack, the moment of the purchase is tenuous at best. Kids, please, definitely do not try this at home! It's usually dark. The dealer is scared and always thinks that you are a cop. You are scared of the dealer. The drugs you are buying could be fake. He might think the money you are using could be counterfeit. Finally, you are both afraid that the other might start shooting.

The first time I was robbed in this "hood"—it should have been a lesson. On the street, a $20 piece of crack is approximately the size of a Tic-Tac. There are hundreds of things that look like a $20 piece of crack, including, as I found out that night, a goddamned Tic-Tac. Macadamia nuts, when crushed up into pieces, look and feel exactly like crack. You could have one in your hand all night and still think it was crack. You could even bite down on one and still not know. The texture is exactly the same. The only way to tell, after biting it, was to wait about three seconds. If your mouth failed to get numb and the taste did not make you sick to your stomach, it was bogus. By that time, the culprit had long since disappeared into the shadows. I spent a great deal of money on nuts back then. I have also bought hundreds of dollars in wax and once spent $50 buying a guy's pulled tooth. At least I *assume* it was his tooth—but who knows?

One night I was getting high with a friend. When the drugs ran out, his dealer would not answer his phone. I told him about the new neighborhood I had discovered. We got in the car and drove approximately twenty-five miles from his house in Woodland Hills. When we got to "that" neighborhood, my friend was scared—as well he should have been!

We were not afraid of the police, as they never ventured into these neighborhoods after dark. It had cost me a great deal of money in trial and error to find a corner with a "reliable" dealer. My friend could not wait, so he pulled the car over—two streets before I told him to! It looked to be as good a street as any in that neighborhood, assuming you are there to buy crack or get robbed. We got both.

Three young men came up to the car. One of them asked me how much I wanted to buy. I told him a "dub"— street slang for $20. Immediately after I made my purchase, the man was gone. Before I could pull my hand back into the car, one of the two remaining men grabbed at it. He told me to open my hand and give him the rock. I refused.

Then, before I could tell my friend to hit the gas, the guy was burning my hand with his cigarette. Still I refused to give up my precious drugs.

I could not take my eyes off the guy who was burning me with the cigarette. So without turning my head I screamed at my friend to floor it. The car didn't move. Instead, I heard my friend say (in an extraordinarily calm tone of voice), "Give me a second, Danny. I am being robbed over here."

With the number-2 man still trying viciously to pry my hand open (by any means possible), I turned to see what was happening to my friend. A third man was at his window. I have no idea where he came from, but he sure got there in a hurry. He was leaning in the driver's side window. He was pulling on my friend's gold chain with one hand while holding a straight razor at his throat with the other. My friend was acting so calm I almost started to laugh at it all. Before I could focus on my buddy's dilemma, I felt an extraordinary pain in my hand. I had almost forgotten about my immediate problem, but the pain helped to remind me quickly. One of the young men was holding my arm by the wrist while the other guy was biting me on the knuckles. They were coming out of the woodwork!

The pain was too much to bear, so I relented and opened my hand—and they were gone like jackals in the night. My friend was not as lucky. His gold chain would not break. The robber was pulling frantically, then he started to scream at my friend—almost as if it were his fault! He was yelling, "I am gonna cut your throat."

My friend was still amazingly calm. He told the guy if he would just relax, he would take the chain off! My friend reached up very slowly, making sure not to bump the hand with the razor, and he took his chain off. The man then took the chain and, with one hand, put it in his pocket. He was still holding the razor in his other hand, and it was still on my friend's throat. Then he reached back in the window and grabbed the keys out of the ignition. Of course we thought he was going to steal the car. He did not. He threw the keys down the street in one direction and ran in the other. At first we were too afraid to get out of the car. We were sure we would be killed. Soon a crowd started to gather. We knew if we sat there, we were going to be robbed again at any second. We got out of the car, ran down the street, and retrieved the keys. When we got back to the car, we noticed all four tires had been slashed. They took our keys and slashed our tires. These guys were definitely urban overachievers.

We drove out of that neighborhood on the rims.

My buddy said he would never go back there again, but it was he who stopped at the street, so it was his fault. Guess what? I was back the next night. After about a month of going to the same dealer without an incident, I was robbed again. This time I was not robbed of drugs or money but of a little piece of my soul that I can *never* get back.

That night I parked my car about a hundred yards away

from my dealer, as I always did. This was done so I could look around before I made a commitment to pull into the cul-de-sac of crack. I saw my dealer standing there. Everything looked and seemed as fine as a dealer alley can be. Just as I was about to pull forward, a man, seemingly in no hurry, walked out from the alley across the street from the dealer. He quietly walked across the street and shot my man point blank in the chest.

The life I had been leading should have passed in front of my eyes at this very moment, but it did not. I heard stories about people being shot. I have seen bodies in funeral homes and the results of a killing on the news. I have also seen thousands of shootings in movies and on television. In the movies, when a murder is committed, the guy who gets shot is usually knocked off his feet and the trigger man runs from the scene. With such great training as that, I thought I knew what to expect if it was ever to happen "in the real." None of this happened. When the dealer was shot, he did not move. He just stood there for a moment (which was just seconds but it seemed like hours), a surprised look on his face. He did not fly backward from the recoil. He simply fell forward toward the gunman. I expected to see a lot of blood. I did not. The man fell into a three-feet-wide patch of grass located in between the sidewalk and the curb. If there was blood, and I can only assume there was, the grass and ground quickly absorbed it.

The shooter also did not act as I expected. He looked around casually and strolled back into the alley from which he had come. I also did not act as I would? should? have expected. I did not run. I just sat in my car for a few minutes, waiting to see what would happen next. What did happen next was far more appalling then the shooting itself. . . .

Within seconds, people had surrounded the dead man's body. They were there so fast I could not even see where they were coming from. At first I thought they just wanted to see a dead body, as the kids did in the movie *Stand By Me*. This was not a movie and these people were quite accustomed to seeing dead bodies. They were there to pick his pockets of crack and cash. I drove away. Why did I say this incident cost me a piece of my soul? I do not mean that because of what I had just witnessed. It was because of what I did later. In a small and odd way, I had known the dead man. I only knew him by his street name, "Ghost." Within a week I was back on that same corner buying drugs. Although I never got a good look at his face, I am fairly certain I was now doing business with the man who shot "Ghost."

So, now you know—I lost all touch with "human" reality and "human" feelings because of drug addiction. Crack is not the breakfast of champions.

Chapter 13

CHECKING IN TO MOTEL HELL

Around this time, because of my events with "the boys in blue," I was also becoming the darling of the now-infamous "troubled sitcom kid" talk and tabloid shows. This was the mid-1980s and the first round of those topics. Every time one of my acting peers overdosed, got arrested, or died, I would become the national TV video poster boy and spokesman. Of course, the first to call was Geraldo. *Would I do the show?* Sure. *Was I clean?* ABSOLUTELY. *Could I be there in two days?* Book the flight. Hey, it was first-class travel, free food, an AFTRA payment to keep up my dental insurance, and a VIP suite in New York.

I answered so fast that I did not take into account some of the obstacles to my traveling. There were no problems with a ride, money, or a place to stay, as the show would take care of all that. My problem was "big." We are talking 160 pounds (to be exact). It was my dog, a Great Dane named Alexander Haig. Al was, by now, my only true friend. It really was nice, but it also was the reason why I had no one to watch him. Al had proven his loyalty, and I would return the favor. I would not put him in a kennel. I called the Geraldo people and told them of my dilemma. "No problem," they said. They could take care of everything.

They couldn't. They did find a hotel that would take a 160-pound dog. They even made arrangements with the airlines. There was one problem even the great Geraldo could not fix. Al was afraid to fly. When we got to the airport, Al went crazy. Even if they made those carrier things big enough for Al, I could not afford one. We just marched into the airport with Al on a leash. When Mr. Haig started to snap and growl and drool, everybody in the terminal got scared, including me. I had never seen him behave this way. Al was a brindle, which means he was orange with black stripes, and he looked like a tiger.

The airline refused to take him unless I had him sedated. I made arrangements to take a flight the next day and took Al to the twenty-four-hour pet care next to my house. I was surprised how easily they gave me drugs. They must have thought all dog lovers are just good folk.

They took Al in back, weighed him, and prescribed him tranquilizers according to his weight. They gave me eight blue pills, which they lovingly referred to as doggie downers. Their directions were simple. Once I arrived at the airport I was supposed to tilt the dog's head back and cram the pills down his throat. Then I was told to walk the dog around until the effects of the pills became apparent. I then was to stuff Al in the container the airline had already been kind enough to provide. No sweat. I went home and went to bed.

I woke up to the ringing of the phone. It was my sister. She had been out of town but was back. Thank God! I told her of my dog dilemma, and she said "no problem." She would watch Al while I was away.

When the limo arrived, I grabbed my backpack and jumped in. We got to the airport in plenty of time for me to have a drink—or five. When my margarita arrived, I reached into my jacket pocket so I could get out the extra dollar to pay for the double. As my hand came back out of my pocket, there was a little package I had completely forgotten about. "Oh, yeah," I thought. "Doggie downers." I feel you should now know that I did not make a rash decision. I thought very carefully and weighed my options before making my next move.

My thoughts? My dog weighs 160 pounds and I weigh 160 pounds. Oh yeah! This is safe. Always one to follow doctor's orders, I did exactly as the vet had said. I tilted my head back and crammed the pills down my throat. The only deviation from the prescription was the double margarita chaser I used to swallow them. I then proceeded to walk around the airport until the effects became apparent. They did. I hate to admit it, but once the K-9 Quaaludes kicked in, I had a pretty good buzz. I got on the plane and the flight to New York went off without a hitch. It was a smooth flight save the fact that I had an overwhelming desire to lick myself, but what guy hasn't thought about that at one time or another?

Of course I did a great job on the show, of course I was charming, and of course I was high. I was also broke, my dealer was dead, I was wishing I was—and then? I did the only thing that there was left to do—I became homeless and did more drugs. It was 1988, and by 1988 things had gotten very bad. To be honest, things had been bad for years. In 1988? They just got worse. Here is a partial list of some of the events of 1988.

I could no longer afford my $640 a month mortgage and was forced to sell the little home I had bought in the Valley. I tried disguising my desperation as motivation, but to no avail. Real estate guys can smell blood a mile away. I had about $40,000 in equity but ended up with only $23,000 after the sale. There were two reasons for the financial loss.

1. I really needed the money.
2. If you have ever seen the show *COPS*, you know the condition in which we "druggies" keep our homes.

It actually was a pretty good deal. Being a drug addict (with no money) might have been degrading, but being a drug addict with $23,000 was downright dangerous. I went on a world-class bender. After five days and nights without sleep or food, I finally passed out. When I woke up, I knew

I had to do something or I would run through the remaining $19,000 in no time. I did what I had always done. I relied on someone better than myself. This time it was my good buddy Scott Dahlgren. I asked him if he would take the money and keep it away from me. Not only was he kind enough to do this for me, but he also asked me to stay with his family. It was great. Scott, his mom, his dad, his sister, and me, the junkie. Just like the Cleavers.

The Dahlgren family never made me feel unwelcome, but I knew this could not go on forever. Scott had opened a checking account and essentially put me on an allowance. What Scott did not know was that I had forged his signature and gotten an ATM card. Just like when I was a kid and had a court-appointed accountant, I was stealing my own money. Unfortunately, this was one of the few skills I had. The ATM card would give me only $300 a day. Often I would get $300 at 11:59 P.M. and another $300 just two minutes later, at 12:01 A.M. Technically speaking, it was "the next day." At a rate of $300 a day, I would have spent about half of my remaining fortune by the time Scott got the first bank statement, thus tipping him off to my shenanigans.

I wasn't too worried. I knew that when he found out what I was up to, one of two things would happen. He would tell me to fuck off and throw the remaining money in my face. He could also do what only a best pal would do: try to save me and really buckle down on me. He chose the latter, forcing me to come up with ever more inventive

ways of stealing from myself. As hard as Scott and others
tried to help, you just cannot stop a guy bent on his own
destruction. Soon the money was gone. I truly believe that
Scott and his family would have let me stay indefinitely. I
still had my pride—but only because I didn't find a plausible way to sell it. I moved out.

Moving took me no time at all, since I had zero possessions. Long ago I had sold or traded away everything I had.
This included all the musical instruments I had from the
Partridge Family days. I moved into my new digs: a 1971
BMW 2002. Living outdoors was interesting and a little bit
frightening. Reading books and watching movies had prepared me. I knew there was a homeless underground, a hut-
less village of like-minded people banding together for the
common good.

Bullshit. Homeless people have the good sense to avoid
each other. If they ever do get together in a pack, the charm
quickly wears thin as everyone immediately starts stealing
from one another. Homelessness is the textbook definition
of "every man for himself." They say there is "honor among
thieves." Well, those thieves must be successful in their
trade! Trust me, when you are broke and on the streets,
whatever the other guy has in his shopping cart looks way
better than what you have in yours.

If I was going to live on the streets, I was going to live
on streets with which I was familiar. I moved to Hollywood. I found a spot to park behind Mann's Chinese Theatre. During the day I would spend a lot of time in front of

the theater. They say you cannot judge a person until you have walked in their shoes. If this is true, I may now be able to judge every celebrity who ever left a footprint in that most celebrated pathway at least seven times. I was still famous at Mann's. I would take pictures with the tourists and sign autographs. It was strange. I was the biggest star these people had ever met—and I was a big deal to them. When the day was over they would go back to their hotels and call home to say they had met me. They had no idea I would walk around the corner and go to sleep in my car.

Every now and again, in my post office box, a residual check from a TV show I had done would show up. On those nights I would sleep in a cheap motel. Such was the case when I moved into the Hollywood Hills Motel. The Hollywood Hills Motel is located on the corner of Sunset and LaBrea. It has since been abandoned and boarded up, but it is still standing there. I drive by it almost every day and it's a stark reminder of my former life.

In the worst ghettos in America, there are usually some hardworking people mixed in among the criminals. This was not the case with the Hollywood Hills Motel. It was 100 percent bad people. Pimps, whores, hustlers, and drug addicts. You would think I would have fit right in. I didn't. In a place that held every sin and sinner known to man, I was told to leave. The manager said that I was too much trouble.

I had found the motel through a girl I had simply met on the street. I was on a pay phone. Next to me, on the other phone, was a beautiful Japanese girl speaking in her native tongue. I wanted to meet her. When she hung up I asked her, in my "best" Japanese, "What time is it?" She answered in English. That was a sure sign I did not speak Japanese as well as I used to! We got to talking, and it turned out she was a drug addict too. I thought this young lady must have been rebelling against her traditional Japanese parents. My theory was proved correct when she told me (in a thick accent) that her name was Lilly. It was a name she could not even pronounce. Lilly took me to her room at the motel and we got high. Lilly and I lived in a bottom-floor room for about two weeks. I never asked Lilly her occupation, but it seemed dubious at best.

She would leave the room at around ten in the morning penniless. She would return around noon with two or three hundred dollars. Lilly also never ventured out after dark.

One day, on one of her sojourns, Lilly came back with a man and told me to leave the room. I could not believe it. Not only had I paid for the room, but also what is more important, I thought Lilly and I were a team. We were kind of a stoned and hygienically questionable Bonnie and Clyde. This was apparently not the case. When Lilly asked me to leave, I was shocked. A hooker was kicking me out! I refused to go. This was my room and I was staying. We started screaming at each other. The man or, more likely, customer, wanted no part of this, and ran. Lilly went to the motel manager's office to complain.

The manager called the room. She was a terrible

woman. She told me to get out. When I refused because I had paid for the room, she said that she didn't care. It was Lilly who had signed for the room. Still, I refused to budge. The manager then told me she had come into our room (at night, while we were sleeping) and had taken photos. They were pictures of me, with Lilly, surrounded by drug paraphernalia. If I did not vacate the premises, she would take them to the press. I did not believe her until Lilly came back with copies of the pictures. I also could not believe she thought I would be intimidated by this hollow threat. I had been trying to sell a story about me to the tabloids for years—without any interest. I stood my ground. Her next move was to tell me she was sending Gus over to forcibly extricate me. This threat got my attention. Gus was the security guy at the Hollywood Hills Motel, so he *had* to be tough. I had never seen him fight, but every junkie, hooker, pimp, and hustler who lived there did exactly as Gus demanded. Gus was fond of showing the scars he had earned from gunshots. Nobody fucked with Gus. I was scared.

I still did not want to leave "my" room, but I also did not see any reason to get hurt. I would simply outsmart the great Gus. I stripped off all my clothes as fast as I could, and I got into bed. The theory being a man, lying naked in his bed, surely must have possession of the room. Gus used his key and burst in the room like a freight train. I am sure he expected to find the room empty, as I would have left in a hurry in an attempt to save my life. I think he was a little shocked to find me lying in bed watching TV. His surprise did not last long.

He casually walked over to the nightstand, grabbed my keys, wallet, and clothes, and threw them out the door and into the parking lot. This turn of events was completely unexpected. These were all my worldly possessions, and I knew that the other guests of the hotel would descend on my goods like rats to fresh garbage.

Without thinking, I ran from the room and into the parking lot, completely naked. I grabbed my stuff and bundled it up under my arm and headed back to my room. The door was not only closed, but Gus was standing in my way. I marched right up to him. He stood there with his arms crossed in front of him, blocking my way, smirking. I thought about it. The fact of the matter was I am a black belt and a full-grown man. With Gus's arms crossed the way they were, there was no way he could stop me from hitting him, if, in fact, I took my shot. I did.

I dropped my bundle and tagged him right on the button. Gus was not impressed—and proceeded to kick my ass. At the Hollywood Hills Motel, anything could happen. When Danny Partridge got in a fistfight in the parking lot while naked, I think the bar was raised on weirdness. A record, I believe, that still stands today.

While stomping me Gus also said some nasty things that I personally thought were uncalled for. Like, "Get your honky ass out of here" and my favorite, "Don't let me see your face again, you Howdy Doody–lookin' motherfucker." I don't think Gus was a racist. I just think there are certain "mandatory words and phrases" that must be used when a big black guy is kicking a little white guy's ass. I made it to my car, crawled in, and drove off—if not into the sunset, at least onto Sunset. I went back to my old stomping grounds behind the Chinese theater and started licking my wounds. The next day I was happy to find that I was not hurt at all. As long as you don't count my *dignity*, and since I had none, I was unscathed.

I decided to go back to the motel and apologize. I wasn't really sorry (of course), but by now these were the only people I knew. Someone once said, "The hell you know is better than the hell you don't know." Back in those days, that is the only hell that would have me. When I pulled into the parking lot of my discontent, I was more nervous than ever. There was Gus and the horrible manager lady. They were standing there as if they were waiting for me. I pulled in and parked across three parking spots. There was plenty of parking, as most "guests" at the Hollywood Hills Motel did not own a car.

I stopped and opened the door. The plan was, if Gus ran over and tried to kill me, I could drive away before he got there. They just stood there and stared. I thought it might be a trick. I would get out of the car, walk over to them, and before I could say I was sorry, Gus would make sure that I was even sorrier.

I just sat there for a while. Eventually someone had to

make the first move. I realized it would have to be me. I left the car running, and I walked the last mile. When no one attacked, I made my appeal. I told them how sorry I was, and that it would never happen again. They continued to stare. At first I thought they might want more flowery prose. Then it dawned on me. I could only infer by their silence that they had never heard an apology before—and didn't know what to make of my strange and foreign ways. The next move was theirs. The horrible manager lady explained that Lilly had company but I could have the room upstairs. It was as if nothing had happened. I guess washed-up sitcom stars fought naked in their parking lot every night.

After a few days, Lilly and I were getting high together again. This time I understood the parameters of our friendship. If I had drugs we were pals. Often if Lilly thought I had drugs and wasn't sharing, she would offer sex. I turned down her invitations. Not because I was sure she was *riddled* with disease, but I had no interest. When you first start doing coke, half the fun is the sex. When you reach the point I had, sex is the last thing on your mind. Even if I could do it, and I was not confident I could, I would rather have had a root canal.

Soon things were back to abnormal. I would go and check my post office box in hopes of finding a check. Sometimes, if I did not get one, I would stay with Lilly if she "didn't have company." She had company quite often.

Since she never went out after five, if she had overnight company—and she thought he might leave before morning—Lilly would pay for my room. Lilly didn't like to be alone.

Life settled down to whatever it was going to be. I waited around, curious as to how all this would turn out. Soon I got a disturbing message. My mother was in town from Philly and she wanted to see me. I could not let this happen. I may have taken leave of most of my senses, but unfortunately, I was still aware of what I looked like. It was not, as they say, a very pretty sight.

I had lost fifty pounds and had dark circles under my eyes from sleep deprivation. Worst of all, I was covered with burn marks. I had become such a crack addict, I could no longer wait for the pipe to cool down before taking my next hit. I would pick up the pipe that had been heated to a lovely red glow by my blowtorch. When my fingers would hit the glass, I would hear a sickening sizzle. Then I would put it to my lips, inhaling the smoke of crack and burning flesh.

There was a knock at the door. It was my mother. I still do not know how she found me, but what could I do? I invited her in. We both tried to act normal. She sat on the corner of the stained mattress. We made small talk. She tried as hard as she could to not notice the stains on the carpet and walls. She also tried as hard as she could to speak to me as if I were still a person. I had sunk so low that I looked as if I belonged there. My mother, on the other hand, was out of place and I wanted her to go.

When she left, I immediately got my stash out to get high. There was another knock at the door. Crack-heads are always paranoid so I jumped up to hide the drugs again. It was Mom again. I was not happy to see her. Not only had my looks not improved, but also now she was interfering with my only pastime. I was rude. "What do you want?" I asked her, as insolent as in my youth—but with far less appeal. She looked at me for quite a while. Finally she said, "I want you to know that I love you." "I love you too" was the best I could do without inviting her back in. I tried to close the door. She stopped me. She looked at me again. With a real tear in her eye, she said, "Danny, it's very important that I tell you I love you—because you are going to die soon. Although it will break my heart, I want to know before your funeral that the last thing I ever said to you is that I love you." I pondered this for a moment. Finally I came up with an appropriate response. "Okey-dokey, Mom, I gotta go." That was the best comment I could muster. She left. I didn't think much of her loving, concerned Mom display. The Bonaduces have always been a dramatic group, and in my opinion Mom just wanted to make a great exit.

No sooner was the door closed than I went to retrieve my drugs again. Appropriately enough, they were in the medicine cabinet. Before I could open the door, I caught a glimpse of my reflection in the mirror. I was a skeleton. I had burn sores on my lips from the hot crack pipes. I smelled. I hate it when my mother is right. Sure enough, she was—I was dying. I was twenty-eight. I also decided it was time to go home—to Mom. I then checked out of Motel Hell.

Chapter 14

I'M GOING HOME TO MOTHER

THE ROAD TO PHILLY

Just because I had come to the conclusion that I was, in fact, dying did not necessarily mean that I would do anything about it. Looking back at the way I lived my life, it seems that dying was at the top of my list of priorities . . . but not like this.

In my "mental" movie, I die in a hail of gunfire or in a high-speed chase, not as an O.D. in a whorehouse. I had to make a move—and that is just what I would do. I would move to Philly. I would move in with my mother. If my mother was less than receptive to my homecoming, I would remind her of that time-honored tradition: "Save the life of a man and you must let a drug-crazed freak live in your basement." I told my mother of my plan, and, as always, she was there for me. She is no fair-weather family member. There was one problem. I had, by now, been taking drugs for so long that I had no idea what would happen to me when I stopped. Showing up at Mom's front door screaming in a drug daze "get these spiders off me" just did not seem like a cool thing to do. She was a woman rapidly approaching her golden years and that's just not fair.

I decided to take the train. The logic here was that if I flipped out, I would do it in front of total strangers and not my dear old Mom. I bought a ticket, boarded the train, and looked for my room. I had not been on a train since I was a kid, and I naturally assumed when you bought a ticket for a train ride that lasted five days, you got a room. Not so! Unless you ask for a sleeping car, you only get a seat. By the looks of me, no one was going to ask me if I wanted the more expensive accommodations. I couldn't afford it. If I remember clearly (often a problem for me), I rode the whole way in the bar car. Even without the benefit of drugs, I did not sleep for three days. When I finally passed out, I didn't move until Philly. When the conductor finally woke me, it was with very overenthusiastic shaking. You could see that some of my fellow travelers were surprised. Apparently there was some pretty heavy betting that I had passed away in Chicago. There was a rush to get off the train and I got caught up in it. Without a moment to think, I was standing on a street corner in the City of Brotherly Love. I was terrified. I had no idea how to act normal. I just stood there. There were no drugs to score, no one was chasing me, and there was no emergency of any kind. "What the hell do real people do with themselves?" I called my mother.

When we arrived at the house my mom shared with her sister Jacqueline, old memories stirred. This was where I would spend my summers when *The Partridge Family* was on hiatus. This was the same front yard where, in 1972, literally hundreds of kids would gather to see the great Danny Partridge. Now, in 1988? I think we all agreed that it would be best if no one saw me.

My hope, if I had one, was to live in my mother's basement like some great redheaded troll whom no one ever saw but was only rumored to exist. Children would dare each other to ring the doorbell but run before the hobbit answered. My mother and aunt had other plans. I was moved into a very nice guest room. It had a wonderful silk quilt on the bed that I remembered from childhood. This would not do. Being a freak in the basement was easy—and an appropriate torture.

Being in the guest room made me—well—a guest. Just as another famous Philly boy, Mr. Benjamin Franklin, so aptly put it two centuries before, "House guests and fish stink after three days."

Was I supposed to have some responsibility in the home? Did I have to pitch in or—God forbid—even get a job? Mom and Aunt Jack put my fears to rest. Nothing would be asked of me. Being Danny Partridge (and its aftermath) had given my mother and me a lifetime of wild experiences. It was clear that letting me out would only cause sorrow—it might, in fact, cost someone bail money. I could rest and do nothing to help. Of course, being the man I am, so "full of pride," that was totally fine with me.

New plan.

I would stay in my mother's house until she and my aunt became old and feeble. I secretly hoped they would hurry. I would then take care of them until they died. In appreciation for my undying devotion, they would leave me the house, which had long ago been paid off, and then I could finally become the troll that until that day came I could only dream of becoming. We got into a comfortable groove. My aunt was a tenured professor with twenty-five years in as the head of the journalism department at Temple University. My mother ran the Boeing Airline Corporation employee newspaper. I slept.

As a teacher and a writer, they had amassed an impressive library. As two working women, they were gone all day. I would wake at the crack of noon, open all the doors and windows so I could smoke in the house, and settle in to watch a little TV.

Standard schedule for me was: wake up, from 12 P.M. to 1 P.M. was *Bonanza*. From 1 P.M. to 2 P.M. it was *Magnum, P.I.* From 2 P.M. to 3 P.M. it was back-to-back *Barney Miller*. *Bonanza* and *Magnum* were mere time passers, but *Barney* was probably the best-written comedy since *The Dick Van Dyke Show*.

Around 3 P.M., I would move into the library. It had

cherry-wood shelves that went to the ceiling filled with hundreds of fine books. It had a large desk and a comfortable chair. All I needed was a smoking jacket (and of course permission to smoke in the house) and I would have never left that room. Around dinnertime, they would come home and tend to my care and feeding. It was perfect. We would discuss the day's events at length. My mom and aunt would speak of the mundane. Like the fact that my aunt had been forced to fail a Chinese exchange student for plagiarism. He would be sent back to China and suffer total and abject humiliation. My mother's conversation was no more exciting. She would say things like "Today a plane load of people fell from the sky—and I had to cover it."

I, on the other hand, would dazzle them with my wit. I would tell them that Hoss's real name is Eric, Higgins is really Magnum's boss Robin Masters—and that it turns out that Wojehowicz is impotent. I liked being boring. I had never tried it. It turns out I am quite good at it. For over six months things went along just like this.

Eventually I became brave enough to venture outside. I went on a tourism excursion, ended up at a shopping mall in King of Prussia—and again, my life was turned upside down, but this time (for a change), I didn't do it!

Chapter 15

THE EAGLE HAS LANDED

Philadelphia is, of course, full of history. I decided, after having been there six months, that I should at least see *some* of it. I went to the Liberty Bell, Independence Hall (where the Declaration of Independence was signed), and the home of one of my heroes, Benjamin Franklin, at 318 Market Street. After a few hours of History Channel–style culture, I noticed something unsettling. Bars now surround all the sights at the birthplace of this great country of ours. It was time to go.

I got back in my mom's car (which she was kind enough to keep filled with gas) and headed to more "remote" monuments. Valley Forge. It's the place where George Washington froze his balls off when he stopped the British from reaching New York. Valley Forge is only about twenty miles outside downtown Philly; it might as well be a world away. It was beautiful. Rolling hills as far as the eye can see.

I sat down in what I assumed to be the middle of the park and let it all sink in. I imagined the cannons firing, the freezing men, and the discomfort George must have felt from his improvised dentalwork. By the way, contrary to popular belief, George's teeth were not made of wood but were ill-fitting hand-carved dentures made from hippopotamus ivory by his dentist, John Greenwood. George was very vain and often had his dentist with him on the field of battle.

On the way home I noticed a large shopping mall and decided it would be safe to check it out. After all, what are the chances that I would run into a crack dealer in King of Prussia, Pennsylvania? Once in the mall, it was clear to me that even though Hollywood had forgotten me, Philly had not. This was the first time I had been among people (I was not related to) in several months, and it was strange. I was still a has-been, but I was a has-been from Philly, in Philly. "A local boy made good," if you will. The people at the mall were happy to see me.

Everyone thought they recognized me from *The Partridge Family* but they were wrong. *The Partridge Family* had ended some fourteen years earlier. Since then I had been, as they say, "rode hard and put away wet." At this point, any redhead could have been the guy from *The Partridge Family*. Fortunately, it was me.

These people were really recognizing me from the talk shows and the tabloids, but they didn't know that. At best they knew that I had had some kind of trouble but could not remember what it was. I appreciated that. I enjoyed the attention for a while, but soon the weirdness set in. It wasn't quite as strange as signing autographs in front of Mann's Chinese Theater and then sleeping in my car in their parking lot. The fact remained, I was signing autographs and living with my mother. Once again the shame washed over me, and once again it was time to go.

Before I could make my exit, a chubby man with red hair descended upon me. He said his name was Woody. He was loud and abrasive. I should have immediately known he was a disc jockey. He was one-half of the *Welch and Woody Show* on a radio station named Eagle 106. "Please," he asked, "would you like to be on my show tomorrow?" Before I could think better of it, I answered in the affirmative. On my way home, I started to regret my decision.

I had some very good experiences with disc jockeys in the past. Jonathon Brandmeier, Howard Stern, Mark and Brian, and a few others around the country who showed some real talent. This guy didn't look like he played in their league, and a "wacky" disc jockey can be hard to take. The next day I showed up at 7:30 and went on the air.

I put on the headphones. Before anyone spoke, Welch and Woody played "Come on, Get Happy." So far, it was like every radio show I had ever done. I hoped things would get better. They didn't. Welch and Woody asked me every question I had been asked by wacky disc jockeys for the last twenty years. I gave my stock answers and they laughed hysterically. Intermingled with their inane questions, my answers, and their laughter, they also played a litany of strategic sound effects. If the question had to do with sex, and they all did, in the middle of my answer they would play a loud "BOING" sound effect that was supposed to imply an erection.

When it was over, the Welch and Woody radio show amounted to a four-hour "dick joke" with a couple of good old fart sounds to top it off. Don't get me wrong. I am not judging Welch and Woody. Not only did I participate in what can only be decried as remedial radio, I was the head "dick."

As I was getting ready to leave, I half expected everyone involved to lower their heads in shame, too embarrassed to look at one another. It's just like that feeling you would get when you remember that you took your clothes off at the company Christmas party (or is that just me?). To my amazement, they continued to laugh hysterically. It was done with that disc jockey cackle one often hears on radio shows when you aren't funny enough to deserve it. They actually liked the crap they were putting out and thought of themselves as comic geniuses.

I was depressed. Philly is not only my hometown, but it is a major market and a fairly sophisticated city. How, I thought, was it possible that these high school pranksters were popular? There was a silver lining to this cloud. I decided right then and there that showbiz, in any form, was beneath me—and I would never venture outside (in public) again. Of course, I would also be the better for all this.

I walked down the hallway toward the exit smug in my superiority. I was then stopped by Dave Knoll, the prematurely gray general manager of the radio station. I really didn't want to talk. I just wanted to go home, take a shower, and wash the whole tawdry experience from my memory. Dave grabbed my arm and casually said, "You're pretty funny—want a job?" I was insulted. I was incensed. I was hired. I ran home to work on some high-quality dick jokes.

So now I am a disc jockey. I didn't know that much about the species, but there didn't seem to be all that much to learn. The best of them seemed to be just regular guys with a quick wit or a certain charm. The worst of them, like the two I just got hired to work with, seemed to prosper by doing things badly. Bad impressions. Bad jokes. Bad timing and extraordinarily bad manners. I could do that—or so I thought.

I didn't start on the air right away. First I was given a long speech by the station's program director, Charley Quinn. He explained the dos and don'ts of radio. He spoke to me for what seemed like hours. To be honest, I glazed over. It had been years since I had been employed, and I had completely forgotten how to pay attention to things that, well, bored me.

I may have been less than receptive but I was pleased to see his enthusiasm. The fact that this man obviously loved his work impressed me, just not enough to keep me awake.

I was just about to nod off when Charley said something that got my attention.

"In closing," he said mercifully, "just remember this one thing: If you're having fun, they're having fun." To this day, that is the best piece of advice I have ever been given about radio and I remember it daily. Thank you, Charley!

Charley was also kind enough to tell me the truth about my hiring. I would be given a six-month contract. I would be paid $15,000. The station would get a lot of publicity for hiring "bad-boy Danny Partridge." When the six months were over, I would be let go to "pursue other interests." In other words, I would be their "dancing bear." Other men might have been insulted by the lack of faith in their talents. Not me. I had not made $15,000 in showbiz in the last fourteen years. I was thrilled. I started as the third man on the *Welch and Woody Show*. On the very first morning, the phones rang off the hook.

When I arrived at 5 A.M., the show staff was already there. The producer had already been there for hours, cutting out the important parts of the newspaper, running videotape, and editing audio tape (which in those days was done with a razor blade and Scotch tape). It was laborious and time consuming.

An office building is an eerie place when it's totally empty. When the show started, I forgot about everything else. I was focused. The show started at 6 A.M. and the phones started right away. There were *Partridge Family* questions. There were Hollywood questions. Some people just wanted to chat. I could tell right away this was going to be great. Best of all, I was following my new boss's instructions to the letter. I was having fun. A lot of it.

The show moved along at a furious pace. There was a great deal of laughter. This time some of it was real! People would ask me questions, I would tell stories. We would take more phone calls. Every now and then, we would stop what we were doing only to play a song, take a break, or do what (in the radio business) is called a benchmark bit. A benchmark bit is a piece of alleged comedy or content that would happen on the same day at the same time, say, for example, Mondays at 7:20 A.M.

The logic was, if people enjoy the bit, they know they will hear it every Monday at 7:20 and tune in. Seven-twenty A.M. is the most important moment in radio because that is the time the most people are listening. Seven-twenty A.M. on Thursdays is the most important 7:20 of all. Thursdays are when the rating diaries are due. Ratings, in radio, are figured out from diaries listeners fill out and return to the ratings company. They cover an entire week and are supposed to be filled out every day. No one ever does that. They fill them out the day they are due, so if a radio station can get your attention at 7:20 on Thursday, it might get credit for the whole week.

So, if your favorite station is giving away $1,000,000, it's no accident that it is on Thursday morning at 7:20.

One of Welch and Woody's benchmarks was a thing

called "Leave It to Beaver" with Clint Eastwood as "The Beaver." As much as I hate to admit it, it was very funny. One of Woody's few talents was that he could do a dead-on Clint Eastwood. The only drawback with this was that Woody's Clint was so good, it made Woody think he could do other impressions. He was very mistaken. The only thing sadder than a truly bad impression is a ventriloquist who moves his lips.

The bit went like this. Welch and Woody would find a scene in the old *Leave It to Beaver* series in which a lot of people were talking to the Beav. Then they would edit out Jerry Mathers's voice and substitute Woody's "Clint" saying all sorts of provocative things. I guess you had to be there, but it seemed funny at the time.

When the show was over, I felt the best I had in years. It was incredible. Not only had the show been great, but, it was also obvious, it was the start of a whole new career for me.

At ten, we opened the door to the soundproof studio for the first time. I was shocked to see the offices teeming with people. As I walked down the hallway, people stopped to congratulate me or say "welcome aboard." The general sales manager stopped me to tell me some of the strategies he had for marketing me to the sponsors. That's when it hit me. I had not had a serious conversation with a grown man in a very long time.

I had stopped interacting with most people about a year prior. I had been holed up in my car or in a seedy motel room or in my mother's guest bedroom. As he talked, I started to feel faint. My face got hot, my ears burned, and I was actually getting dizzy. I could no longer hear what the man was saying but when his lips stopped moving, I said, "Sounds great," shook his hand, and made it to the door. Another milestone. I had spoken at length to half a dozen real people with real jobs, and not one of them knew I was crazy. I would keep this "fact" my little secret for as long as possible.

Once outside, I literally jumped for joy. I just got a last-minute reprieve from the Governor of Has-Beenville. My peers were the Brady bunch, Eddie Munster, and the kid from Lassie—and none of them ever got a second chance (whether they deserved one or not). I could not believe my good fortune.

I decided to go downtown and have a drink. As soon as I parked my car and started to look for an affable drinking establishment, the impact of my new career became apparent. Everyone knew me. The program director got his wish. Before I went on the air, my new job had been covered by all the local press, *AM Philadelphia,* and *PM Magazine.* The story had been picked up by the Associated Press, and I had done some national television interviews. I had been a disc jockey for just a little over four hours and I already was (arguably) one of America's best-known radio broadcasters. "Real-name" DJs make millions—and I made $15,000, but I didn't care. Fifteen thousand dollars was

This photo
was taken in
Birchrunville, PA,
in 1959.
I was one
year old.

My brother, Anthony, and myself playing piano at Pop's house in
Havertown, PA (1960).

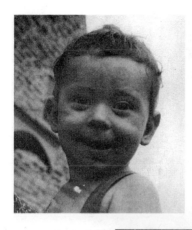

A visit to French Creek, PA, on a family picnic in 1961.

My first pair of cowboy boots. This photo was taken at Christmastime in Havertown, PA, at Pop's house (1961).

This picture was taken at an old schoolhouse that we had connected to our home in Birchrunville, PA (1961).

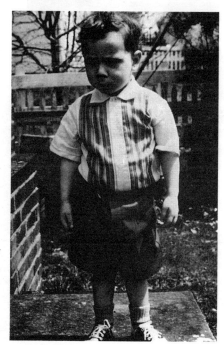

Outside of my house in Broomall, PA (1961).

This photo was taken when we first arrived in CA, late 1964.

On the set of the television version of *Cat Ballou* (1968 or 1969) right before television legend Jerry Paris flipped out at me.

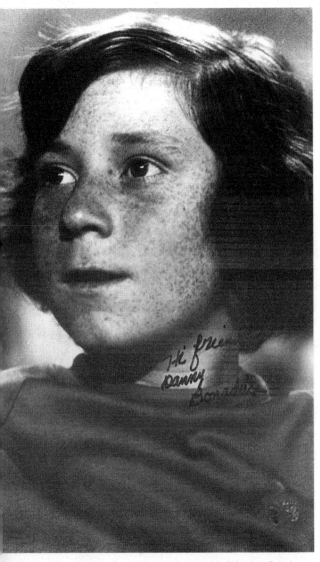

Hi friend
Danny
Bonaduce

Publicity photo (1970). I would sign thousands of these at home and then hand them out at appearances.

A road trip with the family to Solvang, CA (1969).

Me again in 1971 in Los Angeles.

Partridge Family episode at Marine Land Water Park (1971). In the background you can see the whale tank where I was caught performing unauthorized whale shows.

Me on the set of *The Partridge Family* in 1973.

Partridge Family publicity photo (1971 or 1972).
© ABC PHOTOGRAPHY ARCHIVES

At the Steel Pier in Atlantic City in 1973. I was appearing in my own show, singing songs from my 1973 album.

Los Angeles family party (1976) at my father's house. From left to right: Joe Bonaduce, me, and Celia Bonaduce.

Backstage at the Joan Rivers show, from left to right: Paul Petersen (*The Donna Reed Show*), some nurse lady, Todd Bridges (Willis on *Diff'rent Strokes*), and me as I raise a toast in honor of my first nationally televised urine test. I came back clean (1988 or 1989).

The first time Gretchen and I got married, November 4, 1990. In the center is Minister Don. We still owe him six bucks.

The third time I married Gretchen, on May 4, 1991, in Phoenix, Arizona.

Backstage at *Jerry Springer* (1994). Gretchen and I wait to hear about my "Random Acts of Kindness."

Donny Osmond and I square off in Chicago in 1994 at the China Club for charity. He makes the lamest tough guy face I ever saw.

The first episode of my daytime talk show *Danny!* with semi–*Partridge Family* reunion (1995). From left to right, Ricky Segall (Little Ricky), Jeremy Gelbwaks (first Chris), Suzanne Crough (Tracy), Brian Forster (second Chris), me, Gretchen, Dave Madden (Reuben Kincaid).

Pretending to interview one of my idols, Evander Holyfield, for my New York radio show on Big 105 (1998).

Behind the scenes of *C'Mon Get Happy*, the *Partridge Family* movie. From left to right: Psychic Gary Spivey, me, Shawn Pyfrom (the kid who played me), and my daughter, Isabella, who had a crush on the kid who played me. Everything about this picture is wrong (1999).

At home in Los Angeles with my wife and daughter. One of the tabloids was doing a story on how well I was doing. This photo was taken from that shoot (1999).

Dick Clark and me at the 2001 National Association of Professional Television Executives convention being interviewed about our new show by Pat O'Brien from *Access Hollywood*.

Not only did I make it back to Hollywood, but I'm 40 feet tall and naked. (Billboard in LA with my radio partner, Jamie White) (2000).

Promotional shot of my new TV show, *The Other Half*, left to right: Mario Lopez, me, Dick Clark, and Dr. Jan Adams (2001).

© KEVIN FOLEY-NBC

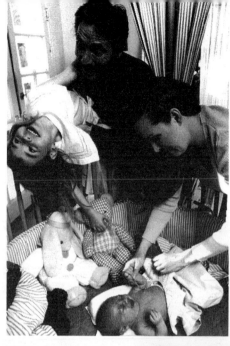

A family shot of my daughter, Isabella, me, Dante, and Gretchen, which was taken for The Learning Channel's *A Baby Story* (2001).

My son, Count Dante, and me. This picture was also taken for The Learning Channel's *A Baby Story* (2001).

more than I had made in years, but far more important? It was the fact that I was once again "a celebrity."

The press did make a big deal about my drug busts. At first, I was embarrassed—but soon I found out that no one really cared. It was the '80s. Everyone had a drug problem, and the few who didn't? They knew and cared about someone who did. People patted me on the back and said things like "Congratulations on turning your life around." How could life possibly be this good? I certainly knew I didn't deserve it, but who am I to question the gods? I ducked into a quiet little bar and ordered a shot. The bartender recognized me (which was nice). Then he said my drinks were on the house, which was even nicer—as I had not yet been paid.

Soon the word spread that I was at the bar. All sorts of people came in to meet me and buy me drinks. By two in the afternoon, I was totally lit. There were at least fifty people in the place and I was holding court. These people may have been happy to meet me, but I was far more pleased to meet them. They had changed my life. Yesterday, all I wanted was to grow old and die as the freak in the basement. Today I was again a *star*. If you happen to be one of those wonderful people who were in that bar on that fateful day, thank you from the bottom of my heart.

Fame is a lot sweeter the second time around. When I got the job on *The Partridge Family*, I didn't know what to expect, and then I got famous—and I thought it was my right. I didn't know it was my *privilege*, and I most certainly did not know how much I would miss it when it was gone.

I may not have had a job in years, but I still knew how showbiz worked. One of the truest things ever offered about fame is "always leave them wanting more." I did not want to overstay my welcome. These people thought of me as a local guy who went to Hollywood, made it big, and decided to come back to his roots.

I had no desire to inform them of the ugly truth. I had indeed gone to Hollywood, made it big, been given the chance of a lifetime—and screwed it all up. Philly is a wonderful town, and I would go back there in a second. Unfortunately, at the time, my sole motivation for going there was that no one else would have me.

I made a grand exit, walked around the corner, jumped in my mom's car, and headed for home. I didn't make it fifty feet when I got pulled over. I was drunk. Fear, as I have learned on several occasions, will sober a body up in a big hurry. The fact that the lights had scared me sober is not to say I didn't look insane. I started to sweat and hyperventilate. My fingers were wrapped around the steering wheel so tight that I could not let it go.

My heart raced as the cop walked up to my window. It seemed at the time that his walk from his cruiser to my car took hours. I had time to think about the ramifications. I had just been on TV the night before as "the comeback kid," and now I was going to be carted off to jail as a drunk. I would be a national laughingstock for the second time.

Ten minutes earlier I thought I had proved author F. Scott Fitzgerald wrong. There were, I thought, "second acts" in American lives. Now it was turning out the bastard was right. I couldn't help thinking that the "F" in "F. Scott" stood for "fucker."

Most men, when faced with this kind of calamity, wonder what their families will say. My first thought was then—the same first thought I would have on subsequent arrests—*"What the hell is Howard Stern going to say?"* When the officer finally made his way to my window, he did not ask for my license and registration. He took one look at me and asked, "Are you all right, sir?" I was not. Here we go again! I had been given the highly coveted second chance and I was going to piss it away. All I could think of was how stupid I was and that I deserved the humiliation that was most certainly forthcoming. I started to feel sorry for myself. I came to the conclusion that when I went to jail this time, it was going to be far worse than last time. I already had been given one pot of gold and pissed it away, in the process learning all the evil that excess can bring. Now I had been given pot number two, but instead of learning from my mistakes, I was doing the absolute worst thing you can do. I was *repeating* them.

Sweat started to drip out from between my hands and the steering wheel that I could not let go of. The officer then asked the big question: "Sir, have you been drinking today?" I answered so fast, I don't think I even let him finish his question. "No," I said without looking at him.

I could have come up with something better than that,
but I was terrified. I could have gone with the standard
"Yes, sir! Just a couple of beers at lunch!" or I could have
tried to be cute and gone with "No, why? Do you want to
go have a few?" I could have also said, "Yes, I just left
church and had some sacramental wine!" For Christ's sake,
with all of those potential stories, I had to come out with a
"Noooooo, Officer!"

I have found that cops are very philosophical when it
comes to criminals. They know that without us they themselves would be out of work, but they hate liars. He didn't
bother to ask me to breathe into his hand or touch my
nose. It was more than obvious that I was wasted. He told
me to get out of the car. We had a very short conversation
and then he put the cuffs on. The next words I would hear
would become very, very familiar.

"Sir, I am placing you under arrest for driving a vehicle
under the influence of alcohol."

Before he could read me my Miranda rights, a carful of
kids came by. They had seen what was going on and drove
around the block. They cheered my name and yelled something to the effect of "Hey, Partridge, at it again??" The
officer took another look at me and put two and two
together. "Jesus Christ, you're the kid from *The Partridge
Family*! What the fuck is wrong with you?" I started to cry.
I told him how I was celebrating the "birth of my new
career" and things had just "gotten out of hand." He had

seen some of the news about me. He said, "Boy, you sure don't need this." Then he told me to be careful, took off the cuffs, got in his car, and drove away.

It was over. I was free. I still had my new job. My mother was not once again embarrassed, and best of all? Howard would not be calling me an asshole tomorrow morning. I counted my blessings and swore to God I would never drink again. Take note: Thank you, Officer, whoever you are!

When I got home I tried to take a nap but was far too excited by my new lease on life to sleep. I decided to have a drink. I would like to take this opportunity to personally apologize to God. I know it was you who saved me. On the other hand, it was you who made me an asshole. I know that some of you reading this must be having a hard time with the fact that one man can be given so many chances and continue to be so stupid. Please keep reading. I promise you, I get a lot—as Archie Bunker would say—"stupider."

For the next several years, it is safe to say I put the "more" in moron.

It was about 5 P.M., and I started to get ready for the next day's show. I went to the store (on foot) and bought every magazine I could find that was geared to the radio station's demographics. I bought *Mademoiselle*, *Redbook*, and *Cosmopolitan*. I was surprised to find out most of those magazines are pure smut. There were articles like "How to Cheat on Your Husband," "How to Date a Married Man," and my favorite, "How to Have a 20-Minute Orgasm."

Please, tell me that those magazines are full of crap! If you add up all the orgasms my wife has had over the last ten years, it comes out to about six minutes—and that is if you count the fake ones (and I do). On the other hand? It was very informative. It was like reading the other team's playbook. I read and read and read. Then I watched the news. At 2 A.M., I went down to the offices of the *Philadelphia Inquirer* and got the paper hot off the presses. I was ready.

When I got to work, I was scared—but also very excited. I really felt I could do this job. Even without *The Partridge Family* thing that was obviously my "in," I felt I could actually be a fun and informative DJ. So, I'm sure you can imagine my astonishment when I found out I had been fired.

At first I thought they had found out about the drunk-driving thing—but they hadn't. I was fired for an equally good reason. It seems the morning show at Eagle 106 in Philadelphia, the #5 market in the country, was called the *Welch and Woody Show*. Not the *Welch and Woody and Danny Show*. These guys had worked too hard to let some Danny-come-lately come in and steal their thunder.

Just like when I got the job on *The Partridge Family*, I did not know that I was starting at the top. You don't begin your career as a DJ in Philly. If everything goes your way, you might be lucky enough to end it there. You start your career in Topeka doing overnights. A thousand bad jokes and a million wacky sound effects later, if you are really good, really lucky, or really filthy, then and only then do you get to go to a market the size of Philly.

I was told I could stay on the show but that I would only read the news from then on. At a quarter after the hour, I read the news for the first time. At twenty after the hour I was fired for the second time. It seems that on a top-40 station you don't really do the news, you imply it. The news had to be done in exactly ninety seconds. I can complete very few tasks in ninety seconds, none of them well.

I was moved to weather. FIRED. Those of you in Southern California may find this hard to believe, but most of the country takes the weather very seriously. Day two of my new career, and I had already been fired three times. This might have frightened mortal men, but not me. I had a contract. This went on for a couple of days. They tried everything to keep me on the show while simultaneously keeping me off of it. I tried traffic, entertainment, gossip . . . everything. No good. I started to get concerned. If I was bad at whatever it was they wanted me to do, they fired me. If I was good? They still fired me!

We had a meeting with the station's GM. He had a solution. He gave me my own show.

Chapter 16

NOW I'M GETTING PAID TO STAY UP ALL NIGHT

They gave me my own shift, 10 P.M. to 2 A.M. To say it went badly is an understatement of gigantic proportions. If James Cameron is looking for his next disaster movie idea, he might want to listen to tapes of my first few years on the air. I will try to spare you some of the more mundane moments, but anything as godawful as my first shift deserves some explanation.

I had been a guest on plenty of radio shows (and did a pretty good job), but now there was no one to talk to. I had no idea how to start a conversation with myself. Again I got just what I wanted. Again I had no idea what to do with it. I knew all the big-name radio jocks had one thing in common. They were controversial. The show was about to start and still I had no clue what I was to do. I decided to do what every jock before had done to introduce me. I played *The Partridge Family*'s "Come on, Get Happy" theme song. Before I went on the air, I made a promise to myself. I would not rely on my *Partridge Family* past. I also told myself that I would not even take any calls on the subject. The show hadn't even started and I was already playing the friggin' song and just begging for someone to call about Susan Dey's eating habits. The theme song ended. The "On the Air" light came on—and I spoke.

"Good evening, ladies and gentlemen . . . I'm Danny Bonaduce and welcome to the show. Give me a call. No controversy too big—and none too small."

Thank God the phones rang or I might have spent my entire career rhyming. My first caller said he had a controversial subject to discuss. Something that had been "bothering him for years." "Thank God," I thought. I spent the next four hours discussing that, if the Professor was smart enough to make walkie-talkies out of coconuts, why couldn't he patch up the SS *Minnow*?

Can you believe I have been allowed to continue in this profession?

The next day I was called into the program director's office. I was sure he was mad at me for last night's show content, or at least the lack of it. I was almost right. He was not mad at me because of what I talked about. He was mad at me because I talked at all.

I did not know it at the time, but top-40 stations become jukeboxes after 10 A.M. I was supposed to play somewhere between eleven to fourteen songs an hour. The only talking I was supposed to do was to introduce songs.

When I got in the door of the programming director's office, he slammed it closed and immediately started to scream at me.

The conversation went like this:

PD (SCREAMING):   What's your name?
ME (perplexed):   What?
PD (still screaming):   What's your fucking name?
ME: Danny.
PD: What's your last name?
ME: Bonaduce.
PD: Good. Now, who sings "Please Don't Go Girl"?
ME: What???
PD (screaming again):   Who sings "Please Don't Go Girl"??
ME: I have no idea.
PD (red-faced):   The New Kids on the fucking Block, that's who.
ME (scared):   Right. . . .
PD: How can you not know this? The New Kids on the Block are our goddamned bread and butter.
ME (depressed to realize somehow that New Kids equaled sustenance):   Okay.
PD: Now . . . say it!

ME:	What?
PD (screaming):	I'm Danny Bonaduce, and here are the New Kids on the Block. . . .
ME (freaking out):	I'm Danny Bonaduce, and here are the New Kids on the Block. . . .
PD:	Good. That's your fucking job: I'm Danny Bonaduce and here are the New Kids on the Block. If I ever hear another word out of you *besides* that, you're fired. . . .

I left the office. It had been quite some time since someone yelled at me as if I were a child, and I did not care for it. That night I sought my revenge in a novel way. I did exactly as I was told. I'm sure most of you saw this coming—from at least a mile away.

When my shift started, I played *The Partridge Family* theme song. When it was over, I said, "Hi, I'm Danny Bonaduce and here are the New Kids on the Block," then I played "Please Don't Go Girl." When the song was over, I played "Paradise City" by Guns N' Roses. To introduce the song I said, "Hi, I'm Danny Bonaduce . . . and here are the New Kids on the Block." You guessed it. No matter what I played, or what breaking news came in, all I said was

"Hi . . . I'm Danny Bonaduce, and here are the New Kids on the Block." When listeners would call up and ask me, "What the hell are you doing?" all I would say was "Hi, I'm Danny Bonaduce . . . and here are the New Kids on the Block."

When I look back on that night's events, I actually feel a small twinge of regret. Not that I did the whole "Hi, I'm . . ." thing, but that my act of revenge was so obvious. I was surprised. When I arrived the next day, I found I was not in *any* trouble. The boss had not listened to the show—and nobody told him what I had done.

For the next couple of weeks, I played all the music I was instructed to but soon I found it impossible not to talk. The "greats" of radio did not play songs like "Bust a Move" by Young MC; they talked. They talked about things that interested them and moved the listeners in some way. I had to try. Soon I was only playing nine songs, then eight, then seven, and so on. Every time I did not play a song, I tried to make up for it with a topic I felt strongly about. I tried my best to make a statement.

When the first ratings came in, the statement was clear. I sucked. I was in dead last place. I was beaten by the Christian radio station, which *was* really saying something. No one I knew thought Philadelphia even *had* a Christian station. I was scared. I had very little time left on my contract, and it would only have cost the station a few grand to let me go. The main reason they did not let me go was that the press kept rolling in. A prime example of this was when

Eagle 106 and our main competitor were fighting for the affections of Paula Abdul. She could not decide which station's event she would play. That's when my boss whipped out copies of both *People* and *US*. He opened the magazines to full-page color photos of me wearing an Eagle 106 T-shirt. Charlie (the programming director) told Paula she should play our show because "we are God's chosen radio station."

Eventually she did decide to play our "event." It was at some mall over the state line in New Jersey. At first, I felt stupid, but then I heard I was also going to be making an appearance at "God's chosen" mall. They hated me on the air, but I was getting the station press and now a national name. I was a walking logo and now a celebrity calling card.

Logo or not, when my contract was up, I was sure I— and it—would not be renewed. I went to have a drink at a hotel that was right across the street from our radio station and most of the other stations in Philly. While at the bar (getting a head start on licking the wounds I knew were imminent), a man came over and introduced himself. He was the general manager of Q-102, our main competition in the local top-40 format stations. Even though I was sure I would be unemployed tomorrow, at the time of that conversation, I still worked for Eagle 106. That fact made me somewhat uncomfortable talking to him.

Actually, I wasn't sure how to feel. He told me he had four kids, one age twelve, one fifteen, one seventeen, and one who was nineteen—and the only thing they agreed on?

It was how much they hated my show. Now I knew how to feel. I hated him. It turned out he was just taking a very long walk to compliment me. He said I talked too much and that the kids want to hear the hits. "You," he said, "belong in mornings." With that he walked away. As soon as he left, my boss walked up to the bar. He was not happy to see us chatting. He wanted to know why I was "talking to the enemy." Of course, I left out the part about his kids hating me. Then I told him all about the guy's thoughts: "I belong on a morning air program."

The next day I was once again called into the boss's office. I assumed that I was about to be given my walking papers. I wasn't mad, as he (long ago) told me that this day would come, and I really was bad at my job. Luckily I had not moved out of my mom's house yet. I waited for the boom to come down on me. It was more "boon" than "boom." Not only did he say I could keep my job, but he offered me a small raise: 400 percent to be exact. He gave me $75,000 a year, which was three times what I had made from the *Partridge Family*.

Chapter 17

I'M BACK AND I AM BAD

So now I'm back and I'm bad. Sure! There are probably some people who think becoming a local late-night disc jockey (after having once been the star of a number-one TV show) is not the same thing as making it back.

I disagree. I was now a grown-up with a real profession. I was never an actor—and I never claimed to be one. DeNiro is an actor; I was a showoff. If you don't think there is a big difference between a child sitcom performer and a real actor, you are mistaken. Take Gary Coleman, for example. One of the most beloved child performers of our day. A showoff, nothing more. Just because we all loved Gary does not make him an actor.

If you disagree with me, try this little test.

Imagine, if you will, Gary Coleman in your favorite scene from *Taxi Driver*.

"You talking to me? You talking to me? There's nobody

else here. You must be talking to me. What you talkin'
about, Willis?" Do you get my point?

As for being bad? I had that part down. My new job also
gave me something I had never had before: a goal (unless
you count trying to see how high I can get without dying as
being "goal-oriented"). In spite of the gigantic raise in pay,
my show was no more popular. If the man in the bar was to
be believed, I belonged on the air in the morning. Now,
that was something to aspire to. Until my show improved
(or became popular) my plan was to keep my head down
and go unnoticed. This was not to be. Now that I was getting real money, people were watching me—and I mean
every move I made.

A small incident happened early in my career, but it is
one of those things that has followed me to every station I
worked in over the past twelve years. Everyone has one of
those stories. Great stories like "What! You actually got
your necktie caught in the copy machine?" Then there are
the oh-no situations, like when you meet the new and very
hot girl in the office—and you decide to let your boss know
"you want to boff the new hottie who just started": Then
you find out that "hottie" is the daughter of your boss. Let's
face it—we all have a little "legend" that follows us around.

This is mine. Actually, it doesn't just follow me—it pre-
cedes me!

I was working the 10 P.M. to 2 A.M. shift. All I really did
was play records and answer the phones, basically cruising
for girls. The girls on those request lines actually treated me

as if I were a rock star. Even though I counted my blessings nightly, my fragile ego got in the way.

My overinflated sense of self was not helped at all by the fact that lots of people, not just the female callers, were starting to treat me like a rock star. A lot of businesses, especially nightclubs, like to have a radio station broadcast from their venue. Normally, a live broadcast from a nightclub was hosted by what is known as "the street team." The street team is usually a bunch of high school and college students wearing the radio station's T-shirts and handing out cassettes.

Now *I* was in demand. A real DJ and a TV star all in one. Nightclub owners loved it. Not only did the station make a lot of money for my appearances, but also I was paid $300 an hour with a two-hour minimum. Everybody was happy. The station was happy. The clubs were happy. The patrons were happy. And I was very, very happy.

I may have been a shitty disc jockey, but in my soul I was an entertainer. I did not just hand out cassettes. I put on a floor show. I sang. I danced. I told jokes. I even did some of the magic tricks my grandfather had taught me. I was a hit and I reveled in my newfound celebrity. One night, after one of my bar appearances, I was heading back to the radio station at about four in the morning. I had decided to sleep at the station that night because there was a mandatory meeting at 10 A.M.

In my attempt to win "employee of the month," I was

going to sleep in the conference room. I figured that before the meeting started, somebody would wake me up and I would be the first one there. When I got back to the station and pulled in the parking lot, there was a girl waiting outside the main door. It was freezing and she wasn't wearing very much. She told me she was my biggest fan and had been waiting all night—in the cold—just to meet me. I was flattered and invited her up for a tour of the station. When we got to the conference room, she noticed the little campsite I had made in the corner.

We made use of it.

The next thing I know, the young lady and I are waking up in a room full of people. The meeting had started. The poor thing let out a scream, grabbed the blankets and her belongings, and ran out of the room, leaving me naked on the floor. The damage had been done. So why add to my embarrassment by running out after her? I merely got up, casually walked over to the conference room table, and leisurely took my seat. Of course, I did all this as naked as the day I was born. Then I looked up at the boss and said, "If I knew all your meetings were this exciting, I wouldn't have missed any."

This little episode followed me for years. Every time I would go to work at a new radio station, when we would get to the conference room, there would inevitably be a little bed of some kind with my name on it. After the first couple of times I started to expect it. I always acted shocked. It's like finding out about your surprise birthday party in advance. You don't want to blow the fun for all the people who worked so hard on it.

The next day I was sure that I would be in a great deal of trouble. Nothing could have been further from the truth. I was a *hero*. Disc jockeys high-fived me in the hallways. I can think of no other profession in the world where behavior like this not only goes unpunished but can really jump-start a career.

At least my wild ways did not involve drugs or excessive alcohol . . . yet. They didn't have to wait long. More than anything, I just wanted a normal life. That was harder to get than I realized. I was making $75,000 a year in salary plus another 50K or 60K in appearance money. Sometimes I was making $2,000 a week, paid all in twenties. It was time to open a bank account. No easy task.

They wanted a lot of things I didn't have. Like a driver's license. I had not been in possession of any kind of identification in ten years. They also wanted a previous address. I wrote down "the intersection of Hollywood and Highland, behind the Dumpster." They did not find me amusing. I continued to give my mother my checks and throw the ever-growing wad of twenties in my sock drawer. Things were going along great and I thought I was truly happy for the first time in years.

Then I took a wrong turn. Literally. I was coming home from an appearance at one of the many nightclubs on the Delaware River. Philadelphia is a wonderful town, but for some reason, our Founding Fathers decided to surround the place with housing projects. To this day, they are some of the worst I've seen, and I saw them up close and personal.

Within (what seemed like) seconds of my wrong turn, I was in the middle of no man's land. I was lost. I was at a stop sign when I saw a group of young men standing on a street corner. It was a scary corner—and they were even scarier men! I had spent so much time in neighborhoods like this, I never gave it a second thought. I rolled down my window to ask directions. Before I said one word, a man had already descended on my car.

He leaned in my window and asked, "How much ya want?" He literally had my life in his hand. And I gave it to him. I didn't think about my new wonderful life for a second. I bought all the crack he had. The second I made the purchase, I hit the gas. I was frantic. I couldn't believe I had done it. I was lost, in a terrible neighborhood, and it looked very much like I was about to throw my life away again. When I got back to a neighborhood I recognized, I rolled up my window. I felt sick. I was almost crying and I was saying out loud, "Just throw the stuff out the window, don't do this to yourself again."

For all my dramatics, I didn't even slow down. I drove the car directly to the first 7-Eleven that I saw and purchased a roll of tin foil to make a pipe. I took my first hit right there in the parking lot. Even though I still had several hundred dollars on me, I went to the seediest motel I could find. (It's too difficult to disable the smoke detectors at a decent hotel.) Besides, I needed to save my cash. As much as I didn't want to, I knew I would be going back.

Chapter 18

BACK ON CRACK

Once again my life was spinning out of control.

Just as when I sold my home, I was the worst thing there is to be—a drug addict with access to money. Unlike the time I had sold my home, this time it did not look as if the money was going to run out. This time I would have to die. That probability no longer appealed to me.

They did not want too much from me at work. I would play a few songs and, every so often, let the listeners know what time it was. I could also hide my ever-increasing erratic behavior from the people at work. It was easy—I barely saw any of them.

Because the cocaine would numb my mouth, I was no longer able to speak clearly on the radio. I was a better junkie than I was a disc jockey. I knew I had to figure out a way to keep my job without actually speaking. To a normal person, this dilemma might seem insurmountable. To a drug addict? This was nothing more than a small problem, and a simple one for me to remedy.

Of the eleven songs an hour I played, I only had to introduce four or five of them individually. Twice an hour I would read a short weather report and tell the time. I came to the conclusion I could record everything I had to say (for a four-hour radio show) in less than ten minutes. Introducing the songs was easy, as were the weather reports. Recording the time was a little tricky. By the third hour of the show, my time checks were as much as twelve minutes off. No problem! The next night I simply recorded several different versions of the time. I played whichever one was the closest to correct.

Hiding my addiction from my mother was not nearly as simple. She noticed the weight loss right away. Soon my symptoms were more obvious than my being on another crash diet. On one occasion, I woke my poor mother up at four o'clock in the morning just to tell her there was a woman living in my closet. It did not take my mother very long to realize it was fruitless talking sense to me. She dutifully got out of bed, went into my room, and very brutally ejected my imaginary friend.

As my drug consumption grew more and more voracious, my radio show actually got better. I no longer tried to be cute or clever. I just played the songs and told the time. Believe it or not, I was also starting to become popular. I also did a number of local television shows. Somehow or other, I got away without getting caught or looking high when I was on them. Being so close to New York, I also did a lot of national talk shows. Doing national talk made me more of a local celebrity. Being a celebrity made me a lot more in demand for local personal appearances. Appearances meant more cash. And by now I'm sure we all know exactly what *more* cash meant.

It also got so busy, in no time I was turning down talk shows. Too many were calling me for appearances. I was now missing too much work. It was not because of drugs! I've never missed a day of work because of drugs. Well? I actually did but only if you decide to count the days I spent in jail. That is the only way that statement doesn't hold up so well.

So, what happened next? Let me give it to you as a question. What do spring break, getting fired, Geraldo Rivera, drugs, and the Daytona Police Department have in common? That's easy—me!! Before that great day came—the one, years later, where I finally quit taking illegal drugs—I actually did take some remarkable and flat-out insane steps to stop. All were failed attempts. This is my favorite trying-to-quit story because it contains one of the strangest ways I ever got high—and shows the farthest length I ever went in order *not* to get high.

I know hundreds of ways to get high and only one way to quit. Some of the wildest ways I ever heard of to get high I learned in NA (Narcotics Anonymous). At my very first meeting of NA, a girl got up to speak. She told of how her nose had collapsed from years of cocaine abuse. Then, to prove her point, she put a Bic pen through her septum. She continued to speak as if this weren't the weirdest thing any of us had ever seen. It was nice to see a bunch of former hardcore drug addicts could still be appalled. She wasn't done.

Pen still in place, she said since her nose and sinuses collapsed, she had to find new and inventive ways to take cocaine. Thankfully, she said, she was too afraid to use needles. The best alternative, she said, was to go to the health food store and buy large, empty cell capsules, fill them with cocaine, and insert them in her butt. "It was a great high," she said. The only drawback? The numbing effect the coke had. It once was a popular anesthesia. The coke made her lose control of her rectum, and she now had to wear a diaper. We all just stared at her. We could see the pen through her nose and we were all imagining the other.

That's when I realized that drug addicts may be single-minded, but they could come up with some pretty inventive ways to achieve their goals. You'll be pleased to know that I never tried that girl's method. I have done a lot of things, but I can say without fear of a presidential contradiction, "I did not insert."

The strangest thing I ever did to get high—and then stay clean—revolved around Geraldo Rivera. Just the fact that I know Geraldo is bizarre to me, but this particular occasion with him really stands out. It was in early March of 1990. I got a call from one of his producers. They wanted me to be on Monday's show. It was Friday. I immediately agreed because I loved the daytime talk-show circuit, in particular *Geraldo*.

I left Philly on Saturday and arrived in New York. I felt well rested and downright frisky, even though I had partied the night before. Once again, the fact that I don't get hangovers had made sure there were no immediate ramifications for my evil ways. Of course, I wasn't done. At this point in my life, any extra energy I had always went to drugs. I wanted coke. I didn't have a connection in New York, as I had spent very little time there. A connection was not really needed. The concierge, in even the best hotels, would get you blow or anything else in the late '80s/early '90s. I also refer to that era as "BG"—before Guiliani. So, I got the blow and partied all night . . . again.

As the sun rose on Sunday morning, I was running out of drugs. The only problem I believed I had at the time was, if I kept going out and getting more coke, I would end up going on *Geraldo* without having slept in two days. That does not include the fact that I would be seriously "jonesing." I didn't really care that much about my reputation. By now I was already known as sitcom's favorite kid addict. I was, on the other hand, starting to make a living doing these talk shows. I did not want to screw that up. I also knew I would *not* be able to stop myself from doing drugs—right up until show time.

As my drug use got worse, I realized that I had completely lost the ability to disguise my increasingly erratic behavior while under the influence. I knew my weakness, so I took steps to prevent it. While I still had enough cocaine left to last me several hours, I sent for a bellhop. When he arrived, I gave him $20, an envelope, and stern instructions. I told him, under no circumstances, was he or *anyone else* to bring me the envelope until 7 A.M. Monday—no matter what I said.

I knew that I was acting bizarre—and that he was suspicious, but so what? I was show people. I was supposed to behave this way. He took the envelope, the $20, and his orders and left. With part one of my plan to be good now behind me, I moved on to part two. The next thing I did was to take another big hit of blow. I had to make sure I did not need to leave the room until the full plan was in effect. I got undressed and ready for bed, knowing full well I would not sleep. Once naked, I got out my overnight bag and threw it on the bed. The bag contained only willpower. I removed the clothes I had brought for the show and threw them over a chair. Underneath the jeans, shirt, and jacket was my salvation: two pairs of handcuffs and twenty-five feet of light chain.

My plan, which must be obvious by now, was to chain myself in the room. In that way I was making it impossible for me to go out and misbehave. The envelope I had given the bellhop contained the key to the cuffs. I know this must seem way over the top to any functioning human being, but to be honest, I thought the whole thing up while stone sober. The plan had merit and I put it into effect.

Step 1: Find the object I would chain myself to. I settled on the steel bed frame.

Step 2: Measure the distance from the bed to anything I might require. Namely the bathroom and the bar.

Once I was satisfied with my surroundings, I went for it. First another hit. Then I went into the bathroom and got a small washcloth. I wrapped it around my ankle and secured it there with duct tape I had brought with me. This was all to prevent chafing from the handcuffs. I had some experience with this, and it is more than a little annoying. One end of the first pair of handcuffs went around my right ankle. The other end went onto the chain. One end of the second set of cuffs went through the other end of the chain and then to the bed. At first I was proud of my ingenuity. I knew my plan would work, but as night came and the blow went, I started to get nervous.

Around 6 P.M. on Sunday night, the drugs were running perilously low and my emotions, high. I started to panic. I started to snort smaller and smaller lines, and every now and again I gave a good hard tug on the chain. I was not going anywhere without that goddamn key. Needless to say, by 8 P.M. the blow was gone. The only flaw in my plan had just come to light. I have to admit, in my heart, I always knew it would. I called downstairs for the bellhop. He had gone home. I asked if he had left an envelope for me. He hadn't. I asked when he would return to work. I was told 4 A.M. Monday. That was eight hours from now. *SHIT!* If you have ever heard the expression "he paced the room like a chained animal," I was the dictionary definition. I paced. I pulled. I screamed and I made all sorts of promises to God. I think the promises to God worked—even though he must have known I was lying. The next thing I knew, there was a pounding on my door. It was 7 A.M. Monday. Somehow I had fallen asleep. They say "God works in mysterious ways." Helping a chained-up junkie may not be one of his biggest miracles, but it is certainly one of his quirkiest.

Besides two unforeseen minor miscalculations, the scheme was a rousing success. I felt great. I was feeling like the smartest cokehead in the world. I went to get the door. That was when I came face to face with the first of my plan's shortcomings. During the night, the cuffs had slipped off the washcloth and had worn a huge abrasion into my ankle. It burned like crazy. The next mistake was I had failed to take into account the fact that I could not pull my pants on over the chain. I didn't think ahead about any of this. I thought I would just hide behind the door and accept the envelope with my liberation inside.

New problem. The door was down a short hallway. When I opened the door, there would not be any possible way to hide the chain from the bellhop (who would naturally be curious). So what? I had made it. I tipped him again, took the key, unchained myself, and got dressed.

When we taped the show, I had no hesitation in telling Geraldo how I had been clean for over a year. Not only did I get away with it, but I was also a hit. No one would ever be the wiser. I guess God got mad at my lack of sincerity. The night before the show finally aired, I was busted for drugs in Florida. Poetic justice at its finest. Geraldo broke into the middle of my I-am-a-changed-man speech with news footage of me being led away in a new set of hand-cuffs. This pair was obviously not my own.

So, how did I find myself on a plane to Daytona in the first place? It was easy! I got a call from some cable show catering to teens. They wanted me to go to Daytona Beach, Florida, and cover spring break. This sounded like fun, so I agreed. It was good for my radio station, as they liked the press I was getting, so they gave me the time off. I ended up getting more press than any of us bargained for. I was thirty years old and I had never been to the ultimate collegiate rite—"spring break." It should have been fun. Thousands of scantily clad young women whose sole motivation seemed to be to do things they would be ashamed of in years to come. I could not have been less interested. I wanted drugs.

The problem was that I was in a new town and I didn't know a soul. No sweat. As I've told you before, a drug addict can figure out almost anything if it means getting high. I had a novel approach to scoring drugs in unfamiliar surroundings. I would watch the local news. I would wait for a certain kind of story that, unfortunately, I knew was coming. When I heard it, all my questions would be answered. I was waiting for the news anchor to say something to the effect of "there has been another drug-related shooting on the corner of Kings Street and Third." The second I heard it, I would jump in a cab and demand to be taken to Kings Street and Second. The only problem with this tactic? There were so many drug-related shootings in the news and, of course, these reports were always about the very worst neighborhoods. Often cab drivers would refuse to take me to my desired location. That is exactly what happened on March 12, 1990.

The best my cab driver would do was to drop me off two blocks away and give me directions to walk the rest of the way. Knowing that no cab would drive into that neighborhood to pick me up, I offered my driver $50 to wait for me. He took my money but said he would only wait twenty minutes. He said he knew I was never coming back . . . and he was right.

As housing projects go, this was one of the nicest ones I've ever seen. Sure, there were gang members and people with guns—but I wasn't terribly afraid of being killed. I remembered something sad that "Ghost" had told me before he departed this world. I told him about being robbed one night, and I said, "I was sure they were going to kill me." He told me not to worry because "we only rob white people down here, we don't kill them." His logic, although tragic, seems to be true. He went on to explain, "If we kill each other, nobody cares. If we kill a white guy? We have to deal with the cops all night." "Ghost" went well above the call of duty to send that lesson home. I went in and out of his neighborhood hundreds of times with very few scars to show for it. "Ghost," on the other hand, was shot to death. He was right. Nobody seemed to care much.

I wasn't in the Daytona projects for more than thirty seconds when a young man walked up to me and asked how much I needed. I told him $20 worth and the transaction was made without incident. When I turned around, I could see my cab was still waiting for me. I know this sounds ludicrous, but I had a sense of accomplishment and couldn't wait to show off for the cab driver. Before I could take one more step, however, night became day. It was the police helicopter spotlight. The cab took off. I thought about running, but within moments, plainclothes policemen were coming at me from every possible direction. I'd walked right into the middle of a stakeout. Unless you've been a "bad guy," you have no idea what it means to be busted.

I did not need a lot of time to think about what was about to happen. I was going to go to jail. The press was going to surround the place. I was going to be humiliated. I was going to lose my job. Howard Stern was going to call again. This wasn't like the last time I got busted. That time? I didn't care at all about going to jail. As a matter of fact, I had kind of looked forward to the three hots and cot (jail slang for three square meals and place to sleep). This time was definitely going to be a major problem.

After contemplating every possible scenario, I expected the police to be upon me immediately. They weren't. When I looked up they still seemed to be far away. They appeared to be running in slow motion, like the women of *Baywatch*, but without the jiggle. When one cop got close enough to tell me what was happening, it turned out they really were moving in slow motion. About ten police officers had stopped approximately 100 yards away from me to draw their guns. They were inching toward me, screaming different commands at the same time. *"Get down, face on the ground, spread eagle."* It was hard to tell what they were saying, but I knew what they wanted! (I'd been there before.)

I assumed the position. When they finally did reach me, one officer pressed his gun firmly to the side of my head. I was (as they say) "hooked and booked." At first, I thought they were being a bit overzealous, but then I realized I was probably the only person in a square mile who didn't have a gun. I'm lucky they didn't shoot me. Once the panic was over, it took them only seconds to recognize me. They had a good laugh and put their guns away. While riding in the back of the patrol car, handcuffs digging into my wrists, the police made the obligatory "we got Danny Partridge" radio calls.

When we got to the holding tank, the press was waiting. Their holding tank was an interesting contraption. It was not only spring break in Daytona Beach, but it was also biker week. With thousands of out-of-control coeds and an equal number of out-of-control bikers, they had to break out the portable police stations. I was taken for processing to a vacant lot. In the middle of the lot was a large cage on wheels. It looked exactly like one of those old-fashioned circus lion cages in the Bugs Bunny cartoons. I would spend the rest of that night on display with a dozen or so other criminals, for all the world to see. It was an interesting mixture of humanity in the holding tank. There was a Harvard boy, a homeboy, Hell's Angels bikers, and two coeds (who spent most of the night vomiting and urinating on themselves). The bikers did the same thing—they spent the night vomiting and urinating on the coeds. I chose teams well and buddied up with the bikers. They seemed to love me . . . too much.

Thank God the police could see inside the cage. I had heard from my pal Todd Bridges that ex–child stars were going for a whole carton of cigarettes back then. I knew what to do. Calls were made. Bail was made. I went back to Philadelphia. When I got home, I was met at the airport by more press. They yelled out a bunch of questions. I just kept walking.

> **NOTE TO CELEBRITIES WHO ARE BUSTED:** When walking by the news cameras, never pull your jacket up over your head. That only serves to make you look guilty. We still know it's you under there.

Chapter 19

HIGH, MY NAME IS DANNY . . .

The next day I was called into my boss's office. He told me, if I wanted to keep my job, I would have to go to rehab. Later that day I hired a lawyer in Florida. He told me, if I did not want to go to jail, I would have to go to rehab—so I went to rehab. Rehab was a terrible experience for me. First of all, there are no drugs there. I know, "no drugs at rehab" sounds like a gimme—but quite honestly, I was a bit surprised. If you think about it, I went there to quit drugs. On the other hand, I went to Weight Watchers to lose weight, but they still let me eat something. Even the drive to rehab was terrible. I went to one about 100 miles outside Philadelphia, near a small town called Reading.

Reading, Pennsylvania, is known for its outlet shopping malls. There is nothing lower on a junkie's list of priorities than outlet shopping. Except, maybe, going to rehab.

I took the two-hour drive to rehab with my mother and

aunt. It seemed longer. The silence was broken only by me, reading the tabloid stories about my arrest. When we arrived at rehab, things went bad right from the beginning.

I knew I would be staying for thirty days, so I packed two suitcases. One had clothes, the other was full of books. A man (who claimed to be my counselor) met me at the front gate. He was a dumpy little man with a bad attitude. He was poorly dressed and didn't smile. He demanded that I open up my suitcases. I asked why. He told me it was none of my business and that I had no rights here.

As soon as I began to comply he explained his motivation anyway. Apparently he was looking for perfume, cologne, and NyQuil. All of these things contained alcohol.

Seeing my dejected look, he acted as if he had caught me at something. The real reason I looked so depressed? It was because it had just dawned on me that I would be spending the next thirty days with dozens of really stinky drug addicts. I also knew they would keep me up all night with their hacking because someone had confiscated their "runny, sneezy, achy, so-you-can-get-some-rest medicine."

When he opened the first suitcase, he found a dozen or so books. He immediately threw the bag into the backseat of my mother's car. He said, "I'm sending them all home, as there are no books allowed here but the big book." I had no idea what the "big book" was, but I thought it had to be huge to replace the 2,500 years of literature he had so cavalierly tossed aside. When he opened my other bag, he found a paperback, which he immediately tossed on the ground. I could stand no more disrespect. People had worked hard on those books, even the paperback. I told him, "If you touch another one of my books, I will cut your heart out." He stood up very quickly and told me to get back in my car and go home.

Being kicked out of rehab, before I had even checked in, meant probable unemployment and possibly prison. I begged his indulgence. He said I could have one more chance, but threats of violence were taken very seriously here. This was nothing more than a failure to communicate. He thought "I'll cut your heart out" meant that I would somehow penetrate his sternum, remove his still-beating heart, and show it to him before he died. (Not unlike some Aztec priest or my favorite kung fu myth.) In my family, saying "I'll cut your heart out" is exactly the same thing as saying "Please stop that."

After being given a reprieve, he pointed to a little office at the top of a hill. That was where I would officially check in. I grabbed my surviving possessions and marched onward and upward. When I got to the office, I was met by at least a dozen or so drug addicts who were already waiting to check in. They were all standing around taking handfuls of drugs. It was very depressing. It was not the fact they were taking drugs before checking into rehab, but the fact I had neglected to bring any. If you think bumming a guy's last cigarette is a tough request, try getting some drugs from an addict a mere five minutes before he checks into rehab. Even by my standards, these people were ingesting an impressive amount of chemicals.

When one of them would pass out (or overdose), two large men in white coats would come and carry them in. It was the rehab "express aisle." Not only did "their way" of checking in seem like a lot more fun, but it also involved a lot less paperwork. Ahhh, rehab! I had not only been told by my employer to go to rehab; my attorney had warned me to go as well. I had to look at my stay there as being "more than mandatory." Now that I had seen a dozen or so prospective clients getting wasted, I was reminded that this was a completely "elective procedure." Now, for the last time, I truly regretted my own attempts at sobriety. In I went!

After much paperwork I was finally admitted. It turned out I was not being admitted to the actual "rehab" part of rehab. First I had to go through detox. Detox is, of course, short for detoxification.

I had not been getting high since my arrest (which was a week or two earlier), and I told them so. They didn't believe me. Apparently someone had tipped them off to the fact that drug addicts lie. This was probably the first time I had told the truth in about five years, yet I was still quite offended that they doubted my veracity. It wouldn't really have mattered if they believed me or not. Crack-heads get special treatment. They needed blood samples, stool samples, and urine samples. I don't think they really needed these things; it was merely a precursor to the humiliation therapy that was forthcoming.

I stayed in detox for four days. On day five, I was admitted to rehab and taken to my first group therapy meeting. It was depressing. A bunch of grown men and women, crying, screaming, throttling pillows, and blaming Mommy for just about everything. I was about to walk out. How bad could jail be compared to this? Just as I was about to leave, a beautiful young blond woman (whom I had noticed at the start) got up to speak. She said, "Hi, I'm Susan and I'm crossaddicted." All at once came a cry of "Hi, Susan, we love you." It was so much like a movie, I laughed out loud. I was still planning on leaving, but I thought I'd stick around to see just how awful the life of a gorgeous twenty-five-year-old could be. She told a very touching story. She said that she had a self-esteem problem that manifested itself in having sex with anyone who asked.

I decided to stay.

As my luck would have it, the two big no-nos of rehab were sex and drugs. If they had a rule against rock 'n' roll, I would have left the place on the grounds of it all being downright un-American.

My first night in rehab was spent in a dormitorylike room with a young man named Ryan. He was from a wealthy family, was of ambivalent sexuality, and this was his fourth trip to rehab. We talked for a while. He was a New England preppy type who spoke with a lock-jawed accent like Thurston Howell III. As he told me about his life of privilege, all I could think was "This kid had it all and threw it all away." I wanted to kill him. Then I realized, we had almost the exact same story. That realization was distressing, to say the least. I had only been at rehab long enough to despise and ridicule it. Having an epiphany was the last thing I wanted.

Early the next morning there was a general assembly. To my surprise, they announced that Ryan had been expelled. Apparently he had been caught with drugs. I was very upset. The things he shared had meant so much, but they would have meant a lot more if he had shared his meds. In rehab, as in life, "all things are relative."

In my world to be expelled meant that you were thrown out and told never to return. In rehab, being expelled meant you were thrown out and told never to return until your parents coughed up another twenty grand. Ryan was back two days later. I was happy to see that the rules were flexible.

Right from the start, I was diametrically opposed to the philosophy that surrounded me. For example, I did not then, nor do I now, believe that drug addiction is a disease. I have seen people with diseases. Their symptoms are usually something to the effect of coughing, sneezing, and throwing up black stuff. This is, of course, my own humble opinion, but I have never known a disease whose symptoms force you to get in your car, drive downtown, and exchange money with bad people. Call me crazy, but if your disease

cannot be detected—with the thorough use of a ther-
mometer—then you're probably not sick.

Predictably, my personal opinions did not ingratiate me
with the staff or the clients. The staff taught their lessons by
rote, much like an eighth-grade biology teacher. The
clients took solace in being told over and over again that
their "disease" was exactly like cancer—and that they had
no power over it. At first, all I wanted to do was keep my
head down, go unnoticed, do my time, and get the hell out.
After a while, I could not hold my tongue in my mouth
over what appeared to me to be staff-sanctioned lunacy.
Maybe it's just me, but I think a rehab's sole objective
should be to teach you how *not* to take drugs. "Just say
no!!" The counselors at rehab went well beyond this rudi-
mentary philosophy.

For example:

Women who were perceived to pay too much attention
to their appearance were taught the great lesson of humil-
ity. They were forced to go without showers, makeup, and
hairbrushes. If this were not enough, they were then forced
to wear men's clothes. The same was true for men. If any
counselor perceived a man to be overly interested in his
appearance, he not only had to go without hair care products but was forced to dress in drag. Just when I thought
the place could get no crazier, I was introduced to the bear.

The bear was a big brown teddy bear. There were many
of these teddy bears as there were many addicts in need of

"visual lessons." "He" (the bear) was a very serious tool to teach responsibility. If you were thought to be irresponsible the counselors assigned a bear to you. I found this amusing. If a few were found to be irresponsible, that meant, by definition, the staff at the rehab had deemed the rest of us "responsible." "Responsible junkie"—that seemed to me to be an oxymoron at best and a terrible breach of common sense (and security) at worst.

Here's how bear therapy worked. Once you were branded as irresponsible, you were given a large brown teddy bear. The criteria for being marked as irresponsible, by the way, seemed arbitrary at best. It didn't matter. Once you were given the bear, the bear was yours. There was a special ceremony for the "giving of the bear." An assembly was called. All the counselors were there. All the addicts were there. We would beat a friggin' drum.

You could be given the bear for up to two weeks. You were never to let the bear out of your sight. The counselors told you—in all earnestness—that you were to guard the bear with your life. Then the culprit would be named. Some poor slob would then get up, march down the aisle, and receive his overstuffed, cuddly little scarlet letter. As the poor bastard was walking the last mile, fifty or so addicts were encouraged to boo and hiss.

It astonished me to see that many of the clients took pleasure in humiliating the so-called irresponsible. I noted one particular woman who was yelling the *loudest* at the poor man with the bear. She was the same woman who in group admitted locking her kids in the car while she drank in a bar for ten hours. All the guy with the bear had done that day was fail to take out the trash. Once given the bear, your day was not over. You were forced to stand, holding the bear, as if it were your child. The staff then instructed the entire auditorium, a room full of drug addicts skilled at ripping things off, that it was their duty to steal the bear away at the first sign of neglect.

There were some ground rules for stealing the bear. We were not allowed to wrestle the bear away from anyone. We had to wait for the "bear bearer" to take his eyes off the bear. Then and only then were we allowed to steal the bear and bring it to a counselor. If someone lost the bear, obviously they had not learned their lesson. They were then burdened with the bear for another week. There were also rules for "bear care." If the person whose responsibility it was to care for the bear tried to outsmart the staff and clients, it was considered a "no-no." If you somehow tried lashing the bear to your body, by using a belt or a rope, this was to be immediately reported to a counselor. *This was considered bear abuse.*

I had to watch as a grown man walked around for weeks at a time not only holding a bear but often in drag! Some had to do it with a sign hanging around their neck reading LIAR. All this, and they had to keep an eye out for forty or so drug addicts putting all their attention into stealing the bear away from them. If stolen? It added more humiliation to this guy's already shitty day.

I was never given bear therapy. I volunteered for kitchen duty and did it well. I had volunteered for kitchen duty my first day. This happened right after a heroin addict brought me my dinner—with his thumb in my soup. Even though I was never given the bear, there were plenty of other things left to annoy me—namely the counselors. The sole requirement for becoming a counselor was to have five years of sobriety. There was no real doctor in the bunch (from what I could tell). My main problem with this? There are a lot of people, such as myself, who become drug addicts because they are assholes who only became interesting as the levels of their chemical dependency grew. Take away their drugs and they are once again reduced to being assholes, except now they are assholes with a mission.

If you think ex-smokers are annoying, wait until you are locked in a room with one of these guys. It seemed to me that some of these people got as dangerously addicted to the rehab experience as they had ever been to drugs. I imagined that some of the counselors probably had been capable of having an interesting conversation at some point in the past. Now they only spoke in bumper-sticker slogans. A man with a beard, long hair, and a tattoo of a Harley-Davidson (with the slogan "Born to Ride") told me, with a straight face, that I needed to get in touch with my inner child.

Getting in touch with one's inner child was not just a philosophy at rehab. It was an actual physical process we were forced to endure. To get in touch with our inner children, my group had to get down on our hands and knees (in a large circle) and draw pictures. Of course, it was in crayon. They had to be of our "secret happy place." Furthermore, if we were right-handed, we had to draw the picture with our left—and vice versa. If this was not bad enough, once the drawings of our happy places were completed, we were forced to describe them by using the voice of a three-year-old.

At this point I would like to tell you that I flatly refused to subject myself to this. I can't. Failure to complete any task was grounds for immediate dismissal. As I've already told you, getting kicked out of rehab, for me, meant jail. I drew a sailboat. "Getting in touch with your inner child" was high on my list of *hated* slogans. I was not much more fond of being told "You need to take a swim in 'Lake You.'"

Being told to take a swim in Lake You was probably the dumbest expression—but it was not my least favorite, as there was no physical form of it. You just sat there looking confused. My least favorite was being told "You need a hug." The reason I found this slogan to be so egregious was, the moment someone said it, actual physical hugging was sure to follow.

I am not now nor have I ever been a hugger. In fact, I am quite suspicious of anyone who offers hugs to anyone who is not a relation. If I am having a bad day, there are usually several things that can make me feel better. None of these include being embraced by a stranger. During my stint in rehab, not only did I have to endure getting or giving hugs to total strangers, some of whom had open sores, but also the counselors actually rated the hugs. If, for example, you were to simply pat someone on the back while hugging them, you were perceived by the counselors as "being dismissive." The whole hugging process would then start anew.

I was sure these people were Moonies. I did not like the way anyone was treated, but, as you can imagine, I didn't like the way I was being treated most of all. It also seemed *imperative* to the counselors that I blame being an ex–child star for all of my troubles.

Much as I cannot equate voluntarily taking drugs to having cancer, I cannot convince myself that being "rich and famous" is a bad thing or the cause of my problems. In my opinion, the only thing cooler than being a child star would be being a child rock star, like Hanson. (Although I must admit I'm betting that little Zack is going to go bad.)

One day in group, I was told to act out strangling "Danny Partridge" to death. I would've been happy to do it for fun—or even to win at a game of charades. It was their motivation to this mandatory melodrama that I objected to. They were insisting that I was not taking drugs to get high but in an attempt to kill "Danny Partridge." Over and over they insisted if it were not for *The Partridge Family*, I wouldn't be in rehab. No matter how strongly I disagreed, they would have none of it.

It did not help my case that Adam Rich, "Nicholas"

from the TV show *Eight Is Enough*, had been busted on the same day I was. To bolster my point that early television success had nothing to do with my current circumstance, I asked them if they would indulge me by playing a little game. I asked them to think of every television show or movie they had ever seen. Once done, I asked them, "Can you think of any that did not have at least one child in it somewhere?" They could not. Then I asked them, "Out of thousands of movies and television shows with children in them, how many ex–child star screw-ups can you name?" Out of the thousands of ex– and current child performers, they could name only five "total losers." Me, Nicholas Bradford, and the entire cast of *Diff'rent Strokes*. I thought my case was won. They were unmoved. I was in denial. They kept at me. Finally I said, "Look, if you guys are right, how come I'm the only ex–child star here but there are nine dentists? Nobody thinks they got in trouble because they were ex–child dentists."

I don't know if my logic prevailed, or if they just got tired of fighting with me, but they moved on. Danny Partridge was not killed that day. Little Danny may not have died that day, but that is not to say there wasn't plenty of carnage.

I was sad to see, that in early 1990, all the groovy "therapies" from the '60s, '70s, and '80s were still alive and well. Which is more than can be said for my group's imaginary victims. There was a lot of primal screaming. People acted out choking Mommy, and shooting Daddy, and any brothers and sisters (who were perceived as getting more attention than they deserved) also got what they deserved. High school bullies and love interests met especially bloody ends. I was now absolutely positive this place was dangerous.

Years later, when I watched the videotapes of the tyrades of David Koresh and the Branch Davidians shooting, through the flames of Waco, I immediately thought of rehab.

I had stopped voicing my objections to their behavior because I had been told I was getting dangerously close to being expelled. My only hope was coming in two days. That's when I was scheduled to have a progress meeting with the staff, my employer, and myself. My intention was to get through the next forty-eight hours any way I could. Then, at the meeting, I would expose the charlatans for what they were. My employer, being a bright man, would see through their facade, take me home with him, and give me my job back. I would later worry about my problems with the prosecutor of Daytona Beach.

When the day came, I was sitting in the office with three high-ranking members of the rehab staff. We just stared at each other. We had become adversaries. Finally, my employer, Dave Knoll, walked through the door. I truly like Dave. He not only did not fire me when I got busted, but he also paid for my rehab. The moment he walked in, you could tell the power structure had changed hands.

Dave was a very striking figure in his $3,000 suit and his prematurely silver hair. He looked and acted as if he owned the place. This was going to be easy. My plan was to let the counselors speak first. I figured if they spoke to Dave the way they spoke to everyone else, he would certainly see them for what they were. They would have hoisted themselves on their own petards.

It didn't work out. The moment Dave's ass hit the chair, the shit hit the fan. I immediately started screaming at the poor guy. I must have ranted for a full two minutes without inhaling! I was foaming at the mouth the entire time. "Dave, get me out of here, I'll never do it again! These people are crazy! They're trying to brainwash me! They are a dangerous cult! People are killing their mothers." I went on and on. The staff sat stoic with just the hint of a smirk. Dave looked on in horror. I would be staying. After Dave left, I was sent back to my room. Once there, I would have plenty of time to ponder the things Dave would be telling my coworkers about my behavior. I also figured that on his long drive home, he would rethink his goodwill gesture of not firing me.

I had been in rehab for two weeks and every day I hated it more. Things were about to get worse. A couple of days after my outburst, I was summoned again to the office. When I entered, I saw the same staff members who had borne the brunt of my verbal attack. They sat in the same spots and wore the same little smirks. I knew this was not going to be good. We sat silently for a few moments. The head man looked down at some papers, shook his head, and looked up me. "Danny," he said, "we don't think we can help you here." I could not have agreed more, but I was surprised to hear them say it. I had already come to the same conclusion—long ago—that they could not help me. I thought they couldn't because they were a group of smock-wearing morons who passed off bad parlor games as therapy. This was the first time the staff and I had agreed on anything. Unfortunately, I could not admit to it. Again I was forced to consider the ramifications of getting kicked out of rehab. I had only one option. I started lying.

"Oh, no. This has been a wonderful experience! I'm really getting in touch with my higher power. I took a quick dip in Lake Me, and just yesterday I hugged my inner child. Now I'm dangerously close to completing Step Seven." As soon as the words left my mouth, I was afraid I'd gone too far. The first few things were easy to get away with. I mean, how could they tell if I had taken a swim in Lake Me? It's not like my hair should be wet! But if they asked me about Step Seven? I was busted. I had no idea what Step Seven was. There are twelve of them, you know! It was all very confusing.

Even though, in my gut, I agreed wholeheartedly that they were useless, I was still stunned by their reasoning. They told me they didn't think they could help me because I was not a drug addict. I couldn't believe it. The only positive thing I had learned in rehab was that I was, in fact, a drug addict. I was just like all the other drug addicts. No better, no worse. Now these draft dodgers were trying to take even *that* away from me.

There was, of course, a bright side. If I could just get them to write a letter that read "To whom it may concern, Danny Bonaduce is not a drug addict. Love, the rehab guys," I would show it to the judge, not go directly to jail, pass go, and collect life. Unfortunately, they weren't done with me. They told me that drugs were not my primary addiction. I, they said, was a sex addict. I was shocked. I was amazed. I was downright proud. For a man, or at least this man, being accused of being a sex addict was the same thing as if they had said, "Danny, we have figured out your problem. Your penis is just too damn big." Even if it's completely untrue, which unfortunately it is, you just want to agree. "Thank God you figured it out. My giant penis has been the bane of my existence. You have no idea how difficult it has been just to get suits made. Now excuse me while I go brag to all my friends about my giant penis problem."

Of course I said nothing of the sort. I just sat and nodded. The man went on to explain how he had come to this conclusion. When I first checked in, those two long weeks ago, I had filled out lots of forms and questionnaires. One of the questions was "How many sexual partners have you had?" I had put down 300 to 500. This may seem like a lot, but if you think about it, it really isn't. I had gone through puberty "rich and famous" in Hollywood. In a recent interview with *Maxim* magazine, Charlie Sheen says he has had sex with 5,000 women. Therefore, if I had had sex with 500 women, I barely had Charlie's agent's commission on his sexual partners.

I had no idea of the ramifications to being labeled a sex addict, aside from the obvious bragging rights. The next day I had an appointment off-site to see a psychologist who specialized in sex addiction. I may have been thrilled at the prospect of leaving the grounds for any reason, but I did not want to see a psychologist. I had had my fill of people playing doctor. I don't mean to offend psychologists, but I have had the pleasure of seeing several psychologists and psychiatrists over the years. I prefer psychiatrists. Let's face it, if the government doesn't trust you to write prescriptions, you're not a real doctor. I usually put psychologists somewhere between massage therapists and feng shui artists.

The moment I arrived at the psychologist's office, I knew I was in trouble. In her waiting room, she had a dozen or so framed plaques hanging on the walls. Inside each frame was some motivational saying. These were the same plaques they sell in airline magazines to too-tired executives who hope to impress their bosses with clever gifts. After a short wait, she called me in. We had a very nice talk.

Thinking that being a sex addict would get me out of rehab (not to mention jail), I really played up to her. Then she dropped a bomb. Sure enough, she was going to recommend that I leave rehab. Unfortunately, she was also going to recommend that I immediately be admitted to a facility in Montana that specialized in sex and love addiction. She went on to say that my stay in said facility would be no less than six months. My plan just seriously backfired.

Somehow I had talked myself out of two weeks of rehab

and into a six-month stay in Sodom. I talked her out of a recommendation. I cannot tell you how I talked her out of her recommendation. I am still not sure of the statute of limitations on terrorist threats. I toughed my way through the remaining two weeks and even readied myself for the graduation ceremonies.

Graduating rehab was as strange as everything else had been. First, there was the outdoor bell-ringing ceremony. For the bell-ringing ceremony, everyone in the place, counselors and clients alike, would line up and stare at you. You would stand next to a bell, which you would have to ring six times. Each time you rang the bell, you would have to publicly explain why and for whom you rang it.

For example:

RING.
"I ring this bell for my mother who has always been there for me."
RING.
"I'm ringing this now for my higher power who has come to heal me."
RING.
"I ring this bell for my inner child who I did not mean to touch inappropriately."
And so on.

After the bell ringing, we all went inside. Once inside, the graduating class would stand on one side of the room while the remaining members stomped their feet, clapped their hands, and sang "We Will Rock You." Then, some poor junkie would be forced to act out the itsy, bitsy spider song. The significance of the itsy, bitsy spider song had always escaped me. Nevertheless, I was upset. Until my graduation day, I had always been chosen to play the spider. The new guy was better.

Now came the "London Bridge" thing. All those staying in rehab would clasp hands and make a bridge. All those leaving rehab would walk underneath. Everyone would sing, "London Bridge Is Falling Down." The relevance of this ritual was easier to ascertain. You see, London Bridge would never fall. I believe this was meant to imply either we could accomplish anything or that London had some damn fine architects. Ironically, the real London Bridge ended up being disassembled and shipped over to Arizona, a fate I too would eventually face.

Chapter 20

HIGH, FRIED, TRIED, FIRED, AND HIRED

I had made it. I was out of rehab. It was the summer of 1990. Unfortunately, I was not out of the woods, I was just entering the forest.

Rehab had a lasting effect on me. Six hours, to be exact. I would like to say that the idiot move that I was about to make was a direct result of rebellion against my treatment at rehab. I cannot. No, the idiot move that I was about to make was a direct result of the fact that I am an idiot. Certainly I had not enjoyed my stay at the dryout farm. I can admit, without fear of contradiction, they did me no harm. I was just as screwed up leaving as I was when I went in. That night I told my mother I was going to meet a girl who had also graduated from rehab that day—and we were going to study the big book. It was a half-truth. I was, in fact, going to meet a girl who graduated rehab with me that day. We were not going to study—we were going to get high.

If getting high only one day out of rehab wasn't bad enough, it had to be under truly bizarre circumstances. When I arrived at the girl's house, it turned out her father was a mortician. She and her family lived above the funeral home. We got high on crack and weed in her basement among the cadavers. The next day I realized I had a court date in Florida—in about a week. I knew they were going to make me take a drug test, so I decided to straighten up. Rehab may not have had a lasting effect, but I have always found fear to be the truly great motivator.

When I got to court in Florida, I was asked to put my hand on the Bible and swear to "Tell the truth, the whole truth, and nothing but the truth." I was terrified. The judge asked me if I had taken drugs since my arrest. I was sure I would open my mouth and, entirely against my will, the truth would indeed pour out. After all, I was under oath. I looked the judge square in the eye and said, "No, sir." It's amazing how easy it is to commit perjury when it's *your* ass on the line. I was fined $1,000 and given 100 hours of community service. I had avoided going to jail. Later on, when I asked the court clerk about my community service (and how to go about it), all she said was "Don't ask me, just write us a letter when you're done."

I went back to Philadelphia. Not only did I get my job back, but all the press was now back with a vengeance. My contract was about to expire. I would probably get a raise.

If you happen to be playing "Danny Bonaduce, the Board Game" at home, here is the score tally. I have now escaped going to jail twice (when I should have gone), and there is a distinct possibility that I am about to make more money for the effort.

Just so we're clear, the previous paragraph is not an attempt to show you how clever I was. I am merely reporting on the life of Danny Bonaduce who at this point in our story is nothing more than a liar and a cheat. If I had a choice between going back in time and going to jail or feeling the shame I do at this moment, it would be a toss-up . . . believe me.

I know it would have been better for this book if I had said "If I had the choice between feeling bad and going to jail, I would gladly go to jail." The fact of the matter is, this book is my attempt to come clean. So let me be honest. I am indeed ashamed, but I am also in my very nice house in the Hollywood Hills and no one is trying to make me their bitch.

I went back on the air with much fanfare. My boss told me not to say *anything* about my arrest or subsequent stay in rehab. I was not happy about his decision. My two least favorite words in the English language are "no comment." Things continued on like that for a few more months, and I settled back into my "routine"—work, drugs, work.

Philly was a city of many "firsts" for me. It was where I got my first radio job, it was where I first realized my drug-taking was not a hobby but an uncontrollable habit. It was also where I first believed that I might be crazy. Don't get me wrong. People had been telling me for years that I was crazy, but it was in Philly that a medical professional backed up their claim.

One night I was driving to the radio station with a young lady named Debbie. I had been dating her for months, and she was really a sweet kid. On this particular night, we had been fighting over some trivial matter that escapes me now—but at that moment it must have been very important to me. I may not remember what it was about, but I am quite positive that I was right. Unfortunately, she wouldn't listen to reason. I thought I could sway her to my way of thinking by the sheer power of logic so I crashed her car into a cement barrier. Not only did this fail to sway her but she also got downright snippy over the fact I had just totaled her new car. She immediately told me, "If you don't go to a psychiatrist, I'll never see you again." In hindsight, I didn't really care what this girl thought of me. On the other hand, it was a really nice car.

I found a psychiatrist in the same office complex as the radio station. I thought that would make things simpler. I was mistaken, and things got complicated in a hurry. I really didn't want to see a psychiatrist, and I had every intention of being aloof and tight-lipped. The funny thing is, no matter what you plan, you always end up spilling your guts. I told him about the violence, about the arrests, and, of course, about the drugs. At the end of our first session (which I was sure I didn't need), he told me he wanted to see me five times a week. I told him I was a lot crazier than I was rich and I could not afford his recommendation, so we settled for once a week.

After I had seen him a couple of times, I was ready to quit. Nothing had changed and he was expensive. Just as I was about to break the news to him, he broke the news to me. In his opinion, I was "bipolar." He misunderstood my stunned expression for ignorance and explained, "It's another name for manic-depressive." He then told me I should be on lithium and then he wrote me out a prescription for it. You might be surprised by my reaction, but I was actually thrilled.

All I knew about bipolar disorder was what I had read in books or seen in movies. In biographies of people with bipolar disorder, it was obvious they had some serious problems. In novels and in films, the characters were always painted as real nut jobs who were clearly dangerous to themselves and to others. I knew even less about lithium. In movies, once they medicated a character with it, they seemed to become zombies. Needless to say, I suddenly liked the idea of taking lithium. My motto in life has been the same as the DuPont Company: "Better living through chemicals." All bipolar disorder meant to me was I got to take more pills. Cool! I soon had to weigh out the pros and cons of taking lithium. The cons—or more appropriately, the con—was needles.

Unfortunately, I was not allowed to take lithium until I felt better. There were rules about how you take it. My doctor, who was overly concerned with my well-being, explained, "If you want to take lithium, I have to have the lithium levels in your blood taken once a week." Huge down side. I can honestly tell you the only reason I never became an intravenous drug user is because I am deathly afraid of needles.

If needles were the only con, there were several pros— and I will list them for you.

PRO # 1: If I was crazy enough to be put on lithium, then I had an excuse for all my past bad behavior.

PRO # 2: If the lithium worked (and I was sure it wouldn't), that would mean an end to the drugs, the violence, the failed relationships, and, of course, jail time.

PRO # 3: If the lithium didn't work and I got busted again (which I was sure I would), it wouldn't be my fault. I would just tell *Hard Copy* "I'm not responsible! I'm crazy! Just ask my doctor!"

PRO # 4: I had paid a king's ransom for pills that made me act like a zombie. Not only were these drugs legal, they were covered by insurance!

I decided to suffer the slings and needles of outrageous fortune and tough out the blood tests. Unfortunately, being on lithium is not like it is in the movies. It had no effect on me at all. Once again I decided to sever my ties with the doctor on the next visit. Then I thought of something. If this doctor is willing to give me one kind of drug, who's to say I couldn't talk him into giving me another?

At my next appointment, he opened with "How are you doing, Danny?" That's all I needed. "Not very well, Doctor. I'm having an overwhelming urge to take drugs." I had his attention, so I continued. "You see, Doctor, the problem is that I just don't sleep and soon my mind starts to wander to the idea of taking drugs. If you would just give me some sleeping pills, preferably Halcyon .25 mg, I could put myself to sleep before these terrible urges have a chance to take control."

He responded exactly as I knew he would. "Danny, I cannot, in all good conscience, give narcotics to a man with your background." Here's where I made my move. "You're absolutely right, Doctor, and believe me, I'm more afraid of having drugs in my house than you are of giving them to me." I continued, "What I was thinking, if you could write me a prescription for only three pills per week, there would not be any way I could abuse them, and hopefully, in a few months—I wouldn't need them anymore."

This was a two-pronged attack:

PRONG # 1: I was right. There is no way I could abuse three pills a week. I once beat all my friends at go-cart racing while on 70 mg of Valium.

PRONG # 2: By telling him the "in a few more months maybe I wouldn't need them" line, I had implied that I was on the hook for a lot more sessions—and therefore, a lot more money.

I had him. He wrote me a prescription for three pills. We finished the session, shook hands, and I left. On my way out, I stopped by the receptionists desk, borrowed a pen, and casually wrote in a "0" after the "3" on the prescription. I walked across the street to the pharmacy and cashed in my ticket for thirty sleeping pills. The only problem was, after a few weeks of doing this, I had to start finding mom-and-pop–type pharmacies that were not hardwired into a main computer. It seems big pharmacies love to call the DEA.

As fate would have it, I soon started dating a girl who worked in a pharmacy and just loved my radio station. Stealing T-shirts, CDs, and concert tickets from the promotions department in exchange for drugs was far less time-consuming and much less expensive than seeing my doctor. So, my doctor and I parted ways. He didn't appreciate my decision to depart and warned me: "Your behavior will get out of control and you could lose more than just your job." I hate it when people are right!

The night before my contract expired, I decided to have a "little party" at the radio station. After all, I was once again "A Star." Let the truth be known: I got a little "tipsy." To my surprise, I also got a little "fired." I was shocked. After all the things I had done, I was actually being fired just for having a couple of drinks? It was like being fired for stealing office supplies! Actually, I was finally getting what I deserved.

The next day, when my boss officially told me he was letting me go, I broke down. I said the same sad, stupid things. "Please, I will never do this again. Give me one more chance. I am sooooorrrrry." Dave was unmoved. I continued to beg. I told him, "After being arrested and going to rehab only to come back and be fired for being drunk, it would ruin me. I will never work again." Dave rolled his eyes. He then said something sad—but unfortunately true—about the radio business. "Are you kidding?" He said, "This is radio! You'll probably end up doing mornings over this!" This is a terrible commentary on my chosen profession. He was right. I had my own morning show by dinnertime—even though I had no way of knowing at that point of the day.

Thus far, my entire radio career had been a fluke. I didn't even have an agent, so I started cold calling. Earlier that morning, when Dave was firing me, he had also been kind enough to give me the phone number of the top radio agent, Lissa Miller. I had called her as soon as I got home. She wasn't in. I left a message. When I finally got home, there was a message from her. We had never even spoken, but she already had secured me my own show. Ten years later, she is still my agent and she is still that good.

So, the Philadelphia part of my life was now over—for the second time. I had yet to meet my mystery agent, Lissa

Miller, or the new employer she had so quickly found for me. I was very excited, and the occasion finally happened. The meeting took place in a first-class lounge at Chicago's O'Hare Airport. It was just the three of us—me, Lissa, and the station owner. When I finally met Lissa, I thought she was overbearing and abrasive. After spending some quality time with her, I was sure of it. The man who owned my new radio station was named Fred Webber. The radio station was "Power 92" in Phoenix, AZ. As for the contract? There was a lot of fine print but the gist of the deal was this. I would be paid $75,000 a year to anchor a "morning zoo"–type radio show. Like I said, there was a lot of fine print. I didn't care what it said, and I signed the contract. All I knew and/or cared about was, I was going back to work. So, I moved to Phoenix. Nicer weather, lousy drug connections.

Part of the deal with the Phoenix station "fine print" was I had apparently agreed to be drug-tested twice a week, every week. I was happy about it. I was going to start a new life in Phoenix. When I got back to Philadelphia to coordinate the move, I did exactly what you might expect. I made bad decisions. I figured, if I'm going to start a new life in Phoenix I should probably get high on some rock day and night until I get there. That's just what I did.

My mother and I had decided to drive to Phoenix together. On the morning of our departure I had not slept in days. I got in the car and promptly fell asleep before we had even left my mother's driveway. The next thing I knew, I woke up in Phoenix. I'm sure we stopped at hotels along the way, but I remember none of it. My poor mother had driven us all the way across the country. She stayed a couple of days to help me settle in, then flew back to Philadelphia. I was on my own again, but at least I was working.

I was ready. Phoenix was beautiful. I'd slept for a week. I felt great, and knowing I had to take drug tests every seventy-two hours, I knew this time I would make it. The night before I was to go on the air, Fred sent one of the station employees over to my hotel. He wanted her to show me around town so I would sound "local" when I went on the air the next day. Let me change the name in order to protect the wicked, so we'll call her "Banger."

The fact that she had a wacky radio name was a huge strike against her, but I didn't care. She was cute. She showed me all the clubs and points of interest—and we had a very nice time. Later that night, back at my hotel room, we mutually decided that she had had way too much to drink and should not drive home. One thing led to another—and soon we were kissing. Not long after that, we were naked and kissing. Suddenly she stopped, pushed me away, and said, "Maybe we shouldn't do this" and "I don't shit where I eat." I looked at her and said, "That's fine with me. If you are going to shit, I really don't want to do it anyway." We laughed. We did it.

Soon after, I got my own apartment and "Banger" dropped by unannounced. As soon as I opened the door, she saw my very attractive Japanese cleaning lady. I can only assume she thought I was dating this woman. She reached in her purse and, without saying a word, pulled out a small spray bottle and I was Maced in the face right smack in the eyes. I was left screaming in pain on the floor. "Banger" walked out, slamming the door behind her. The cleaning lady was kind enough to bring me a wet towel. She washed out my eyes.

We did it.

The next day at work, "Banger" hit me over the head with a metal chair. She started following me around. Next she was screaming at me in public and physically attacking me at work. I didn't know what to do. I had never been around anyone more screwed up than me. I went to the boss. I told him what was going on. He was not at all surprised. He'd had exactly the same problem between "Banger" and another disc jockey. His solution to the problem? If I didn't handle this immediately—he would fire me.

Things mellowed out after a while. But I would have rather been hit over the head with another metal chair every day than to muscle through what was coming. In the small print, I had agreed to call myself Danny Partridge on the air. Humiliating, sure, but I had figured a way around it. Or so I thought. My real first name is Danny. My plan was to go by my first name alone. Thereby fulfilling my contract obligations without becoming a total laughingstock. It didn't work. Fred caught on in a hurry. He told me that if I didn't call myself Danny Partridge at least four times an hour I would be fired. I had only been living my "new life" for two weeks and I had already been Maced, hit over the head with a chair, forced to call myself Danny Partridge, and had my job threatened twice.

So far being drug-free was not what it was "cracked" up to be. I was starting to get depressed. The only reason I wasn't back on drugs was that I was still waiting to be tested. I may not have been getting high, but I was starting to drink a lot. One day, after work, I had a slight breakdown. It was only about eleven in the morning but I just couldn't take it anymore. I was drinking tequila straight out of the bottle. Soon I was crying, tears rolling down my face. I went out on the balcony, looked up at the heavens as if demanding God's attention, and screamed at the top of my lungs, "I am thirty years old and I am still Danny Partridge!" I wanted to fall on my sword.

Of course, guys like me don't deserve a soldier's death, so I passed out and went back to work that next day. Calling myself Danny Partridge was certainly humiliating but it was only the beginning. I was on a rap station. Soon I was given a list of mandatory slang expressions. From that moment on I said things like, "Yup yup yo, homies. This is Danny Partridge busting out the freshest jams, here's Bell Biv DeVoe. Power 92 has the 411 on the R&B tip. Peace out. . . ." I may have gotten out of going to jail, but God was surely getting even.

Life went along like this for a couple of months.

"Banger" was not being pleasant to me, but she was no longer actively trying to kill me. Calling myself Danny Partridge was horrifying. Using unfamiliar slang that made me sound a lot like someone's father trying to prove he is still a "hep cat" was embarrassing but by this point in my life, I had swallowed my pride so many times I was getting used to the taste. But where the hell was that drug test? It had been two months. I should have taken sixteen of them by now. Still, the requests never came.

After two months without taking a drug test I started to think it was merely a formality. Maybe Fred had put it in my contract only for insurance purposes, or perhaps to look concerned. Once I was convinced I would not be drug-tested I, of course, fell off the wagon. I decided to get high. I didn't know where to get drugs but that had never stopped me before. I watched the news. Sure enough, someone was reporting live from a drug-related shooting. As soon as they gave the address I jumped in my car. I scored the crack and got high for forty hours straight. Friday through Sunday. Finally, late on Sunday, I got some sleep. Monday, I went to work as if nothing had happened. Immediately after the Monday show I was called into Fred's office. Fred was sitting there along with my program director, Steve Smith. The second I walked in the door Fred said he wanted me to take a drug test.

How could he have known? Was he having me followed? I had no time to ponder these questions. I panicked. I could feel my face get hot. I started to drip sweat. When I say I was dripping sweat, this is not an expression. As I tried to act nonchalant, sweat drops were literally pouring off my nose and chin. I hadn't said a single word and they already knew I was lying. I would prove them right the moment I opened my mouth. "I can't go today. I have a plane to catch. My mother is sick. My father is dying. My dog ate my homework."

Fred, true to form, told me if I didn't take a drug test right then and there he would fire me. This was a serious problem. If I refused to take the test, Fred would fire me. If I took it, Fred would fire me. The fact that I was fired for refusing to take a drug test would surely make the news, and Howard Stern would have my ass. Once again I would be a laughingstock and probably unemployable. I wasn't sure, but I also thought that refusing to take a drug test could possibly violate my probation in Florida and send me to jail. On the other hand, if I did take the drug test and failed, which I knew I would, I would still be fired. It would still make the news and would definitely violate my probation and I would surely go to jail.

I could hear my mind screaming "Think, think, think!" I couldn't believe it. For the life of me, I could not think of a single way out. I agreed to take the test. Of course, I really wasn't going to do it—but I figured the drive to the hospital or the wait in the doctor's office might give me time to come up with a plan. It did. Unfortunately, the plan sucked. Steve asked me if I wanted to ride with him. No, I told him (sticking with my lies). "I have a flight to catch afterward." As I followed Steve to what turned out to be a private laboratory that specialized in employee drug screening, I noticed that he was driving very fast.

That's when I came up with my plan. I would crash. The plan was simple and logical! I would hit a telephone pole or brick wall or some other unmovable object. The trick was I would have to make sure to be going fast enough to do myself serious bodily injury without killing myself. I picked out an object on the horizon, unbuckled my seat belt, and tried to prepare myself. Just as I was about swerve I realized there was a huge flaw in my plan. If this was going to work, I had to be seriously injured. Broken legs, broken ribs, maybe a head injury possibly rendering me unconscious. The real problem was that Fred had written permission from me giving him access to my bodily fluids. The hospital would surely take blood. I would be in the hospital. I would be hurt and I would still be drug-tested and busted. I told you the plan sucked.

Before I could think of something else we pulled into the laboratory. Steve and I walked inside, made ourselves known, and sat in the waiting room. Steve looked very uncomfortable. He told me how embarrassing this was for him and that he was sorry. Steve was then, and still is, a very nice man, but at that moment, I had no time to worry about his feelings. The room in which I would go to be tested was only fifty feet away. Even a brain as well versed in trickery and deceit as mine could not possibly come up with a scam during a fifty-foot walk in full view of everyone. I was doomed.

Soon the manager of the lab came out and greeted us. He said that there were some forms to fill out and that he had to ask me some questions. He told me to follow him to his office. Steve Smith got up to come with us. I told him that this was embarrassing enough and I could handle it from there. I didn't know what I was trying to pull, but whatever it was, I knew it would be harder to get away with if my boss was watching. Steve sat back down. I went into the man's office and sat down. In between filling out forms (and asking the questions), he added the fact that he had been a fan of mine for years. He went on to say how happy he was to see that I was doing so well after all I had gone through. "Well," I said, "I'm sorry to disappoint you, but I'm going to fail this test." Before I could stop myself I had told him the truth. This was a serious setback.

When I said that, he looked terribly disappointed. I thought, "What the hell are you so bummed about? I didn't do anything to you!" I was wrong. Without ever having met him, I had already lied to his face. He had seen me on half a dozen talk shows talking about how wonderful it was to be clean. He had believed me. He was proud of me. I had been lying.

He asked me what had happened to make me slip. I did not really want to tell him, but I figured every minute I spent talking to him was another minute out of jail. It was my way of avoiding becoming the lead story on *Hard Copy* again. He seemed sympathetic, but I knew the result would be the same. Drug tests were this guy's job. He had heard every sob story any junkie could ever think of. When my story was over, I prepared for the inevitable. What he then proposed was truly shocking.

He was upset because he had used me as a success story to many of his clients. He said he wanted to help me. He told me if I would meet with him every day and let him help me get clean, he would make sure I passed the drug test. We settled on every three days. Had he asked for a bribe, which I would have gladly given him, I might have understood his motivation; however, he wanted nothing except to help me get clean. I know that many of you are thinking what this man did was bad. That he was an enabler or some such thing—and that I should have gotten what I deserved. Believe me, I agree with you. I should have gone to prison, overdosed, or been shot dead some fifty pages ago.

If I am struck down by lightning tomorrow, I will know that the last eleven years were simply a bonus that I never earned. As for this man, I am sure there is some validity to the theory that what he did was evil. I will always remember him as doing me the biggest favor of my life. If you are reading this, I owe you one.

His plan for how we would rig the test was simple. I would go with the nurse into the examining room and pee in a jar just like anybody else. Later he would pee in a jar and simply switch the labels. His jar was now labeled "Bonaduce." He did not throw my jar away. He labeled it John Doe and sent it to the lab anyway. He wanted to see exactly how dirty I was. When the results came back, Danny Bonaduce was as clean as a whistle. On the other hand, John Doe was as dirty as a frat house. I could only assume (after not having taken a drug test for two months) that I would now have to take them every seventy-two hours. It had to be a direct result of having acted so suspiciously in Fred's office. The problem was the laboratory manager had to continue taking my tests until John Doe came back clean. He did. Cocaine is usually flushed from your system within a week. My tests came back dirty for a month.

Finally my first legitimate test came back clean. Thank God it did! By now Fred had become so suspicious, he switched my testing to another laboratory. It did not matter all that much, because over the last month I had taken at least ten tests and I had figured out how to rig them on my own. When I went to the new lab for my first test I was clean. I took the test while simultaneously making sure they followed the same procedures as the last place. They did. I would go in the bathroom and urinate into a jar. In the bathroom, there was a toilet, a sink, and a towel. These were all the tools I had to work with. It was enough. The only problem with this procedure (that would ensure the legitimacy of my test) was a special piece of thermal paper placed inside the specimen jar that registered the tempera-

ture of the sample. In other words, whatever went in the jar
would be registered on that strip as warm pee or cold pee.
Cold pee was not a good thing.

This was the scam I concocted. Please do not try this in
your drug testing lab or at home—without parental super-
vision! I went to a medical supply store and bought a gross
of the special paper temperature indicators. I learned
enough so that I knew the temperature of the specimen had
to read 99 to 101 degrees Fahrenheit. I also bought fifty
matching specimen jars. I immediately went home and
relieved myself in several of these jars and placed them in
the refrigerator. When the date came when I was called to
take my next test, I took one of these jars and several of
these paper strips with me. I also stayed off drugs in case
my plan did not work.

This was only a rehearsal. When I got to the lab, I filled
their jar as usual. I set it on the counter. Their paper strip
read 100 degrees. Then I pulled my sample out of my
pants' pocket and ran it under hot water. Then I took its
temperature. When I took its temperature, the paper read
125 degrees. I started to panic. I ran my sample under cold
water and continued to take its temperature. I had to use a
new strip of paper every time—because the paper only registered the highest temperature and, once recorded, would
not drop. Finally, when it read 100 degrees, I dropped my
piece of paper into my jar, put their jar—along with my
used paper strips—into my pants' pocket, and made the
switch. The nurse signed me out, and I went home. I did

not sleep this time for days—simply out of fear that I would be caught.

I took several more tests like this, staying clean the whole time. The reason I stayed clean was I had to be sure my sleight-of-hand was working. If somehow my fraud was detected, I would act indignant and take the test again. This time I would demand a witness, knowing full well I could pee with impunity. Once I was sure the results of my tests would be perceived as clean, I would simply bank a dozen or so jars. I called it the "good stuff" and put it in my refrigerator. With insurance like that, I began to get high again.

Life was spinning out of control once more. No one knew it. I probably did not either. I was only getting high on the weekends. I was never late for work. I did good shows and, most important, I was passing my drug tests. I was also enjoying rigging the drug tests. I thought of myself as a criminal mastermind.

With all my medical paraphernalia, I was starring in my own version of *ER*. I was brilliantly devious like Sherlock Holmes's nemesis, Professor Moriarty, and I was getting away with it. In truth, I was an asshole. One day I got called into Fred's office. He said I had failed a drug test! This could not be. There were no drugs in any of the samples I had given them. If I was busted, I knew it had to be for something else. It was.

Apparently there was another test that day that they would randomly do on specimens. This particular test could determine if the specimen was fresh. The results in question did not prove I was dirty. They just came back "inconclusive." I was scheduled to take another test the next day. Of course, I did not know about the freshness test at the time. All I knew at that point was that I had to come up with some answers before test time. I was "dirty" again.

They say "Necessity is the mother of invention." Well, I have to admit what I did next was inventive—even for a cornered junkie. I made a list of everything I thought I needed to know about drug tests. Then I called a major hospital in Los Angeles, California. I asked for the Toxicology Department. When I got a real-live toxicologist on the phone, I told him my name was "David Brown" and that I wanted to talk to him about a movie I was producing. He went for it.

I told him the story was about a college football coach. It was kind of a *Hoosiers* film but about pigskin. I went on to say that one of the subplots was about one of the players on his team. "A good kid is caught up in performance-enhancing drugs. The coach suspects him but cannot prove anything. The coach is right. At the end of the movie the kid dies of a heart attack on the field—and the coach is riddled with guilt.

"So, Doctor," I continued, "what I need to know is, how does this kid keep passing his drug tests?" That is when he started to spill his guts. He gave me a crash course. I found out there are many high- and low-tech ways to get around a drug test. One of the more elaborate ways he told me was that my "character" could have his kidney emptied using a large hypodermic needle. Then he could take another needle, this one filled with clean urine, jam it through his side, and refill his kidneys. I certainly was not going to do that. Even if I could get my hands on all the necessary props, it was not an option. The toxicologist was starting to have a very good time. By now he was even coming up with plot twists. He told me several other things I would never have dreamed of. For example: Drug tests are exactly that. Drug tests. That meant, when I agreed to be tested, they were not allowed, by law, to look for anything else. That meant my "character" could substitute anybody's urine for his own. Man, woman, black, white, young, and old. That interested me. I was starting to come up with a plan.

I asked about storing clean urine in the refrigerator. He told me that under normal circumstances refrigerated urine would work just fine—unless they did this other kind of test on the specimen. He said that they were allowed to perform this test without asking, because it did not disclose what else was in the specimen—only the age of it.

I forget what the test is called, but he said it had something to do with gravity. To pass this test, the specimen could be no older than a few hours. I thanked him for his time and hung up the phone. I thought I had my answer. All I needed was drug-free urine that was no more than a few hours old. As a bonus? That urine could be donated by *anyone* on the planet. The bad news? Out of the eight billion people on the face of this Earth, I did not know anyone who could fill the bill.

In fact, I did not know anyone in Phoenix—period! Any of my acquaintances back in Los Angeles or Philadelphia who would even *entertain* the idea of doing a pee for me were easily as screwed up as I was. The time for my makeup test was looming ever closer. I was getting nervous, but I was not in a panic—yet. As I said, I had the answer. I just did not have all the pieces of the puzzle.

Then it dawned on me. When I first arrived in Phoenix, I got a lot of press. One of the stories compared me to the Phoenix—you know, the mythical bird that rises from the ashes. I was the Phoenix who had "risen from the ashes" of drug abuse. I was not ashamed of this lofty comparison. Remember, when I arrived in Phoenix, I also believed I had "beaten" drugs. I, of course, was again mistaken. When that story came out, one of my coworkers (I will not say who) remarked he had found the article about me "particularly interesting." It seems he had never taken drugs, had a sip of alcohol, or even had a cigarette.

Now I had my guy. All I had to do was talk him into it. I could not get him that night, so I had to wait until I saw him the next morning. My test was scheduled for immediately after the show. Now I was starting to panic. During the show, I asked the "man who would be pee" to join me for lunch. He accepted. Then I marched into my boss's office and told him I could not make it at 11 A.M. I then promised I would get to the laboratory before the end of the business day. That was fine with him.

At lunch, after some small talk, I told "my man" of my dilemma. I went on to explain that he was the answer to all my troubles. Before I had a chance to beg on bended knee, he agreed to my proposal. He actually seemed excited about doing something naughty. I do not think it hurt me that he was working for $5 an hour and all the T-shirts he could wear. I offered him $100 for his troubles.

This arrangement got me through the next several months of my employment at Power 92. Little did I know, I would need more than a jar of clean urine to save me from what was coming.

Chapter 21

LIVING IN PHOENIX CAN BE A DRAG!

They say you have to hit rock bottom before you change your life. Well, I spent so much time bouncing around down there that it would be beyond my capabilities to tell you where and when my bottom was. I do, on the other hand, know the single *best* day of my life. It was the day I met my wife.

I know, I know—it sounds sappy, but it's a great story. It gets *really* sappy later. The nicest part about Phoenix was meeting my wife, Gretchen. Gretchen and I have been married since the day we met, and that was over eleven years ago. So, how did I meet this marvelous woman who changed my life? I was set up on a blind date. Amazingly, I arrived on time, sober and bearing gifts. I knocked on the door and one of the most beautiful women I had ever seen answered. I introduced myself and she said, "Nice to meet you." Then she did the unspeakable. She leaned back into the apartment, turned her head, and yelled down the hall, "Gretchen, your date is here." I was mortified. I know how these "packs" run, and this could only mean one thing. Gretchen was the "ugly" friend. To my great relief, Gretchen was *very* attractive, albeit in a punk rock/Nancy Spungen kind of way. I immediately found the silver lining to the situation. The girl who answered the door was probably at least a three-dates-till-sex kind of girl, and the punk rocker would probably give it up tonight.

We went out on a double date—the hottie, her boyfriend, the punk rocker, and me. It was a great date that culminated in our being thrown out of a bar for table dancing and the hottie's date vomiting in a Dumpster. These were my kind of folks! When Gretchen and I got back to my place, I thought, "Why wait?" and I made my move. I wrapped my arms around her and placed my Jägermeister-tainted lips on hers. I was just about to slide into second base when Gretchen slammed on the brakes. She pushed me back and said in all seriousness, "I am a Christian and I am not prepared to do that until I am married." My first thought was "Shit, I'm $90 into this already." After careful consideration, I thought it a reasonable request. So, I got out the yellow pages, found a minister, and we were married by midnight.

The next morning I awoke first—and God had *not* blessed me with a blackout. I remembered *everything*. I did not know what to do! I had always been self-destructive, not just destructive. Now I had altered this young lady's way of life. There she lay, sleeping like an angel—that is, if angels come in smeared makeup and crazy hair. I could not live with the guilt. I came up with a plan. I would be a complete asshole and she would leave me! Then it wouldn't be my fault. When Gretchen woke up, I looked at her and said, "I'm sorry—I don't remember your name." Without a moment's hesitation, she said, "That's easy—it's Mrs. Bonaduce, and don't you forget it."

There she was, cute, naked, and funny. I thought I would give this marriage thing a try. Eleven years later I am still awed by her greatness. Sometimes on the street or at a party, people will come up and make a fuss over me. When I introduce my wife, sometimes they give her a nod. Sometimes they ignore her completely. Although I am thrilled that people want to know me, I can't help but think, "Are you CRAZY?! You just met Joan of Arc and you picked me to talk to!"

Gretchen would soon change my life.

Now that we are in the middle of my life in Phoenix, it will take us back to one of those three questions that I always get asked. Here's the insight on "Did I know the hooker was really a man?" The answer is NO! Now, do not get me wrong. I don't feel that going out to pick up a *real* female hooker will somehow put me in the moral right. I just didn't know! I was newly married and was still a very bad boy. In my home we now lovingly refer to it as "the transvestite incident." This well-publicized incident had nothing to do with prostitution. That fact seemed to escape the legitimate press and Howard Stern alike.

To the untrained eye, the arrest and subsequent trial over the transvestite incident might have seemed like the low point of my life. Au contraire! Jacques Cousteau could not have investigated the depth of my depravity! For the record, I was actually charged with aggravated assault with reckless endangerment. A lot of people, including the judge, thought the violence broke out because I had discovered the true gender of my liaison. The assumption was, when it was "too late," I started beating up on the transvestite as my way of protecting my manhood.

That was CRAP! What did I care? I respect every woman's right to accessorize, but I can assure you his dick did not match his shoes. Darius Barney, "the alleged transvestite," had other fine qualities, aside from his behaving like a lady of the evening. He was an asshole and he was going to get his ass kicked, regardless of his fashion choices. Here's what happened.

One night I went out for cigarettes. I have no idea what time it was—but I can only assume it was late. When I got to the now-famous corner, I saw a tall woman. She had long straight black hair that went all the way down to her waist. She was wearing a tube top, a black leather miniskirt, and fishnet stockings. I have always been a sucker for fishnets. It was pretty obvious she was "working" the corner. I rolled down my window and said something clever like

"How you doing?" She didn't say a word. She made a bee-line for my car, opened the passenger's side door, and hopped in. Not wishing to look suspicious, I put the car in gear and started to drive.

I wasn't quite sure what to say, so I tried to make small talk. She was all business and cut right to the chase. The moments of her companionship would cost me $40. That would have been fine with me, even a bargain—but something was wrong. When she said the words "forty dollars," she sounded a lot like a gay Orson Welles. I turned on the interior lights. In the words of the great Austin Powers, "She was a man, man!" I pulled the car over. I apologized for the mistake, and told him I would take him/her back to his corner. He did not like that arrangement. He told me since I had taken him off his corner, I owed him $40. Once again I explained that this was a simple misunderstanding, but he got belligerent. He started to demand his money. I assessed the situation. He was not carrying a purse.

That meant, even though he had successfully concealed his penis from me, I couldn't see or imagine anyplace where he could hide a weapon. It was as if he were trying to scare me out of my money. It would have been a lot easier just to pay him, but it was now a matter of pride. (Not really. I just enjoy using the word "pride" in the middle of a story about me and a transvestite hooker.)

The conversation got heated and I gave him one more chance to get out of my car. He declined. So I got out of the car. I walked over to the passenger door, opened it, and

grabbed him. I shudder to think of what it was that I
grabbed him by, since he was wearing a tube top. I only
pray it was his ears. As soon as I had successfully pulled him
from the car, I realized what a precarious predicament I was
in. The person I had seen on the corner was not only a tall
man but a big one. Things did not look good. I was now
dealing with a man in a miniskirt and fishnets who outweighed me by fifty pounds.

He pushed me away and then took a step forward.
When he did that, I punched him square in the nose. It was
a bad night and it was about to get worse. As the transvestite hit the dirt, a police car (that coincidentally had been
parked only a few hundred feet away) hit his lights. The
idea of being busted for brawling with a transvestite hooker
was too much, even for me.

I decided to make a run for it. I jumped in my car and
hit the gas. My assumption was that the police would see
what they assumed was a woman lying on the ground and
stop to offer her assistance. They didn't. They were in hot
pursuit of me. Four other police cars and a helicopter soon
joined in the chase. Speeds reached well over 100 miles an
hour. If you are ever in a police chase, remember, Camaros
are an excellent choice.

I was headed for home. I came around a corner in a full
sideways slide. I saw my house, pulled over, and jumped
out. The police cars were nowhere in sight, but a helicopter
spotlight was still on me. I didn't have time to fool around
with keys, so I jumped over the security gates to my apart-

ment complex. I ran into my apartment and closed the
door behind me. I knew the helicopter pilot had seen me
enter the apartment, and I knew he would radio his friends.

I had to come up with a plan in a hurry. I did. Unfortunately, it was a very bad plan. I decided to take all my clothes
off and get into bed. My theory was, when the police burst
through my door, as I knew they would, I would claim that I
had been in bed for hours and insist that someone must have
stolen my car. In my haste, I didn't notice Gretchen wasn't
home—she was out looking for me. When the police arrived
at my front door they were let in by Gretchen, who had just
come home. They told her, "We're looking for a man who
attacked a woman!" Of course, she let them in to look
around. She had no idea it was me! I could instantly tell by
the sound of their voices, if they found me lying in bed
naked, they would kick my ass first and ask questions later.

I quickly devised a new plan. *Hide!* I jumped in my
closet and pulled a pile of dirty clothes over me. When the
police reached my bedroom, they could not find a light
switch. They searched for me in the dark using only their
flashlights. At one point one of the officers pointed his
flashlight directly at me. I was looking directly at him—yet
somehow he didn't see me. To my horror, one of the officers walked directly over to the laundry heap that I was hiding under and jabbed it three times with his nightstick.

Somehow he missed me. The police were leaving my
room when one of the them turned around for a final look.
He saw my hair sticking out. He screamed, *"I got him!!"* and

several policemen poured back into the room. They dragged me out of the closet, stark naked, and proceeded to kick the crap out of me. I was completely subdued but still taking a pretty serious beating. I wondered why, with both hands behind my back, they were continuing to punch and kick me. I soon got my answer. The police had made the same mistake I had. They had also believed that the transvestite was a real woman. Therefore, they had mistaken me for a woman beater. The police in Arizona don't take kindly to woman beaters. So they decided to beat the living shit out of me! I don't hold this against them, even though I didn't do what they thought I did. To be honest? I'd had an asswhupping coming for a long time, and they gladly obliged.

Once they got tired, the police dragged me back downstairs. I was naked and bruised—and I don't mean my ego. Gretchen screamed, *"Stop! That's my husband!"* They were unimpressed. They allowed her to grab a pair of shorts for me; unfortunately, they were hers. As they were dragging me away, now wearing women's pants, I screamed out, *"Tell them, honey, I was here ALL night, right?"* They dragged me back to the scene of the crime. They then shined a spotlight in my eyes and asked the person (whom they still believed was a woman), "Is this the man who attacked you?" "No" was his reply. The cops were at least as surprised as I was. They asked him again, but this time they added, "Don't be afraid, he can't see you with that light in his eyes."

"No," he said again, and then he added, "I told you, it

was a Mexican." I had no idea why Mr. Barney was lying, but I was sure I was going home. Finally, one of the more observant officers noticed that his "lady" victim had outdoor plumbing. The vibe changed immediately. Now they didn't like either of us. Plus, the police were just realizing they had some more serious problems. They just found out their "female victim" was actually a man in a miniskirt. To make matters even worse, one of the police officers finally recognized me. Now they had a very reluctant cross-dressing victim with a bloody nose.

On the other side of the street, they had a relatively popular local celebrity standing on the sidewalk, wearing nothing but women's shorts and a pair of handcuffs. I was also bleeding from both eyes. Worse for the officers was the fact that the victim was still insisting I was not the man. The cops were getting nervous. Mr. Barney and I were taken to separate hospitals for medical treatment. On the way to the hospital Mr. Barney changed his tune and admitted I was in fact the man who hit him. I was taken directly from the hospital to jail. For what seemed like the umpteenth time in my life, I was treated to the "fun" of hearing news stories of my arrest over jailhouse radios.

Normally, under these circumstances, I would have ignored the news and focused my energies on trying to figure a way out of this mess, but this time, the news reports were really ominous. When the reporter explained the "victim" was a Native American who lived at Window Rock reservation, I noticed (for the first time) that at least ten of my cellmates were also Native Americans. They had been picked up on drunk and disorderly charges and they didn't look happy. I was immediately moved to a private cell for my own protection. I posted bail the next morning.

The next thing I know I was the lead story on the national news and in the opening monologue of Letterman and Leno that night. I was also the top story in Phoenix for over a month. I thought this was a tad excessive. In my opinion, it was nothing but a fistfight and a glorified speeding ticket. The tabloids ate it up and ate me alive! I actually did understand the appeal of it all. The little redheaded kid from *The Partridge Family* was busted for smacking a transvestite hooker. It was like Eddie Munster getting popped for lesbian dwarf tossing. It wasn't *really* news—but you have to laugh at it, unless, of course, it is happening to you.

I was charged with aggravated assault stemming from the breaking of Mr. Barney's nose. The reckless endangerment had something to do with running a stop sign at 120 miles per hour while being chased by numerous police cars and a helicopter. The comedy of it all should have stopped when the Maricopa County Prosecutor's office informed me of some unpleasant legal news. It seems when committing reckless endangerment (while on probation from another state), the offense carries a maximum sentence of life in prison. As hard as I tried, I couldn't make that out to be funny—because I (unfortunately) met those requirements. Gretchen wasn't laughing either, but she stayed— God bless her!

There was a light at the end of the tunnel and it wasn't a train coming at me. There was good news and bad news at pretrial. The prosecution had a few holes in their case. It seems Darius Barney had been arrested several times for assault. I, on the other hand, had only been arrested several times for possession of narcotics. Translation: I didn't hurt other people, only myself. I was a much nicer class of criminal. Even with my bad habits, I could still be allowed to mix with polite society. That was not the case with Mr. Barney. The bad news was, I couldn't keep my big mouth shut.

For example:

When the judge said, in court, "Mr. Bonaduce, let me tell you what I think happened that night. I think you went out and picked up a prostitute, and when that prostitute turned out to be a man, you got angry—and assaulted him," I told my lawyer, I wanted to press charges against him for consumer fraud. One reporter, with the *Arizona Republic*, laughed so hard, he fell off his chair. The problem was the judge hated me now, and he was not alone. The *Arizona Republic still* hates me to this day. (Wait till they review this book—you'll see.) The TV and print tabloids referred to all this as "the end of my career." What career? I was a former TV star and as of a few days after this incident, an ex-DJ in Phoenix!

I also referred to Mr. Barney, a Native American, as "Chief Running Both Ways." I was doomed. I was also out on bail, on every form of news that there was, I was unemployed, under indictment, overexposed, and recently married to a very pissed-off wife.

With all the attention I was suddenly getting, I did see a chance for a comeback. I suddenly became the hottest ticket on daytime TV. So I made up a sanitized version of the story and stuck with it. After all, you're nobody in this business until you've lied to Geraldo. For years to come, I was the butt of many jokes, and some of them truly were very funny! Between the pretrial and the real trial, I also had six months to kill. It was during this time that I got many interesting phone calls, including one from an old and dear friend.

Chapter 22

EVERYBODY RUN, THE SITCOM KID'S GOT A GUN

While waiting to go back to court, and most likely to jail, I got a lot of phone calls. Most of them were from Howard Stern. He found my current predicament to be the height of comedy. I also got calls from all the daytime talk shows, CNN, and all the tabloid TV shows. This was very depressing, because my lawyer told me I was not allowed to talk— and we all know how much I like to talk.

I did not know this at the time, but apparently anything you say on television can and will be used against you in a court of law. I was unhappy that I could not talk with Howard. By this time he had become a national phenomenon. A good interview with Howard could mean work. Either through one of his affiliates or, just as likely, his competition.

I was upset that I could not go on the talk shows for several reasons. I really like being on television. I am one of the few people I know who could call his pals to say "I just got busted, make sure you record *Entertainment Tonight*."

Another reason I wanted to go on the talk shows was because they were really being unfair. Not to me, but to my beloved show business. Starting around 1985, the year of my first major bust, and well through 1988, I had done at least fifty daytime talk shows and one prime-time special with Bryant Gumbel and Katie Couric. The subject matter of the shows were all the same: "Ex–Child Stars Gone Wrong." It was always the same cast: me, Dana Plato, Todd Bridges, Butch Patrick (Eddie Munster, *The Munsters*), and Paul Petersen (*Donna Reed*). A better title for the shows would have been "Has-Beens on Parade."

The show line-up (interesting choice of words) looked like some *Love Boat* reunion show gone terribly wrong. All the other ex–child stars would talk about how show business had ruined their lives. I, on the other hand, was of the opinion that show business had not ruined our lives, we had. I did not believe—for one moment—that any of these people truly believed that television was responsible for their downfall. The fact that they were on television to discuss their "theory" weighed heavily in my favor.

I also enjoyed pointing out that "if being a child performer is so carcinogenic as to deserve a Surgeon General's warning, somebody should call Ron Howard, Helen Hunt, and Jodie Foster to tell them to lie down because their days are obviously numbered."

By 1988, the subject of ex–child stars on a rampage

had pretty much petered out. Now, with my latest arrest, it was back—it was 1990 and it was bigger than ever. "We" were "hot" again! Without me there to support my point of view, however, talk-show hosts, ex–child stars, and even psychologists were saying things like "a kid with his own series is just practicing for a future in prison." They went on to say, "Any parent who would allow their kid to go into show business is involved in some kind of child abuse."

I disagreed then, and eventually I would go on to prove my resolve on this issue. I would like to think I didn't go on the talk shows because it was the best thing for my case. I'm afraid that the way my mind worked at the time, I would have gladly gone to prison in exchange for delivering a really good sound bite. The real reason I didn't go on the talk-show circuit in the posttransvestite era was because the court had forbidden me to travel.

The more phone calls I got, the less willpower I had. My "no comment"s were getting longer and longer. In other words? The "no comment"s were turning into thinly veiled comments. My lawyer, a fine man named Richard Gierloff, told me I had to stop answering the phone. I couldn't leave the state, but I could get out of town. I decided to go into hiding. Gretchen and I went to Flagstaff, Arizona. It was Saturday night when we checked into a motel. I turned on the TV and hopped into bed. I was relaxed. Nobody could find me here. I was wrong. On the television was *Saturday Night Live*. There was Phil Hartman on a mockup set of *America's Most Wanted*. He said, "Tonight we investigate a crime wave that is sweeping the nation. Join us as we search for 'America's Most Wanted Ex–Child Stars.' . . ."

I knew what was coming. Onto the stage walked that night's host, Michael J. Fox. He was wearing a bright-red fright wig. He immediately shot someone. The first lines were from Tim Meadows, who was playing Todd Bridges. He said, "Bonaduce, why are you always killing people? I'm tired of cleaning up after you, Bonaduce."

I had to admit two things:

1. It was pretty funny.
2. There was no escape.

I went back home.

By the way, the funniest thing, in my opinion, about *Saturday Night Live*'s "America's Most Wanted Ex–Child Stars" skit was Chris Farley playing a murderous Mindy Cohn from *The Facts of Life*.

The phone was already ringing at home when we got back. When I picked it up, I was very surprised to hear the voice at the other end of the line—it belonged to David Cassidy. I had not heard from him in years. He was pissed. He was yelling at me but at the same time being very complimentary. He said, "Danny, you are the funniest person I have ever known." As soon as I said thank you, he would finish the sentence: "It's time for you to stop being the punch line. Stop being an asshole."

After he calmed down, we talked for quite a while and it was very pleasant. Eventually he told me that the reason he had called was that he wanted to help me out. He was offering me a job. David was going on tour and wanted me to be his opening act. David thought, if I showed up at all the shows on time—and sober—somebody might hire me in a more permanent position and I could get my life back together. I was touched. We couldn't make it on Gretchen's salary (she was managing a car rental agency), and the legal bills were getting huge. God bless her, she was still at my side.

Unfortunately, I had to decline. I had never done stand-up comedy, and, of course, there was the pesky problem of me not being allowed across state lines. David would not take no for an answer. To my absolute amazement, David Cassidy personally called the court. He explained how I really needed this chance—and that he would watch out for me. He went on to tell the court they could hold him "personally responsible" if I jumped bail or broke the law in any way.

What was more amazing to me than David Cassidy being willing to put himself personally on the line for me was the court saying "yes." They actually gave me permission to travel. Looking back, I can only assume that David

Cassidy had lost his mind. I was and I am still very moved and grateful to him for that. Twenty years after *The Partridge Family* had begun, David Cassidy, whom I had looked up to in awe from day one, had turned out to be a most excellent big brother.

Chapter 23

ON THE ROAD WITH DAVID

I could not believe it. I was thirty years old and I was actually on a bus again with David Cassidy.

This time the bus was not a prop but a viable mode of transportation. I also did not need drugs. For some reason or another, this "time warp" was freaky enough all its own and there was no urge. It also helped that Gretchen was with me on occasion. With her, I would not be able to get away with a thing—or even try. Drugs had been scared out of me for the moment, but not the desire. Gretchen watched me like a hawk. While we toured all around the country, David also took his responsibilities as my legal chaperon very seriously. Every night he would bang on my hotel door and demand to come in so I could prove I was not under the influence. I thought he just meant drugs. One night I let him into my room—and he saw a bottle of tequila I had purchased at the store. He totally flipped out.

I know that he only wanted the best for me, but you have to admit there is something kind of funny about being yelled at by David Cassidy. I was so nervous before that first show, I was physically sick. I had never done stand-up comedy before, and to make matters worse, David was insisting that I be sober, and who could blame him?

The lights went down in the theater and the announcer said, "Ladies and gentlemen, Danny Bonaduce." I ran onto the stage wearing a T-shirt with big letters on it that read DAVID CASSIDY'S EX–CHILD STAR WORK RELEASE PROGRAM. I hadn't said a word—and I had already gotten a big laugh. I worked my way through the next ten minutes and, to my surprise, it was not a total disaster.

Finally I got the signal I had been waiting for. It was time to bring on David. When David hit the stage, I was amazed by what I saw. David had the exact same effect on women then that he had had twenty years earlier. There were just fewer of them and they were older. David and his band were amazing. Women screamed, cried, I even think one woman fainted. After a few more shows (when I was sure this reaction was not a fluke), I finally decided to ask David something. It surprised him. "Why the hell are you running all over the country playing small clubs? You're Elvis. You should be in Las Vegas making a hundred thousand dollars a week."

I think David was offended. Not by the comparison to the King, as David is a big fan, but by the fact that I said I thought he should be in Las Vegas. David was still in major rock 'n' roll mode then, but ten years later, he would prove me right after all. Not only did he go to Las Vegas, but he also broke all attendance records for the MGM Grand's new "EFX" show. He would soon star in his own show at the Rio and produce two other shows. The only place I was wrong was about the money. I told David I thought he could make $100,000 a week. My guess is he made double that, easy!

Elvis may have left the building, but he left the door open and David went in.

If you ever have the chance, go see David's show and you'll see what I mean. I may have been right about David's future, but he also proved prophetic about mine. Just as David had insisted, I showed up at all the shows sober—and on time. Sure enough, people started to treat me better. Although no job offers were forthcoming, we did a lot of television and even *Good Morning, America*. But still, no job offers. Then we played Pennsylvania. David and I were scheduled to play Hershey Park. It's an amusement park in Hershey, Pennsylvania, that's owned by the chocolate family. When we arrived, the amusement park informed us that they didn't want me. They did not find me "suitable" for children. It would have been easy to be offended, if they weren't so goddamned right.

I was scheduled to do promotion for the show by appearing on Eagle 106, my old radio station back in Philly. I didn't want to go. Normally, I did all of the radio shows. David only did some. I did all the radio shows because we knew David Cassidy would sell tickets to all the David Cassidy lovers. I, on the other hand, might sell some tickets to people who would not ordinarily go—because of what I liked to call "the freak factor." The freak factor? That is when people would only come to the show to see the freak: me.

Every time we hit a new town, the local press would do a story on us. My arrest record and the fact that I was currently under indictment got more ink than *The Partridge Family* connection. It was much like the people who go to the auto races in the hopes of seeing a crash or slow down in traffic to see a car wreck on the highway. I was starting to believe some people would come out to the show only to see if I would blow my brains out or overdose right on stage.

I particularly did not want to go to Eagle 106 because not only was I not appearing at that night's show, but I was also embarrassed. Remember, it was at Eagle where my old boss had paid for my rehab. I couldn't imagine, under my current circumstances, that he still considered this a wise investment. I went anyway. There was a new morning show: *John Lander and the Nut Hut.*

John was a great guy and I had a wonderful time. When the show was over, I tried to get the hell out of there without seeing anyone. Too late. The moment I opened the door I saw my old boss, Dave Knoll. He walked straight up to me. I was expecting the worst and I certainly was not expecting what he had to say. "Danny, you were great with

John. We've been looking for someone to fill out the show. Do you want the job?" I couldn't believe it. This was the moment I had been waiting for. As quickly as the elation came, it dissipated. I had completely forgotten something. I looked at Dave and said, "Thanks, I'd love to. But I can't. I forgot, I think I'm going to prison." He asked, "Do you think they will let you broadcast from there?" That was all we had to say, and I left. By the way, Gretchen checked; they wouldn't. When the tour was over, we went back to Phoenix and awaited my sentencing.

Chapter 24

THREE HOTS AND
A COT . . . NOT!

When I got back to Phoenix, there wasn't much to do except meet with my attorney. These meetings turned into a pleasant diversion. Richard is not only an excellent attorney but also a fine gentlemen. He is well versed in literature, history, and fine wines. The only flaws in his character are his profession and the company he keeps. It could not have done his reputation any good to be seen socially with me. I do not wish to sound like a consumer reporter for criminal attorneys, but if you ever find yourself busted in Phoenix, call Richard Gierloff.

The prosecutor was playing hardball. Because I had committed this crime while on probation in another state, he was loudly declaring that I was going to prison for years. Finally I caved in. We all agreed that I would plead guilty to a reduced charge: aggravated assault and reckless endangerment. We also agreed that I would go to jail for sixty days. I did not want to go to jail, but I saw no reason to waste sixty days of my life. When the court day came, I packed appropriately. Gretchen and I packed what I called my "prison package." It included a course on Italian and Arnold Schwarzenegger's book on body building. My plan was to emerge from jail buff and speaking a third language.

Outside the courtroom, the bailiff met Richard, Gretchen, and me. He asked about my bag. When I told him what was in it, he told me I would not be allowed to take it with me. I still do not understand, but apparently there are several different kinds of institutions of incarceration. If I were going to prison, I would be allowed to bring possessions. I, on the other hand, was going to jail.

In jail, you are not allowed to bring *anything* with you. Just money. Then you can buy what you need from the jailhouse store. I was just guessing, but I did not think language courses would be hot sellers. I gave Richard my bag and borrowed $100 from him. The bailiff went on to give the complete rundown of what would occur in the courtroom. He told me that my lawyer would get a chance to speak. The prosecutor would get a chance to speak and then I would get a chance to speak.

When it was all over, the judge would sentence me to sixty days in jail. It seemed bizarre to me that we would all get a chance to speak, especially when it was a foregone conclusion that I was going to jail. Then the bailiff said something even stranger. He said, "Normally, when the judge passes sentence on a defendant, I would walk over to

the defense table, place him in handcuffs, and escort him
from the courtroom." Then I learned things would be different for me. He told me, "As soon as the judge sentences
you, you are to get up, walk straight past the judge and into
the judge's private chambers." When I asked the bailiff why
this break in procedure, he told me the judge was doing me
a favor. The courtroom was full of reporters, and the judge
felt there was no reason to have pictures of me being led
away in handcuffs haunt me for the rest of my life. I
thought to myself, "For a man about to send me to jail, this
judge is a really nice guy."

In court, everybody played his part. The prosecution
said I was a menace to society and should not be shown any
favoritism because I was a celebrity. When it was Richard's
turn to speak, he got very passionate. Gretchen later
remarked that he sounded like Perry Mason. He told the
court that I was not being treated any better because I was a
celebrity, but, in fact, it was worse. He went on to say that
the court was reacting to the local news and entertainment
magazine TV show cameras. That to show the world the
court was being fair, they were actually punishing me far
more than the crime demanded.

When my lawyer was done with his speech, I was very
proud of him. That feeling did not last long. We had
already agreed that I was going to jail for sixty days. When
my lawyer was done speaking, the judge slammed down his
gavel and sentenced me to ninety days. Before I had a
chance to grab Richard by the throat and go for a new

charge of manslaughter, the judge added a word: suspended. When I asked Richard what that meant, he said,
"You are not going to jail today." Richard's speech had
worked. The judge suspended my sentence for six months.
He also ordered me to pay Mr. Barney $4,500 to have his
nose repaired, and I had to perform 750 hours of community service. If I could manage to be good for six months I
would not have to go to jail. I have now been good for
eleven years, and I owe that all to Gretchen.

When it was all said and done, I walked over to the
prosecutor to shake hands. After all, the man was just doing
his job, and to be fair, in hindsight, I really did deserve to
go to jail. When I put out my hand, the prosecutor fired
one last parting shot. He grabbed my hand, looked me in
the eye, and said "Don't worry, son, you'll be back."

I don't know if the fact that I have lived my life as a law-
abiding citizen for the past eleven years has had anything to
do with wanting to spite that prosecutor. If it does? Thank
you, it worked!

Chapter 25

WHAM, BAM! I REALLY AM A MARRIED MAN

Gretchen may look like an ordinary person, but it is only a clever disguise. She is a perfect example of what humanity should and could be. There are far too many isn't-my-wife-great stories for me to tell in these few pages. Besides, with my limited vocabulary, I could never do her justice. It would be like saying the Sistine Chapel is pretty. I will, however, try to convey the sacrifice she made for me. After we were married, it didn't take her long to figure out what she had gotten herself into. She married a lying, cheating, then-unemployed drug addict whom she thought was probably going to jail. Instead of running for the hills, which I most certainly would have done if the tables were turned, she set about fixing me.

My family, my friends, rehab, the judicial system, and even my own self had tried to fix me. I didn't think this woman's chances of success were any better. But she laid down the ground rules. She took away all the money. There wasn't a lot, as I was unemployed and $30,000 in debt to a lawyer. I was not allowed to carry more than $5 with me for over a year when we were first together. After a year of being clean, she raised it to $20.

The next hurdle was the sleeping arrangements. I usually sleep very little, maybe four hours a night. Try as she might, the poor thing could not stay awake. I would promise her, "If you fall asleep, I will not leave the house." Gretchen would never tell a lie—but she knew one when she heard it. She knew I couldn't help myself. She came up with the plan. In the end, she had more plans for getting me clean than I could figure out scams for getting high. Her plan for the sleeping problem was to sleep on top of me. This is not as good as it sounds. I would make myself comfortable sitting with a book in my hand or watching TV. When I found a position I thought I could maintain for an extended period of time, Gretchen would drape herself over me and go to sleep. Every time I would get up to go to the bathroom or get a drink, the movement would wake her. She would jump to her feet like a startled cat and demand to know where I was going. I would tell her, then get my drink, sit back down, and the process would start all over again. Gretchen lived like this for two years. Sometimes it would take more than Gretchen's goodwill and selflessness to stop me. Sometimes she had to get tough. Sweet as she is, Gretchen is also far and away the toughest person I have ever known. One night I got sick of her rules and regulations. I went to her purse, took out $20, and headed for the door. Before I could make my escape, she blocked the doorway and demanded to know where I was going. I told her the truth. I was going to get high.

She tried to stop me physically, but Gretchen weighs only ninety-four pounds. I simply picked her up and moved her out of my way, then ran for the car and started it up. When I looked over my shoulder to back out of the driveway, there was Gretchen, arms folded and standing behind the car. It was a standoff, although only one of us was standing. I was in a souped-up Camaro with my foot on the gas. I was sure she would move. I was wrong. I decided to scare her.

I put the car in reverse and started to inch toward her. She didn't give. As the car moved closer to her, she sat down. I got out of the car to see what she was doing. I was amazed by what I saw. She was lying down across the driveway directly in the path of my rear tires. I screamed at her, "Are you crazy? Don't you understand I'm a drug addict? I will run you over!" She looked up at me, almost casually, and asked, "Will you really? Do you want drugs bad enough to kill me?" I was leaning toward yes.

Then, while still lying in the driveway, she went on to explain my predicament. She said, in all likelihood I would be arrested before I even got the drugs, but if I did happen to get drugs, would one night of getting high be worth spending the rest of my life in jail? Until that night, I thought there was nothing stronger than a junkie's desire to get high. It turns out there is something stronger—and I had married her. I slunk back into the house like a whipped dog.

Gretchen's toughness was not restricted to me. One night when we were in New York we were walking through Greenwich Village. A very large African American man walked up to me, said he was a big fan, and handed me a package of cocaine right in front of Gretchen. She immediately started screaming for the police. She was yelling at the top of her lungs "Help, police, this man's a drug dealer." I wanted her to be quiet. At that moment, the only person I was absolutely sure had drugs on him was me. I threw the package into the gutter. Between the "crazy woman" yelling for the police and me throwing away his drugs, this man was understandably upset. He looked as if he were going to come after me. He didn't get the chance. Gretchen started yelling something about drug dealers being the scum of the Earth.

When the man turned to look at her, she hauled off and punched him in the face with everything she had. The man was much too big for Gretchen to have done any damage, but he was shocked long enough for me to throw her in a cab and get the hell out of there. On the way back to the hotel, I yelled at Gretchen. I told her that I could have handled the situation and that she had insulted my manhood. I also told her that she could have gotten herself killed. I acted very angry, but secretly, it was just one more thing to admire about her.

These are, of course, outrageous examples of the lengths Gretchen was willing to go to to help me. Mostly she displayed quiet dignity, inner strength, and a noble nature. In other words, she was really starting to bug me. I envied her character. When I was on drugs, I had the perfect excuse for all my shortcomings. I wasn't a failed actor. I was a drug addict. I didn't have failed relationships. I was a drug addict. Without drugs as my whipping boy, I had to take stock of myself. I was coming up short.

Every day I was off drugs, my life got better. Every day my life got better, the more I knew I didn't deserve it—and it was obvious I had done nothing to deserve Gretchen. I started to hate myself and to resent my wife. What made her so much better than me? The answer turned out to be her faith in God. She had faith and I did not. Gretchen's faith made her fearless. I was afraid of everything. Life would throw me the smallest curve and I would immediately assume the worst.

Gretchen, on the other hand, could face a calamity on a grand scale and all she would do was look at me, smile, and say, "Don't worry, honey, every time God closes a door, he opens a window." This is not just a saying for Gretchen. She truly believes it and it gives her comfort. The best I could get out of it was that God is not terribly energy efficient.

I tried praying but it didn't help. Gretchen tried pointing out parts of the Bible she thought applied to me. At first, it did seem like the Good Book was speaking directly to me. Then I realized anyone could get anything they needed from the Bible. It wasn't that long ago that Charles Manson was sure the Beatles were the Four Horsemen of the Apocalypse. Poor Charlie, everybody knows it was KC and the Sunshine Band.

Then one day (shortly after the transvestite incident) the answer dawned on me. I was a Catholic. I hadn't been to church in twenty years—but that didn't matter. If you're born Catholic, your name never comes off the list. It's like the Book of the Month Club. As a Catholic, I could go to confession. For those of you who are unfamiliar, let me explain going to confession, as I understood it. I could go to church on Saturday and confess my sins to a priest. A priest could give me penance, and if I agreed to his terms, I would be absolved. Absolution was just what I needed. I was very excited. Gretchen was skeptical. When "confession day" finally arrived, I ran to the church down the street. It did not open until ten. I was three hours early. I waited. When the doors finally opened, I rushed inside. There was no one in sight. I didn't even catch a peek at the person who unlocked the doors.

I waited some more. Finally a man emerged from the far end of the church by the altar. He was not wearing the priestly black shirt and white collar, as I had expected. He was a monk, wearing a full-length burlap robe with a hood. For a belt, he had a piece of rope. I wanted to run. How could a man like this possibly understand sins like mine? Sex, drugs, not to mention the infamous transvestite hooker. (That alone counts for at least four of the seven deadly sins.)

I stayed. I was completely serious. I would do whatever it took. After what seemed like forever, the friar walked into the confessional. A little light came on over one side of the booth. I walked in. The church was still empty. He opened a little sliding door between us and I began. "Forgive me, Father, for I have sinned. It has been twenty years since my last confession." There was an audible groan from his side of the booth. I could tell this was not the way he had planned to start his morning. My confession took over an hour. When I emerged from the confessional, there was a long line of impatient sinners glowering at me.

For those of you who are afraid the rest of this book is going to be dedicated to my religious conversion, fear not, my children. It did not take. I have had to come to terms with the fact that I will never be as good or as decent as my wife. It is something I will have to live with, as long as she will have me. As the years wore on, the rules became less strict. I now carry cash and credit cards and come and go as I please. It just does not "please me" to go anywhere.

Looking back on my life before Gretchen, it is obvious to me that I was headed for death. It would have been either by overdose or being shot dead on the streets. I will always owe my parents for giving me life. I will always owe Gretchen for giving me back a life worth living. After a few months of living the clean life, I was beginning to enjoy it.

Everything started to turn around. One day the phone rang. It was Dave Knoll, my old boss from Eagle 106 in Philadelphia. The job he had offered me while I was on tour with David Cassidy was still waiting. I was about to become the wacky sidekick on the *John Lander and the Nut Hut* show. Gretchen and I were moving to Philly.

It had only been about a year since my mother and I had driven across the country from Philadelphia to Phoenix. Now my new wife and I were driving back. The only difference here was this time I would stay awake and do my share of the driving. We packed up our belongings, including our Great Dane, Max, and piled into my infamous Camaro. What a great car that was. Several trips across the country and one very-high-speed police chase—and it never gave me a lick of trouble. Gretchen and I also had no money, so we could not afford to stop at any of our country's points of interest, except one: Graceland.

The tour was very interesting, although I wondered how a person with Elvis's tastes ever made it big. Of course, you have to remember, he decorated the place in the '60s.

We were walking back to our car in Memphis when a man ran up to me. "Hey, Danny, remember me?" he yelled. I didn't. He said, "Come on, man. We had a fight!" That did not narrow it down, but he was not done. "Sure you remember. You were naked." "Gus!" I shouted. "How the hell have you been?"

I was happy to see him, not because we had any good times to reminisce about but because I had told Gretchen about my naked fistfight during my crackhead days in Hollywood and I don't think she believed me. It was good to have corroboration. We made small talk for a while and then I asked him about Lilly, the Japanese girl I used to get high with at Motel Hell. He said, "Oh, somebody cut her throat and stuffed her under a mattress." He said it as casually as if he were telling me she had bought a new car.

Neither Lilly nor I were stellar people, but the fact remained, she was indeed a person and somebody had simply thrown her away. I wondered if anyone cared. Lilly and I had led similar lives. I couldn't help but think how easily it could have been me instead of her. Gretchen thought the same thing. Until that moment I don't think she had any real understanding of just how ugly parts of my life had been. We drove in silence for a while.

When we crossed the Pennsylvania state line, our good moods returned. My plan was, once again, to stay with my mother, who has never failed to be there for me. As soon as we got on our feet, we would get a place of our own.

Chapter 26

ONE PICTURE IS WORTH A THOUSAND DAYS

When Gretchen and I finally reached Philly, I was surprised to see how beautiful it was. I thought I had always hated Philly. It turned out that I only hated *me* in Philly. The place was great. Things were wonderful. Through Gretchen's hard work and the tireless efforts of several law enforcement agencies, I had been clean for almost a year.

I was again making $75,000 a year, and it did not take long before we were able to buy our first home together. It was a charming little place, approximately 800 square feet, right on the banks of the Schuylkill River in Mannyunk, Pennsylvania.

I really was starting to enjoy the fruits of being clean. This time it was also surprisingly easy to stay clean. Not because I had miraculously found some willpower, but because everyone was watching. The Phoenix probation department had graciously agreed to transfer my case to the

Philadelphia probation department. So had the fine people at the Florida probation department.

This meant I was under the watchful eye of the legal systems of three states, all at the same time. They all demanded two urine samples a week. Not to be outdone, my wife insisted that my employer also have me drug tested twice a week. My employer did not want to—and it was not because they trusted me. It was that they just had no drug testing policy in place. I have never seen anyone successfully stand up to Gretchen, and this was no exception. Not only did she get them to agree to test me, but she also had it written in my contract. She was not done. Once she had "test" written in my contract, she told them that the first time they failed to test me, not only was she sure I would take drugs, but she would consider their negligence "a breach of contract." I told you she was tough!

Let me save you the math. Between Philly, Phoenix, Florida, and my employer, it came out to eight drug tests a week, or every day and twice on Sundays. While I lived in Philly, I filled more jars than Kraft. To this day I still have difficulty going No. 1 unless there are people in lab coats watching me.

My first meeting with my new probation officer was quite amicable. Too damn amicable. I sat in the waiting room with the other criminals waiting for my name to be called. When it was my turn, I was escorted to my new probation officer's cubicle. He was a nice enough guy, although he was a very by-the-book man. About halfway through our meeting, the head of the probation department arrived. He shook my hand, told me what a pleasure it was to meet to me, and asked me if I would mind taking a picture with him. After we had taken the picture, and the chief left, I told my probation officer that taking a picture with his boss was going to come back and bite me in the ass.

He did not understand, so I explained. I had been through this before. I told him what would happen. One day that picture of the head of his department (with his arm around me) would be floating around the office. Somebody would go into the head guy's office, throw the picture down on his desk, and demand to know why he was showing favoritism to a criminal like Danny Bonaduce. My new probation officer thought I was paranoid. We would see.

My new probation officer told me that I should complete my 750 hours of community service by collecting food for the Philadelphia food bank. Wanting to get my community service done as quickly as possible, the next day I spent eight hours going door to door asking for canned goods. It was amusing to see the reactions of people when they realized Danny Partridge was at their door demanding nonperishables. Still, I became bored in a hurry.

I explained my problem to my boss and he agreed to do a huge benefit for the Philadelphia food bank. Not only would he guarantee several tons of canned goods, but the station would also cut a check to the food bank for $10,000. This was more food and money than I could hope to collect in a lifetime of community service. I wrote the judge who sentenced me and told him the news. The honorable judge would have none of it.

His thinking was, even though it was a noble gesture, it was just another example of me skirting my punishment. He was right. So, there I was, collecting food for the homeless, working hard, being faithful, remembering where I lived. All of it is good stuff. The best was my starting actually to feel downright good about myself.

One morning we awoke to the most picture-perfect day imaginable. The sun was shining yet it was cold enough to snow. There was an ice floe on the river. I was again failing to find the words to tell Gretchen how much I loved her. It was a perfect Christmas day. My mother and aunt were in California visiting the rest of my family. With nowhere to go, we decided it would be nice to take a romantic drive to Rhode Island and see all the famous mansions on the beach. So Gretchen and I (and our Great Dane, Max) jumped in the Camaro and headed for Rhode Island. We needed to relax.

Around this time, Gretchen was confused: with things going great, why was I feeling so depressed? She recommended that I go and see a psychiatrist. I told her I'd done that once before in Philly. I started to think it "might be a geographical problem." I told her I had not enjoyed my experience with my last Philly psychiatrist, so I picked one out of the yellow pages. Once again he immediately diagnosed me as a manic-depressive and put me back on lithium. Within weeks Gretchen could tell lithium was not having its desired effect; in fact, I was acting stranger by the day. I stopped taking the lithium, and as much as I enjoyed his company, I stopped seeing The Shrink. That's when Gretchen and I decided to take a trip to Rhode Island.

Once there, it was as beautiful as a postcard. Unfortunately, we could not get out of the car for a romantic walk on the beach because the wind chill factor was 40 degrees below zero. We got a hotel room. During the summer, rooms there probably rented for as much as $150 a night. In the dead of winter, it was only $19. For all we cared, it could have been a luxury suite at the Plaza. We were watching the news. All of a sudden, I again felt the overwhelming desire to try to tell Gretchen of my great feelings for her. I told her how not long ago, I did not expect nor did I have the desire to live. Now, I went on, my life was perfect and I owed it all to her.

We kissed. When we turned back to the television, a very sad story was unfolding. The story was about a young person who, as a result of an auto accident, had been left confined to a wheelchair. If that wasn't bad enough, on Christmas Eve someone had mugged him and stolen his wheelchair. I never thought God had anything to do with the fact that I always seemed to wiggle my way out of trouble. After all, why would God ever take a man like me under consideration? This seemed too strange. Just as I was saying what a perfect life I had, this story came on the TV. It almost seemed as if God were daring me to do something "good" for someone else—with no benefit to myself. At first I was going to ignore his challenge. After all, over a bet with the devil, God had completely screwed Job. Furthermore, God once told Abraham to kill his son. At the last minute, it turned out God was only playing a practical joke.

Aside from punning, I have found the practical joke to be the lowest form of humor. It continued to gnaw at me. Finally I could take it no more. I called the news desk and told them if they would give me the young man's address, I would bring him a new wheelchair in the morning. They told me they could not give me the young man's address, but if I would leave my name and number someone would get back to me. I did.

A few minutes later, someone from the news department called back and asked, "Is this *the* Danny Bonaduce?" "Yes," I said, confused by the question. As if, after all the things I had done of late, someone actually might want to impersonate me. Once they were convinced I was the genuine article, they told me if I really wanted to help the young man, I should meet him at his house at 10 o'clock tomorrow morning.

They gave me the address and I hung up the phone. Gretchen kissed me. The next morning, when I arrived at the young man's house, there was a camera crew waiting. I did not ask for nor did I want the publicity. At first, it seemed to cheapen the whole affair. After a moment, I realized giving a handicapped kid a new wheelchair was *better* publicity than I had been receiving over the past several years. I walked in the house, gave the young man a check, kissed his mother, and went on my way. The next day when I returned to Philadelphia, I was surprised to see what I had done was all over the news. *Entertainment Tonight* and *Hard Copy* were running the story. Even Larry King was talking about my selfless gesture.

On the news they were showing the young man's mother. She was crying and saying "I had been praying for a Christmas angel . . . Who knew it would be Danny Bonaduce?" I certainly didn't. I had been called many things, but a "Christmas angel" was never one of them. A few days later I went to my scheduled appointment with my probation officer. He was not in, so I was taken to the head of the department. He had seen the story on television. He also seemed to be touched by my Christmas spirit. He gave me a very touching speech about how I was a credit to the department.

He asked me how I had heard of the young man's plight. I told him I had seen it on the news. He asked me where I had seen it. I told him Rhode Island. Before I could finish the word "Island," somebody in the room (whom I had not seen) grabbed me by the hair and smashed my face into the desk in front of me. My nose started to bleed.

There was a third person in the room (who had also escaped my attention) who grabbed my arms and handcuffed them behind my back. Next, they stood me up and threw me against the wall facefirst. They told me I was going to go to prison for the remainder of my sentence.

Then it dawned on me. When I went to Rhode Island, I had crossed state lines without permission. In Florida, Phoenix, and L.A., I was sure I was going to jail. In Philly, I knew I wasn't. There was no way this guy was going to send me to jail for crossing state lines to buy a kid a wheelchair. It was that goddamned picture. He wanted me to beg.

I did. Begging was not enough. He kept saying he needed another opinion. By the end, there were fifteen people in the room. In other words? Everyone he worked with who had hassled him about that picture was in that room. He did not need anyone's opinion. He was the head of the department. When he felt he had regained his stature, he said he would give me one more chance and took the cuffs off.

NOTE TO THAT OFFICER IN THE PHILADELPHIA PRO-BATION DEPARTMENT: If you are reading this, I admit I am a small enough man to have begged in public to stay out of prison. You, on the other hand, made me beg because you are a punk. One of us should have been better than this. As unpleasant as that day was, much like all my bad days, it had a silver lining. That incident and a few more like it were inadvertently responsible for *The Partridge Family* movie.

Apart from this one incident, I really enjoyed my time in Philadelphia. I not only had fun working with John Lander, a gentleman and a consummate professional, but "wacky sidekick" is a pretty easy job. Philadelphia, being so close to New York, made it easy for me to take the train into town and do the talk shows. (Needless to say, I got permission from my probation officer *first*.) It was on one of those trips that Gretchen punched the drug dealer. It was 1992 and I was becoming a real fixture on the talk-show circuit again. One day I got a call from Larry King. He wanted me to go down to Washington, D.C., and do his show. I was thrilled at the idea. I was the only guest. No whining ex–child stars saying how show business had ruined their lives. Only my point of view, and me. This was the chance I had been waiting for. I almost blew it.

The next day at work I was bragging about my upcoming trip to CNN and my interview with Larry King. John Lander joked that he would give me "a hundred dollars if I found a way to mention his name." Always one to take a challenge (and make a fast buck), I wanted to set the extent of our agreement. I wanted to know, would John give me $100 just to mention his name on Larry King, or would he give me $100 every time I mentioned his name? The deal was set. John would give me $100 every time I mentioned his name.

That night, with permission from probation, I took the train to Washington. I sat directly across from Larry King himself and got ready for my moment. I should have been concentrating on being clever and concise. After all, this was watched all over the world. Unfortunately, all I could think about was the bet.

The floor director gave us the countdown, "five-four-three-two," then he pointed at Larry and we were on the air. Larry gave me pretty much the same introduction I had gotten from other talk-show hosts for the past six years. "Ladies and gentlemen, you know him as the wisecracking little redheaded kid from *The Partridge Family*. After the lights went out and the director yelled cut, he, like so many other child stars, found himself out of work and on drugs . . . Recently he was arrested for assaulting a transvestite prostitute. He is now making a comeback on the Eagle 106 radio in Philadelphia. Please welcome Danny Bonaduce."

Not a stellar introduction, but certainly one I had earned. It would be my job over the next half hour to explain that all the charges against me were true and accurate but that show business had nothing to do with my downfall. I prepared for his first question, which I was sure would be "Did show business ruin your life?"

It wasn't. The first thing Larry said to me was "So, Danny, tell me about your radio show." Remembering the bet, I said, "Well, Larry, it's not my show. It's John Lander's show. It's called *John Lander and the Nut Hut*. I work for John Lander. I am one of John Lander's 'nuts.'" I must have sounded like an idiot. I had only been on the show ten seconds and had already made $400. During the interview, I was able to say John's name four more times while still sounding like a lucid human being. Generally, I did a pretty good job—and Larry said he would like to have me back. Which, by the way, he has . . . five times so far!

The next day at work we played clips from the show. John owed me $800. I was surprised to see John had the money with him. I think he was even more surprised that I took the money. I always took the money. Except once.

Chapter 27

GETTING LOOPED IN CHICAGO

Ever since I got that first call from disc jockey Johnny B. back in 1985, Chicago had kind of adopted me. After my tour with David Cassidy, I actually had a solid comedy act. Soon I put the two together and, since I was now off probation, I was flying off to Chicago from my new home in Philadelphia about one weekend a month. Chicago has a very active comedy scene and dozens of comedy clubs. I think I played all of them. Every time I played Chicago, Larry Wert was there. Mr. Wert was Johnny B.'s boss, the vice president and general manager of WLUP radio in Chicago.

WLUP or "The Loop," as it was known, was at the time the most powerful and prestigious radio station in America. My act, although getting better, was certainly not good enough to explain Mr. Wert's constant attendance at all of my comedy gigs. I wondered what he was doing there.

Eventually I got my answer. He was sizing me up. Thirty days before my contract expired in Philadelphia, I had every legal right to look for other work. I had no intention of doing so. I was very comfortable in Philadelphia and being John's sidekick was enjoyable—and more important, easy. Then Mr. Wert called and screwed everything up. He offered me a job on "The Loop" doing overnights. (That's the shift between 2 and 6 A.M.) It's the worst shift in radio. In hopes of getting more money in Philadelphia, I told my bosses about the offer for Chicago. Their counteroffer amazed me. Apparently, the *John Lander and the Nut Hut* show was doing so well in Philadelphia, they were going to move the show to one of their stations in New York.

They offered me $350,000 to go with it. I called Mr. Wert back. His counter-counteroffer was equally startling. He would give me $90,000. Here was the decision I was left with: Move to New York, the number-one market in America, and make $350,000 for doing the best shift in radio. The other? Move to Chicago, the number-three market, and make $90,000 doing the worst shift in radio. It seemed like an easy choice. That is, until I involved my wife.

Really, I just wanted to tell her about the $350,000 we were about to make. I only mentioned Chicago in passing. She told me Chicago was actually the better offer. It was obvious to me that she had lost her mind. I let her plead her case only to be nice. She said that I was far too talented to be just the wacky sidekick forever. If my show was as good as she knew it would be, I would make the big money soon enough. It was time, she said, to stand on my own two feet. I did not know if I wanted to kiss her or kill her.

In the end, I did exactly what I have done every day for the past eleven years. I did what my wife told me. And just like every day for the past eleven years, Gretchen was right.

Once again Gretchen and I packed up our belongings and our dog, Max, and headed out. As soon as we started driving, I started to have misgivings. For my entire radio career, I had either played eleven songs an hour or been the wacky sidekick. In other words? For the last three or four years, I usually talked on the radio for approximately six minutes per hour. Now I had signed on to a talk station. I had never even heard an all-talk station. I would be expected to talk approximately fifty minutes per hour, in a four-hour show, six days a week. To make matters worse, getting quality guests at three in the morning was going to be tough. I was not even sure I could get callers at that hour.

I started to panic. What the hell was I going to talk about for four hours a night? I couldn't sleep, so we drove all night. I had found some talk stations on the AM dial and listened for hours. The jocks (if that's what you could call them) were terrible. They were either wannabe political pundits or UFO and conspiracy freaks. As the sun came up, Howard Stern came on the radio. He was complaining about how low-life, scum-sucking disc jockeys all over the country were stealing his act. He was telling the truth. After touring the country with David Cassidy and doing dozens of morning radio shows, it was obvious to me there were a lot of people making a lot of money stealing from Howard Stern.

I had found my answer. I too would steal from the king. I planned to listen to the rest of the show and make mental notes of what to steal and how to change what I heard just enough to disguise my plagiarism. The problem was Howard would not move on. He talked for hours about how these disc jockeys would be nothing without him and nobody ever gave him credit. That's what seemed to bother him most. Not that they were stealing, because, as he put it, there are always pretenders to the throne, but that nobody gave him credit. I pulled over at a phone booth. I got out my phone book and gave Howard a call. Howard's producer, better known as "Baba Booey," put me right through. I told Howard that I was on my way to Chicago to start my own talk radio career. Howard said something about Chicago being too cold. I went on to tell him, "I just want you to know I will be stealing your act." At first, Howard started to yell and call me names. He then said I was just like all the other scum-suckers who were ripping him off. I jumped back in and said, "That's not true, Howard." I told him that I had been listening all morning and I reminded him of what he had said: "It was natural to steal from the best [him] and what really bothers you is they do not give you credit."

Howard asked me my point. I told him I wanted to be the first of the many who had ripped him off to give him proper credit. I thanked him for his act and hung up the phone. When I got back in my car and turned on the radio, I expected Howard to be going crazy. Instead he had nothing but kind words for me. Every time he bashed some disc jockey for ripping him off, he would end his tirade by saying "At least so-and-so could try to be honest like Danny Bonaduce." In the end, I never ended up stealing Howard's act. Thank God. Nobody does Howard like Howard. I know, I've heard them try.

WLUP, Chicago, my new radio home, also had a sister station called AM 1000. It was what they call a "clear signal station." Meaning, at night, it could be heard in thirty-eight states and Canada. After my "Howard call," I tuned in the car radio to AM 1000 even though we were still at least a thousand miles away from Chicago and I heard an announcement. A big booming overmodulated voice dripping in reverb came on the air and said:

"HE'S COMMMMMIING."

After the break the disc jockey got back to his program. The next break started the same way. This time the big voice said,

"HE'S DANGEROUS. . . ."

This was starting to get my attention. Sure enough, the next break started exactly the same way. The big voice said,

"HE'S CRAZY!"

This went on all night. I was riveted. Finally, at the end of the night, the big voice put all his adjectives together. This is what it said:

"HE'S COMING.

"HE'S DANGEROUS.

"HE'S CRAZY.

"HE'S OUT OF CONTROL.

"HE'S DANNY BONADUCE."

I was mortified. I had not done anything dangerous, crazy, or out of control in at least two years. Nowadays I was barely interesting. What the hell was I going to do once I got there? When I got close enough to the city, I tuned in "The Loop." Now I could hear the big guns on my station talking about me. Johnny B. did mornings. Kevin Matthews did middays, and Steve and Gary did afternoon drive. At the time, this was the biggest lineup in radio and certainly the most expensive. Johnny B. and Kevin seemed happy about my imminent arrival. The former had given me my start and the latter was instrumental in getting me hired at "The Loop." Steve Dahl, of the *Steve and Gary* show, was not so enthusiastic. Steve wondered aloud, "What the hell is a washed-up ex–child star [who doesn't even take drugs anymore] going to do on the radio?"

I had to admit Steve's question had merit. When we finally arrived in Chicago, Gretchen and I checked in to our corporate apartment. We hadn't exactly hit the big time. Our apartment was approximately 250 square feet, including a kitchenette and a bathroom.

When we pulled the Murphy bed out of the wall, it took up the whole apartment, forcing Gretchen, Max, and me to sleep together in the bed. I don't mean to sound trite, but the fact is, we were very happy there. I kept hearing the big announcements on the radio about my new show. It was scheduled to debut in about a week. In preparation, I read everything, from *Newsweek* and *Time* to *Popular Mechanics* and *Playboy*. I watched all the local news and read all the local papers. At the very least, I would be informed. A couple of nights before my show was set to begin, Mr. Wert invited me to a small dinner party to "celebrate and toast" my new show.

When I arrived at the restaurant on the ninety-fourth floor of the John Hancock building, Mr. Wert, Kevin Matthews, and Johnny B. were already waiting. We talked for a very long time and were having a great deal of fun. Suddenly Johnny B. announced that he hated me. He said, now that I did not drink or take drugs, I was boring. I knew he was kidding and everybody laughed, but I felt there was some truth to it. I pointed out the only flaw in his theory. Raising my beer, I said, "I still drink." We talked a while longer and soon Johnny B. slipped away from the table. When he came back he had a bottle of tequila and a large steak knife. When I asked him what they were for, he said, "If you're still the old Danny, drink this bottle of tequila then kill Mr. Wert." Now I knew he was kidding. Everybody loved Larry Wert.

After a few more drinks, I remembered a trick every Bonaduce can do. The trick is to get someone to put their hand on the table and spread their fingers. I would then "walk the knife" back and forth from their thumb to their pinky and back. To give you an idea of how fast I can do this, I would venture to say, I could jab the knife between your fingers maybe 200 times in under a minute. My sister Celia is faster. I could get no volunteers. I had to do the trick on myself. I had never done this to myself and I put my hand at an awkward angle. I started slowly and went faster as I warmed up. My father and sister were great at this game. Unfortunately, the only way for them to get great was if they ignored the cuts. When I got the blade going *so fast* that it was merely a blur, I really had their attention. Once again I ignored the cuts. When I was done there was a little blood on the tablecloth, even more when I wiped my hand on my napkin.

Johnny B. and Kevin seemed pleased to know that with a few drinks and a little prodding I could still be counted on to be ridiculous. Mr. Wert looked apprehensive. I think he thought something bad might happen. The next day Mr. Wert got a bill from the restaurant for $4,000. Unbeknownst to me, under the tablecloth, I had carved a deep handprint in a very expensive African cherry-wood table. The knife point had gone clear through the tablecloth. Mr. Wert wasn't happy.

So, it was time for the first broadcast of the Danny Bonaduce talk-radio show. I was a nervous wreck. I left my corporate apartment on Elm Street, and walked the two blocks to the John Hancock building. I was already shaking with fear. That, and the fact that, with the windchill factor, it was 20 degrees below zero didn't help. I thought I might collapse in the street.

I tried to concentrate on my upcoming show, but all I could think about was the fact that I had turned down $350,000 a year to do a job I was good at—in exchange for $90,000 a year to do a job at which I was destined to fail. When I reached the thirty-seventh floor, I walked down the halls to the studio. I was met by my new producer, "Shemp." I knew the moment he said his name, I was doomed. I hate wacky radio names. To me, it is the radio equivalent of a stand-up comic who wears funny clothes. I walked into the studio and got ready for the show. I was afraid I would have no phone calls at that late hour. I was happy and surprised to see all ten phone lines were lit up.

When it came time for my show to begin, Shemp played a taped intro he had made for me.

He'd gotten videocassettes of at least ten talk shows I had appeared on or in which my name had been mentioned. He then edited all the talk-show hosts together introducing me. It sounded as if Geraldo, Jay Leno, David Letterman, and Oprah Winfrey were welcoming me to Chicago. It was awesome.

I wouldn't come to fully appreciate the magic of Shemp for several more years. Wacky name or not, he is—by far—the best producer I ever had the pleasure to work with. I know this now—but on that first night I misjudged him. When his intro was over I prepared to take my first phone call. As I pushed the button that would put the caller on the air, I kept thinking, Howard Stern, Howard Stern, Howard Stern. No matter what my first caller said to me, my plan was to find a way to mention lesbians, call the caller an idiot, and hang up. I pushed the button and said, "You're on the air." The caller said, "Hi, Danny, this is Mark from Schaumburg. I just wanted to tell you how proud I am of you. You have come such a long way since Johnny B. called you back in 1985. You are an inspiration. By the way, I saw you and your wife on Oprah Winfrey. She is beautiful." This guy had completely screwed up my plan—thank God! I said, "Thank you." The calls were like that all night. And I'm happy to report that at least one Howard Stern imitator died before he ever got on the air.

Before I knew it my first show was over. For the next few weeks, things went great. I liked the listeners and they seemed to like me. Someone in the press even went so far as to refer to me as "the nicest guy on the radio." Not that my show never got risqué—sometimes it did—but it was never mean-spirited. Even though radio stations are not rated between midnight and 6 A.M., I got the feeling I was doing well. So you can imagine how surprised I was when, five weeks into my one-year contract, Mr. Wert came in the studio and fired me live on the air.

Only five weeks into my new job, some very familiar words were about to be spoken. To be honest, I was not terribly frightened when Mr. Wert told me, "You're fired." I knew I had not done anything wrong, and he had a big smile on his face. Also, I had eleven months to my contract. If he *really* was firing me, he was going to owe me a great deal of money. Furthermore, Larry Wert is a true gentleman. Unlike some of the bosses I have had, he never abused his power. I was fairly certain I was not really fired. I was right, sort of. He was indeed kicking me off the 2 A.M. to 6 A.M. shift. At the same time, he was promoting me to the "very respectable" 10 P.M. to 2 A.M. shift. The moment he told me of my promotion, some of the staff from the station came into the studio from where they were hiding. They had champagne and we had a party live on the air.

Then it dawned on me. A better shift probably meant more money. So I asked him, "Hey, Mr. Wert . . . does that mean I will be getting a raise?" Suddenly the festivities came to a screeching halt and the room got very quiet. Everyone stared at Mr. Wert. It was the only time I have ever seen him look nervous. He told me, "We'll discuss it later," and that it was inappropriate to discuss money live on the radio. For some reason, it was very important for me to discuss it immediately—with the mikes on. Mr. Wert still seemed to be in a good mood, so I persisted. We ended up negotiating my new salary live and on the air. As we went back and forth, we both ended up taking phone calls from listeners—as to why I *should* or *should not* get more money. It was hysterical.

Mr. Wert started off by offering me $100,000 a year. I countered at $150,000. In the end, we settled on $125,000. Not bad. I had been on the job for only five weeks and was just handed a $35,000 raise. The next day Mr. Wert called me into his office. He told me I was never to discuss how much I was paid over the air again. He explained the company we both worked for also owned other radio stations in Chicago. I was now making a lot more money than some of the people working the same shift. Discussing the amount of money I was being paid would make his job much harder when it came time to negotiate their deals. His reasons made sense. When I explained to him why I had done it, he agreed that my motivation also had merit. I said that for the past five weeks, on his radio station, I had discussed, among other things, my past. People seemed particularly interested in the hard times. The drug stories and living in my car had considerable impact. If I was not willing to be as truthful with the listeners when something good happened to me then I was no longer being open and honest about my past, just exploiting it. He told me that he understood and smiled.

When I turned to leave his office he added, "If you do it again, I really will fire you." He meant it. As I said, Mr. Wert is a true gentleman. He is also a hardass when he has to be—but as time wore on, I indeed did get a few more promotions. I eventually ended up doing "afternoon drive"—the second-best shift in radio. It could be construed as the first-best shift if you consider that you do not have to wake up at three in the morning.

About the same time they put me on AM 1000 in the afternoons, they also hired Howard Stern to do mornings. Man, I was really in the big time. After a few months of afternoon drive I was ready to take my first vacation. On the way to the Caribbean, Gretchen and I stopped in New York so I could appear on the *Ricki Lake* show. After I taped the show, I went back to the hotel to gather my belongings and fly off to paradise. I was halfway out of the hotel when I was paged to the front desk. It was a call from Larry Wert. He said, "You have to come home, we just fired Howard Stern."

There are two surefire ways to make sure you have a short life span in Chicago.

1. Say anything bad about the city.
2. Screw with Larry Wert or his boss, Jimmy deCastro.

Howard did both his *first* day. I would have come home anyway, but before I could hang up Mr. Wert agreed to pay any money I lost on this vacation and added that he would pay for the next one. When I got back to Chicago, Mr. Wert laid out his plan. I would substitute for Howard until they found a suitable replacement. In the meantime he would hire some "weekender" to fill in for me. I said, *"NO!"* I had heard too many stories about $10-an-hour weekenders substituting for million-dollar disc jockeys only to have the bosses find out that the $10-an-hour guy was better. I was not taking that chance. I told Mr. Wert the only way I would agree to do it was if I could do both shows.

It was an unheard-of request. No one had ever appeared on the same radio station eight hours a day. Mr. Wert did not think I could do it. I appealed to his inner tightwad. I told him I would do both shows for no extra money. He warmed to the idea. For the next six months I was on the air from 6 A.M. until 10 A.M. Then, in the afternoon, I was on again from 2 P.M. until 6 P.M., five days a week. I should have asked for more money. It was harder than I thought. The fact that my throat constantly hurt was the easy part. The hard part was listening to the legions of rabid and vapid Howard Stern fans that were threatening to kill me. Howard sued. Eventually it was all settled, but in the end? Howard Stern wrote more about Larry Wert in his book than I have in mine. Howard was not as nice. Things continued to go great for me in Chicago.

That is not to say I did not have a fight on my hands.

Chapter 28

DONNY AND THE AMAZING TECHNICOLOR NOSEBLEED

It started at the health club, and I mean *the* health club, Chicago's famed East Bank Club. It was not uncommon to see Oprah Winfrey and Michael Jordan working out there. It cost a fortune to join, so they could keep out the riffraff, but I went anyway. My company had a corporate membership. Having spent most of my adult years stoned, broke, or both, I had not had much use for health clubs, so this was, indeed, a serious perk.

The East Bank Club is not just a gym, although it has all the appropriate equipment. The East Bank Club is a palace of pampering. Along with the saunas, Jacuzzis, tennis courts, basketball courts, massage tables, it has a full bar. I found the idea of a bar at a health club amusing. Do not get me wrong, I drank there, but I was amused the entire time. One day, after working out, I was looking at myself in the mirror when a man walked up behind me and said, "Bonaduce, you are such a poseur."

I assumed it was one of my friends. It wasn't. It was Donny Osmond. Donny and I really did not know each other, although I must assume we had met once or twice over the years. We talked for a while and he seemed like a great guy. In fact (even though this story is about to get ugly), I would like to use Donny Osmond as further evidence of my ex–child star theory. He is living proof that a person can grow up relatively well adjusted in show business. As we talked, Donny told me that he was going to be on the Johnny B. show later that day. He was going on to promote his appearance in *Joseph and the Amazing Technicolor Dreamcoat.* Donny (and the musical) were scheduled to be in town for five weeks. His engagement would go on to be extended for almost two years. This was a testament to his talent.

I told Donny that during his interview, he should tell Johnny B. that he had caught me "posing" at the club. I knew Johnny would get a kick out of that. Sure enough, later that day, when I turned on the radio, there was Donny Osmond talking about my behavior at the gym. Johnny asked Donny a good question. He wanted to know if Donny ever got sick of the fact that all the bad ex–child stars (me) got all the press, while the good ones (Donny) were ignored. Donny said, "Yes."

Johnny continued. He wanted to know if Donny thought he could beat me in a fight. Donny said yes. Then

Johnny asked, "If I were to set up a boxing match, would Donny fight Danny?" Unfortunately, Donny said yes. The next thing I know, I am listening to Donny Osmond challenge me to a fight over the radio. I still believed that Donny was kidding, just playing along. Donny was only a tourist in Chicago. I had to live there and I had a reputation to live down. I couldn't let this challenge go unanswered. I called the show.

I was also trying to play along. Then Donny started to sound serious. Johnny B. would not stop prodding him. It got ugly. I was soon saying things like "I'm going to come down to the studio and knock your giant teeth out and take them home for a souvenir." I went on to say, "I bet Donny thinks fighting with me would change his Goody Two-shoes image." Then I countered, "But, if he insists on this madness, the only thing that would change would be his appearance."

We said some more stupid things to each other, and I eventually hung up the phone. When I showed up for my next shift, I had all but forgotten about it. When I got on the air, however, the only thing everyone wanted to talk about was when was I going to fight Donny Osmond? There was no way out. I hated Johnny B. *soooo* much that day! I thought he was a low-life, scum-sucking, and publicity-seeking disc jockey. In other words, I recognized my own kind.

The fight was set. It was to be held at the China Club. When the 3,000 available tickets went on sale, they sold out in less than ninety seconds. This had turned into a big deal. People were starting to refer to it as the fight of good versus evil. Guess which one I played? It was all anyone could talk about. Donny and I not only got a ton of press in the States, but we also did interviews in Australia, France, and even Japan. The rumor was that Donny was taking this very seriously and training every day. I was having a hard time getting worked up over the fact I was going to have to kick the crap out of a pretty nice guy.

Eventually I started to get nervous. What would happen if I lost? Donny had nothing to lose. Nobody expected him to win. If I lost, I would have to leave the country. One day I was giving interviews about the fight to one of the local television news shows. In the middle of my interview, they ran a clip of Donny training at the Windy City Gym. Lou Duva was training him. Lou is one of the premier names in boxing. The clip was about thirty seconds long, and I'll be damned if Donny didn't look good. He shadowboxed. He jumped rope. He sparred. He was very graceful. I was starting to become scared.

When my interview was over, I asked the news director if I could see the B-roll of Donny's interview. B-roll is the excess videotape they shot of Donny Osmond that they did not show. They would not let me take the tapes home, so I had to watch it right there in the newsroom. I did not like what I saw. He *could* jump rope. He *could* bob. He *could* weave. Donny Osmond was a goddamned athlete. I was starting to sweat.

Then I got a break. I saw something important they did not show on the news. I saw Donny get hit. He did not like it. To be honest, "hit" is a strong word. I saw Donny get touched. Donny's nose started to bleed. He did not react too badly to it, but his sparring was over for today. As they say, I breathed a huge sigh of relief. Even with my martial arts training, I had never been graceful. On the other hand, you can hit me with a bat just to get my attention. I knew Donny was toast.

Finally it was fight night. Donny and I had dressing rooms that the China Club set up in the VIP area. After seeing the tape of Donny getting hit, I had stopped caring about the fight—except about how it could help my career. We were still getting a ton of press. In an attempt to keep that press going, both Donny and I had taken to saying terrible things about each other.

I hoped that we were both kidding. I decided to walk over to his dressing room and let him know I held no ill-will toward him. The moment I walked into his room, I realized Donny was *not* kidding. There were pictures of me all over his dressing room walls. Some had big Xs drawn through them. Some were defaced. Donny also had gone to the trouble of drawing horns coming out of my head. I thought this was pretty odd, but maybe this was just his way of being motivated. There must have been ten people in the dressing room.

I walked up to Donny and said, "I am sorry about all the nasty things I've said about you. It was just hype," and

I put out my hand. Donny turned his back on me and said to someone, "Get him out of here." A gorilla of a man walked up and confronted me. His name was Bobby Hitz. Bobby is only about six feet tall, but he is also about 250 pounds of solid muscle. His knuckles were the size of chestnuts. Bobby walked up to me, looked down, and said, "Mr. Osmond does not want you here. I think it would be best if you would leave right now." I could not get out of there fast enough.

When I got back to my dressing room, I told my friends about the pictures on the wall and of my altercation with Bobby Hitz. I got some alarming news. My friends told me Bobby had taken over Donny's training. Bobby was not only the local heavyweight prizefighter who had fought George Foreman, but that nose of his looked as if it had been broken a dozen times even though it had never been broken at all. When Bobby decided to become a professional fighter, he never wanted a fight to be stopped over "something as trivial as a broken nose." Legend has it, before his first fight, Bobby had all the cartilage in his nose surgically removed. In other words, Donny Osmond was hanging out with a serious bad-ass with bad intentions. Bad intentions are contagious.

Before I walked into Donny's dressing room, my plan was to "carry him" through the fight. I would hit him only enough to win—but I would make sure he did not get seriously injured. Now all bets were off. I would knock him out the moment I got a chance.

When it came time to fight, Donny was introduced first. I could not believe his entrance. I forget what song he used, but the music was blaring. To my amazement, Donny was carried into the ring on a golden throne. He was being carried by the entire cast of *Technicolor Dreamcoat*. They were all dressed as Egyptians. It was quite a sight. It was also, in my opinion, one of the reasons Donny was about to get hurt. Donny had come to a show. I had come to a fight.

I walked to the ring by myself. To show my contempt, I had a cigarette in my mouth. Johnny B. and former World Heavyweight Champion Leon Spinks did the ring announcing. Unbeknownst to me, all the ring girls were transvestites in homage to my "fight" in Phoenix.

NOTE TO READERS: Since the Donny fight, Bobby Hitz and I have become good friends, so I can now reveal to you what Donny Osmond's fight plans were.

Bobby told Donny, "Bonaduce is an animal. The second the bell rings, he is going to run across the ring and attack." He went on to tell Donny about my three-pack-a-day smoking habit. Bobby told Donny just to cover up. "Bonaduce will run out of gas in thirty seconds." The bell rang and the fight started. Just like a trained monkey, I did as Bobby had predicted. I ran across the ring so fast, Donny was barely off his stool when I started punching him, head and face. Just as he had been coached to do, Donny covered. Just as he had been told I would, I pounded away. We were barely thirty seconds into the fight and I could already hear the ring announcers saying, "Somebody should stop the fight—Donny's being killed."

I continued to punch away. As the clock ticked away, my punches became far less frequent and far less powerful. Bobby was wrong. It took me ninety seconds to run out of gas. I could not breathe. I could hardly keep my hands up. It did not matter. It was obvious to me that Donny Osmond was merely looking for a place to fall down. I started to mug for the crowd, as I was the obvious victor. I looked back at Donny to see if he had fallen yet.

He hadn't.

There he was, standing in a textbook fighting position. The son of a bitch wasn't hurt at all. Worse, he looked really pissed. Worst of all, he did not look tired. There is a saying that goes, "Fatigue makes cowards out of men." It could not be more true. I was terrified. I knew my life was about to change. From this moment on, I would no longer be "the guy from *The Partridge Family*" or "the crazy guy who took all those drugs" or even "the guy on the radio." In about two seconds, and for the rest of my life, I was going to be "the guy who got his ass kicked by Donny Osmond."

I contemplated suicide. The bell rang. Thank God we were using two-minute rounds. I dragged myself to my corner. I was breathing so hard—and coughing so much—I could not take water. I looked over at Donny's corner. The bastard had not even broken a sweat.

I was dead. I contemplated fouling. Perhaps an "accidental" head butt—or an "accidental" elbow to the face or a knee into the Osmond family jewels. Unfortunately, even cheating took more energy than I had. I came up with a new strategy. When the bell rang for Round 2, I would use much the same plan that Donny had used in Round 1. The only difference would be that I would not cover up. I would just stand there (with my hands at my side) and let Donny Osmond punch me in the face until he was tired. My theory was not only would Donny Osmond tire himself out, but I would impress the judges by showing that Donny could not hurt me.

NOTE TO READERS: IT WAS A SHITTY PLAN.

I was right about one thing. Donny could not hurt me. Unfortunately, I was wrong about everything else. It became obvious that Donny would never tire of hitting me in the face. It became equally clear that getting repeatedly punched in the head was no way to convince the judges that I was winning the fight. Donny had won over the crowd. People who had come to the fight expressly to see me pound "Mr. Puppy Love" were now cheering for Donny. I decided to defend myself but I couldn't. I could barely lift my hands to cover my face. I supposedly made a comment about his sister Marie that he didn't appreciate, but you'll have to read about that in his book and his "account" of the fight.

The bell rang to end Round 2. I again limped to my corner and collapsed on my chair. It was obvious to me Donny had won the round. One round to go. In my mind, the fight was a tie. One round each. Unfortunately, there was one to go. In between rounds, my wife ran up to my corner and started to yell some very un-Gretchen-like words of encouragement. I was shocked. Gretchen had seen Donny in *Dream Coat* three times—and admitted to me she had a huge crush on Donny when she was a girl. I thought she had secretly been rooting for him. Now she was screaming *"Kill the bastard!"*

When the bell rang to start Round 3, she shouted out her real motivation for her outburst. As I was dragging myself to the center of the ring, I heard Gretchen yell, *"There will be no living with you if you lose this fight."* She was right, but there was nothing I could do about it. I was spent. Donny rushed at me like a madman, just as I had done to him in Round 1. I covered up and waited to take my beating. It never came. I finally looked up to see what was happening and why Donny was not killing me. I could not believe my eyes. In his excitement, Donny had run across the ring *so fast* that he ran facefirst into my glove. He had a bloody nose. This was the best punch of the fight, and it was an accident. Just as in the B-roll tape I had seen, Donny did not want to fight anymore. Seeing Donny's nose bleed gave me a boost of energy, but not much. When the fight was over, the judges declared a draw. The crowd would not have it. They wanted a "clear victor." The deciding vote was given to the referee. He picked me. There was a mixed reaction in the crowd. They had come to see someone be knocked out. It did not matter to me. I was declared the winner, awarded a rather garish trophy, and was ready to go home. To this day, Donny thinks I somehow cheated and is still very upset by the outcome. Donny, if you happen to be reading this, let me say that I have matured enough that I can honestly admit the fight was probably a draw. On the other hand, if you are still mad, let me say this: I have not matured enough to admit that I am *not* willing to do it with you again.

Chapter 29

MOST PEOPLE MAKE ASSES OF THEMSELVES ON TV; I JUST SHOW MINE

The Donny Osmond fight remains the biggest attention-getting moment I have ever had in my radio career, but there were some other moments in Chicago that meant more to me. Some of these moments were downright touching. My appearance on *The Arsenio Hall Show* was not one of them.

One day in 1994, I got a call from Arsenio's people asking me if I would appear with David Cassidy and Shirley Jones. Of course, I immediately agreed. The moment I hung up the phone, I went on the air with the same scheme I had pulled off on the *Larry King Live* show. The question I put out was, "Which one of my coworkers or fellow disc jockeys will pay me—and how much—to sneak in their name during my interview with Arsenio Hall?" This time I wasn't really doing it for the money. I was doing it so my listeners and I could be coconspirators on an inside joke played out on national television that only the people of Chicago would be privy to. I was surprised by who decided to take up my challenge. It was Larry Wert, vice president, general manager, and resident showoff of WLUP.

Mr. Wert not only said that he would give me $1,000 every time I mentioned his name, but he would also give $1,000 to DARE, a drug-use intervention program for young people. It was Arsenio's favorite charity. When I got to the show, it was me, David Cassidy, Shirley Jones, and Arsenio Hall on the set. At first, Arsenio asked all the standard *Partridge Family* questions. We all gave our answers and got a few laughs. Finally Arsenio turned to me and asked me about my new radio show. This was my moment. I told him that until recently I had been a sidekick on someone else's show, but now I had my own show "thanks to a man named Larry Wert." It was Larry Wert who believed in me and I owed my career to Larry Wert.

BANG. Three grand for me. Three grand for DARE.

That was enough. The joke was played, and it was now time for me to try to give a good interview. Arsenio then did something shocking. Instead of asking me a new question, he said, "This Larry Wert seems like a great guy. Tell me more about Larry Wert." Even though I could hear a cash register in my head and I was raking in the dough, I couldn't understand what was happening. Between the two of us, we must have said Larry Wert's name twenty times. We took a commercial break. During the break, Arsenio explained a few things to me. Somebody in Chicago had sent in a fax detailing my entire plan. Arsenio was on to me. All he wanted to know was, did I believe Mr. Wert would really give the money to DARE? I told him yes, I did. When we returned from the commercial break, Arsenio explained to his viewers what was happening and that DARE was getting $1,000 every time we said the name "Larry Wert."

Then, and I'm assuming to my boss's horror, Arsenio started to repeat Larry Wert over and over again. When he was done the total was up to about $40,000. But Arsenio wasn't done. He had a surprise for me. The fax from Chicago not only told him about my plan, but it told him something else about me. It told him that I had Larry Wert's name tattooed on my butt. He asked me if this was true. Unfortunately, it was.

Let me explain.

When I first arrived in Chicago, I was still trying very hard to live up to the madman image that WLUP had spent so much time and effort cultivating. With my arrest record, I couldn't do anything illegal. So I did something just as stupid. On one of my first shows, I got the names of my coworkers, Johnny B., Kevin Matthews, and Larry Wert, tattooed on my butt, along with the radio station's logo. Once I admitted to this, Arsenio said he wanted to see it. This was one of the first television shows I had done in years that didn't dwell on my criminal past, so I made up for this step in the right direction by standing onstage—on national television—with my pants around my ankles and my ass to the camera. Shirley Jones laughed hysterically. David Cassidy looked like he wanted to kill me. I got a standing ovation. Back in Chicago I thought I was probably in trouble—not for taking my pants down, but for costing my boss forty grand.

When I got back to Chicago, I marched into Mr. Wert's office to tell him he didn't really have to pay me, but the checks were already on his desk. Twenty grand for me. Twenty grand for DARE. By the way, I still have the tattoo and proudly display it. It is my red badge of stupidity.

Believe it or not, my childish antics on Arsenio Hall's show? They ended up giving birth to what is probably my finest moment on radio. A few nights after *Arsenio* aired, I was doing my radio show when I got a call from a guy who had seen my performance and wanted to comment on it. I took his call and he said, "Hey, man, I saw you on *Arsenio* and I just wanted to tell you, you are an inspiration." I could not imagine what part of my performance he found "inspirational." When I asked him, he said that he was proud of the way I had gotten off drugs and gotten my life back together. (Oh, yeah, I had forgotten that part of the interview.) All I remembered were my pants being down around my ankles and getting "eye" daggers from David.

I said thank you and was about to hang up when he said something else that got my attention. He told me that he was also a drug addict. Unfortunately, he said he had failed to get his life together—and now he was going to kill himself. He couldn't think of anyone else to tell—so he decided to call me! At first, I didn't necessarily believe him. A lot of crazies call in on late-night radio shows. On the other hand, if he was to be believed, this was possibly the saddest thing I had ever heard. The more we talked, the more I believed him.

His story was tragic, but so are most drug addicts' stories. The only difference here was *this* guy called *me* for help. He told me he was a nurse and that he had recently been caught stealing drugs from the hospital. After they fired him, he went back to the hospital and stole a lethal amount of morphine. He was now going to use that to kill himself. This guy's entire life and the possible end of it were spilling out on radios all over Chicago.

I didn't know what to do. This guy had called me for help. By now I truly believed he was going to kill himself. I couldn't exactly put him on hold. I kept talking to him while I wrote a note to my producer telling him "to call the police and have the call traced." He was starting to slur his words. I was afraid he had already injected himself. He kept saying he was "going to hang up now"—but I kept him on the phone. He had called my show at the very beginning, and now, four hours later, I was still on the phone with him and my shift was ending. Where the hell were the police?

Five minutes before my show was over, thousands of people in Chicago and I heard the police come crashing through his door. The reason for the delay became clear when the law enforcement officer (who had just burst into my caller's home) picked up the phone. He wasn't a policeman. He was a Mountie. The guy was calling from Canada. The Mountie picked up the phone and thanked me for my assistance. He was about to hang up, but I had to know. I asked if he believed that the man was really going to kill himself.

He told me that on the coffee table, next to the caller, was a syringe and what appeared to be enough morphine in it to kill an entire neighborhood. He said he truly believed the man was going to kill himself. He went on to say, "It's not every day someone gets to save someone else's life— you should be proud of yourself." I was.

When my show was over, I called the Mounties back and asked what would become of the young man whom I now, in some way, felt responsible for. I was informed that he would be taken to a hospital and looked after. Over the next few days I checked in with the hospital to see how he was doing. After he was released I lost touch with him. To be honest, after a month or two, I pretty much forgot about him.

But it would not be the last time I heard from him.

Chapter 30

A SPRINGER SHOW, WITH TEETH!

After the suicide call, my life got back to normal, whatever that is. Then I got another call that was going to shake things up again. This time, the call was from Jerry Springer. This was back in the day when Jerry didn't exclusively do "freak shows." Sometimes he did celebrity freak shows. Naturally they called me. Somehow I had become the spokesman for celebrities with deviant behavior. To this day, I haven't been able to shake that claim to fame.

Over the past eleven years I haven't had as much as a speeding ticket. Yet when a celebrity gets busted, they still call me for comment. When Pee-wee Herman got busted, they called me. When Hugh Grant got busted, they called me. Robert Downey Jr. keeps me on many a show—and, of course, poor Dana Plato.

When Eddie Murphy got pulled over with a transvestite hooker, everybody called me. After all, I am the expert!

Being the good guy of bad-boy behavior is nothing to be proud of, but every career needs a hook—and I guess I earned this one. But when they told me it was another ex–child-star-gone-wrong show, I told them I wasn't interested. Jerry's people went on to be quite flattering. They told me I was one of their favorite guests and there was a noticeable spike in the ratings whenever I was on. They asked me if they came up with another topic that was suitable for me, would I then be willing to come on the show? A few days later they called back. They said they had a new idea. The episode was to be called, get ready, "Danny Bonaduce's Random Acts of Kindness." I laughed out loud. I know a Jerry Springer episode called "Danny Bonaduce's Random Acts of Kindness" sounds like something I made up. We actually shot the show, and stranger still, they actually aired it.

I asked them, "Specifically, what acts of kindness are you talking about?" They reminded me of the young man in Canada that I had "saved." I didn't mention that "talking a man out of suicide over the air" made for good radio. I wanted to see what other acts of kindness they had in mind. They told me while researching my name to try to come up with an angle for me, they had come across the story of me buying a wheelchair for the young man in Rhode Island. They really liked the quote from the man's mother calling me a "Christmas angel."

They weren't done. They had found some other things that I had completely forgotten about. Once, while doing show prep right before my show, I read a story about a couple from a small town. On Christmas Eve someone, they believed it was a cult, had tortured their dogs to death. The story went on to say that the couple was unable to have children of their own and that they felt like someone had butchered their kids.

I went on the air and called them. I don't really know why, I just wanted to tell them that "the people of Chicago—and I—felt terrible for them." I went on to say if they wanted, "I would send them two new Labrador puppies to replace the ones they had lost." The woman started to cry and told me not to put myself out. I told her the truth; this was not going to cost me a penny. I assured her that if she wanted the dogs, I was positive a pet store would call the show and donate the dogs. I was right. Seconds after I said it, all my phone lines were lit up with pet store owners. They were willing to donate not only the dogs but also a year's worth of food. The woman accepted.

As you can see, the act of kindness really belonged to the pet store owner. I had done nothing more than feel bad and make a phone call—but apparently Jerry Springer was giving me all the credit. The next person on Jerry's list was an old junior high school friend of my wife's. Gretchen and this young lady had not spoken in years, but she contacted me through the radio station. Once again it was right around Christmas. Don't hold me to the particulars, because this was years ago, and I don't really know these people.

The phone call went something like this. My wife's friend told Gretchen that her husband had been arrested for drunk driving. If she couldn't raise the bail money, her husband would spend Christmas in jail. The young lady went on to say she had seen Gretchen and me on several talk shows talking about how Gretchen had changed and saved my life. The woman told Gretchen how proud and happy she was for us. Then she asked to borrow the bail money. Gretchen could have just said yes (as it is completely true that Gretchen saved my life). Therefore, everything I have (or ever will have) belongs to her. Still, Gretchen gave me the courtesy of asking if we could lend her friend the money. You should have seen the surprise on Gretchen's face when I said no.

I took the phone from my very stunned wife and told the lady that I would not lend her the bail money. Even though I've never agreed with AA or NA "disease theory," I told her if she could guarantee to me she would make her husband go to ninety Alcoholics Anonymous meetings in ninety days, Gretchen and I would give them the money as a Christmas gift. The lady agreed and we sent the money.

Once again I was getting credit for somebody else's act of kindness. This one, and many others, belonged to Gretchen. So here was the show.

- They would fly in my wife's friend and her allegedly sober husband.
- They would fly in the couple with the puppies.

- They would fly in the young wheelchair man and his entire family from Rhode Island.
- They couldn't find the young man from Canada, but Jerry would read the news stories about the incident.
- We would then discuss what a great guy I was.

The fact of the matter is, I am not such a great guy. Truth be known, I was only out bail and wheelchair money. In my estimation, my wife probably gave her friend the money; the pet store gave the puppies; the suicide call made good radio. The only thing I was sure I had done—just because it was the right thing to do—was give the kid a wheelchair. Modesty should have prevented me from doing the show, but I'm in show business—and we just don't do that.

The show was agonizing. There must have been at least ten people crying and thanking me. What does any reasonable person do when someone says thank you? You say "you're welcome," and that should be the end of it. Unfortunately, saying "You are welcome" and moving on to the next guest makes for one very slow and bad television show. People thanked me for an hour. To be honest, some of it was pretty touching. I think the lady and her dogs made me cry . . . but I wouldn't swear to it. The woman from Rhode Island gave her now-famous "Christmas angel" speech. The whole thing was pretty bizarre. It was about to get weirder. For the last segment of the show Jerry had scheduled a psychologist who was going to explain why I felt the need to do this sort of thing. The psychologist was a ruse.

The empty chair on the set was for a surprise guest. This was not the kind of "surprise" guest that makes daytime talk show guests shoot each other. Nonetheless, it was an ambush surprise. It was the suicide caller. We hugged and cried while he loudly thanked me for saving his life. Finally (and mercifully) the show was over. I went home.

The "suicide caller" begat *Jerry Springer*. After the show aired, I got another crazy phone call, and this one was out of the blue. You've noticed that I get a lot of odd phone calls!

Chapter 31

HEEERRRREEEE'S JONNY

Things were going extremely well with my career—and even better in my personal life. They say, if something seems too good to be true, it probably is. That is not necessarily the case. A few years earlier, I had married a total stranger. I was broke and probably going to jail. Now I had a great career, and I had been off drugs for over three years. I was not on probation in any of the fifty states.

Better still, I knew exactly who my benefactor was. Many people (in my position) spend a great deal of time searching for their "higher power." I got lucky. I married mine. As an extra added bonus, my "higher power" happens to be totally hot. I know that may sound shallow, but I am not alone in my desire for physical beauty among the divine. Check out the masters, Raphael, da Vinci, and Michelangelo. They never painted female angels with warts or a drooping eye. So, if my life seemed to be turning out to be too good to be true, it was. Why, then, couldn't the phone call I just received be true? As far as I was concerned, it was! When I answered that particular call, the man at the other end introduced himself. He went on to explain that he was a writer and a producer. If I had heard him correctly, and the man actually said what I thought he said, he needed no introduction.

"It's a pleasure to talk to you, Mr. Demme." He said, *"Call me Jon."*

Sure enough, I was very surprised that *the* Jonathan Demme was calling me. Demme is the Academy Award®–winning director of movies like *The Silence of the Lambs*. That's a very big Hollywood name. I was so excited, I could hardly breathe. I also wondered what in hell this guy wanted with me. So I asked him (and, of course, I rephrased it). "What can I do for you?" What he said next was astonishing. He told me he had been aware of me for some time, and, in the back of his mind, he had always thought that my life story would make a great movie. Just that Jonathan Demme knew I even existed would have been enough for me. I could not contain myself. I covered the phone and started whispering the goings-on to my wife. He was not done shocking me. He went on to say, "The problem with my story is it didn't have an ending."

I wondered where he was going, but if Jonathan Demme wanted to make a movie about my life and needed an ending, dying would be the *least* I could do. He let me off the hook. He said that he had seen the *Jerry Springer* show and now he had his ending. My life had come full circle. I was now helping others. I was still flabbergasted by this conversation, and I was also incredibly moved. But I must admit, the idea of Jonathan Demme, the great man himself, sitting around in his underwear eating chips from the bag and watching *Jerry Springer* made me laugh out loud.

We talked a little while longer. Just before we hung up, he said two more strange things. "Okay, then, with your permission I will get started on this right away and I'll see if I can drum up some interest." The thing that struck me as odd in his final sentence was the "with your permission"— as if there was a chance in hell I was going to withhold it. Maybe he was just being polite. Stranger still was, "I'll see if I can drum up some interest." Jon Demme does not drum up interest. Interest tries to drum up Jon Demme. Maybe he was just being modest. We talked maybe four more times over the next two months. Actually, I talked. He mostly listened.

The thing that astonished me most was how "available" he was to me. I had tried in vain for most of my life to get people like this on the phone. Now I had his office number at Avenue Pictures. I had his cell number. I had his home number. If I called him at his office he got on the phone immediately. If he wasn't in, he called me back within minutes. He wanted me to tell him stories—and I did. I did not tell him everything, because I didn't want to scare him away. People usually do not want to gamble a great deal of

time and money on a guy who is seriously screwed up.
Writers think they make up people like me.

I didn't tell him about things like my chaining myself
up in hotel rooms so I could appear sober on talk shows
then lie about how I'd been sober for years. I didn't neglect
to tell him these stories out of shame or embarrassment. I
didn't tell him because, once you admit to someone that
you used to lie to everyone you knew, they immediately
start to wonder if you are lying to them. I also did not mention any of the psychological evaluations that I have peppered throughout this book. In fact, until now, I don't
believe I have ever publicly mentioned anything about my
seeing a psychiatrist—let alone what the psychiatrist had to
say. No matter what I told him, he never acted shocked or
surprised. Whenever I was finished telling him a story, the
few things he would say afterward were always kind and
complimentary.

One day my phone rang and it was he. He said he had
serious interest in the movie at Fox. I was surprised that
Jonathan Demme was putting this much time and energy
into a TV movie. He said it was time to meet. I flew to California that Friday. I was so excited on the plane ride, I
could barely contain myself. We were to meet at some
fancy restaurant called Pinot on the corner of Sunset and
Gower—the infamous corner where the hookers used to
work when I was on my *Partridge Family* audition years
before. I got there early. I get everywhere early. One of the

many paranoias that plague ex-junkies, or at least this ex-junkie, is being late. If other people are late, they are probably stuck in traffic. If I am late, I assume people think I'm in some seedy motel smoking crack.

I waited at the bar and ordered a soda. I really wanted a drink, and I could have had one. I had been very careful in my wording on this subject with Jon. I never said I was clean and sober. I said I was clean. Which, by the way, I am. I also said I was drug-free. Which, in my opinion, I am—even though I still smoke, consume alcohol, and enjoy coffee. There are some people who think alcohol, nicotine, and caffeine are the same things as drugs. These people are zealots and probably not that much fun to hang around with.

I was standing at the bar when somebody, not too far behind me, said, *"Danny!!"* I turned around, and there he was. Some guy I'd never seen before. His hair and eyebrows were so jet black—and he was so perfectly coiffed—that he immediately reminded me of Dash RipRock from *The Flintstones*. He walked up to me, stuck out his hand, and said, "Great to meet you!" He acted as if he knew me. This was nothing new. A lot of people in my age group grew up watching *The Partridge Family* and often react to me like an old friend. Usually, I like that a great deal. This time I was nervous. I shook his hand and said, "Nice to meet you too." Then he dropped the bomb. "I'm Jon Denny." I could not believe it. Had this guy purposely deceived me? Was he a real writer? The only thing I knew for sure was my dreams of a life story movie were over. After a painfully long silence, I looked at him and (almost yelling) said, "I thought you were Jonathan Demme."

He just smiled and said, "I get that all the time." This guy was five seconds from getting his ass kicked right there in Pinot! I ordered a shot. I did not know what to do. I contemplated leaving, but where was I going to go? I had already flown all the way to Los Angeles—and at my own expense. The restaurant looked expensive, and I had to assume this guy was buying.

As I thought about our past conversations, I realized this was my doing. He had said his name when he first called. When I called his office I only asked for Jon. On a couple of occasions, when he was not home, I even spoke to his girlfriend. This guy had not tried to deceive me. This was an honest although horrifying mistake. After a few more drinks it all seemed pretty funny. It helped my mood a great deal when we started to discuss Jon's résumé.

Sure, he wasn't Jonathan Demme. He also wasn't, as I initially feared, a gym teacher or a real estate agent who thought he had a great idea. He was a real, live writer and producer. He had done some very high-quality television work for PBS, and I had even paid money to see one of the movies he'd produced: *The Object of Beauty,* with John Malkovich and Andie MacDowell. In other words, Jon got things made. If you do not live in Los Angeles, you may not know what being able to get things made means. It is my opinion that there are approximately eight people in Los

Angeles who really get movies made. Everyone else just
runs around.

After dinner I went to a hotel. The next morning I went
home. I wasn't nearly as excited as I had been, but I wasn't
terribly depressed either. After all, things were going well
for me anyway. Being upset because I might not get my
movie made would be like being upset because I didn't win
the lottery twice.

After a few more months of phone calls and faxing, Jon
and I wrote the darkest comedy since *After Hours*. Five
years later, when the movie finally made it to television, it
was no longer the movie we had written. ABC decided they
wanted a movie about *The Partridge Family*. I got a producer's credit and a substantial amount of money. My sole
responsibilities were to have dinner with the new writers
and show up on the set at least once for press. I suddenly
liked producing. In the course of my relationship with Jon
Denny, we have done what we set out to do—we have written and produced. Importantly, we made a daytime talk
show, a movie of the week, a game show, and a series of
specials. Jon is a very talented man and a real go-getter,
and, except for the fact that sometimes he wears shoes that
match his handkerchief, he is a pretty excellent guy.

Chapter 32

I WORK HARD FOR THE MONEY!

When I arrived back in Chicago, I did not have time to mourn the assumed loss of my *Life Story* movie. I was too busy. My bosses had yet to find a replacement for Howard Stern. When I was asked to fill in for Howard, I jumped at the chance. Pulling two shifts gave me something money couldn't buy: legitimacy.

For my first few years in radio, I was considered nothing more than a publicity stunt. Just being hired at a station like "The Loop" gave me a future. Having the people who ran arguably the most prestigious station in America give me four raises within one year helped me to be perceived as a legitimate broadcaster. Doing two shifts a day made me one of *the* broadcasters. I am not in any way comparing myself to the greats of radio of today or yesteryear. I am just saying (as far as I know), it had never been done before in a major market. There are only a handful of disc jockeys who have done both mornings and afternoons day in and day out. The legendary Tom Joyner, otherwise known as "The Fly Jock," was one. Tom did mornings in Dallas and afternoons in Chicago, and did it for years. He actually flew back and forth between those cities, every day. Not to take anything away from Tom, but he did have a couple of things going for him that I did not. First of all, he was working in two cities—but on the same kind of radio station. That meant he could play back all his best bits from his morning show in Dallas and repeat them on his afternoon show in Chicago. The other thing in Tom's favor was that he played a lot of music.

I do not think anyone had been on the same big-city radio station for eight hours a day. I also don't believe anyone has ever done it on an all-talk-format station. Because I worked in the same city and on the same station, more than 60 percent of the people who listened to me in the morning also listened to me in the afternoon. I could not repeat myself. I had to come up with eight hours of original programming every day.

NOTE TO READERS: Before you think that I must have developed a muscle from patting myself on the back, I never said it was eight hours of *good* programming. I am just pointing out that I did it.

That was enough. Good or bad, by now there was no missing me in the radio business. "The powers that be" knew they could count on me. It had been a long time since anyone had thought that of me. I was very proud and, what is more important, so was my wife. Looking back on it, I guess I did miss getting the money. I think every kid in America wants to be a millionaire. I was not even close to it . . . yet.

Eventually, after they finally replaced Howard and I was back down to holding only one job, I became accustomed to the long hours, and, to be honest, I never sleep anyway. So, I thought, "Why waste the extra time?" I took on three new jobs to replace the one I had lost. These jobs paid. I started to work as an entertainment reporter on WMAQ TV, the NBC affiliate in Chicago. I also agreed to (again) sidekick for the John Lander show in New York, by way of a satellite studio they installed in my home. My bosses in Chicago only allowed me to be on the air in New York one hour a day. That was cool.

Next I would do another entertainment report—but this time by phone—to Australia, no less! The toughest part of the Australian job was my entertainment report from that morning had to be rewritten. My WMAQ report focused on local celebrities, and they meant nothing in the Land Down Under. To wrap up my day, I would then go to my "real" job at The Loop.

There were two good things about all this extra work.

1. Soaking up information like a sponge. I was spend-ing a lot of time in a newsroom, reading the gossip

columns, and I was on a current events type show in New York. It not only did not hurt my real job on The Loop; in my opinion, it made the show better.

2. The extra money. All of these jobs paid somewhere in between good and (in my world) ludicrous amounts of money.

The only drawback? I could see that working all these jobs would cause not only fatigue but confusion. I had a very hard time keeping track of what day it was. Worse still, I was having trouble keeping my stories straight. If I had a good joke (or story) in one city or country, I would, of course, want to repeat it in the others. The problem was, by the next morning, I could not be certain on what show I had told what story first! I would have to disregard it. Not one of the shows I was working on knew—or would have cared—that I was working four jobs.

If I went on the air and told a five-minute story that I had told the same audience yesterday, I saw no problem. They would have assumed I was either back on drugs or (what is worse in the radio business) that I had run out of things to say. Gretchen, of course, thought I should quit my three side jobs. Soon enough she would get her way. I needed the time. I was about to get my own television show. Yes, a TV show!

NOTE TO READERS: Before I move on, I would like to tell you a little bit about the best thing (aside from Gretchen) that ever happened to me in my entire life.

It was at this point in time that I first found out I was going to be a daddy. Nine months later, on November 23, 1994, Gretchen gave birth to our daughter, Isabella. I will not bore you with typical father stories, like Isabella is the smartest, the funniest, most beautiful child in the world even though it would be completely accurate information. We left Chicago when Isabella was only one year old. Even Isabella did not become "fascinating" until she was almost a year and a half old. We nicknamed her *"Boo Bear!"* You will meet her soon.

It really is amazing how life changes. I had been free of drugs for several years. I was happily married with a beautiful infant and living in my favorite city in the world, Chicago. I was back, and I was good! I was now the host of my own highly successful radio talk show on WLUP. I certainly wasn't bigger than Johnny Carson, but I was on my way. Chicago and I were also having a love affair. It was everything I had always wanted. Everywhere I would go, people would ask for my autograph like I was a star. Or they would slap me on the back like I was some kind of sports hero. When I walked on the street, people would honk their horns and yell out "Hey, Danny! Great job." I was Chicago's version of Rocky Balboa. I was a parade!

Just when I thought my life couldn't get better, it got better. My new partner, Jon Denny, had recently arrived in Chicago to work on our movie script. After hearing my radio show, Jon decided I should have my own TV talk show. I told you he was a smart guy. He went back to Los Angeles and talked to his friends at Disney Studios about me. The people from Disney's TV division, Buena Vista TV, listened to tapes of my radio show and watched video of a talklike infomercial I had done—and then looked at a collection of my talk-show guest appearances. Sure enough, the two big cheeses there, Mary Kellogg and Suzie Polse, decided to give me a daytime talk show.

I couldn't believe it. I was going to be back on television! There was one problem. They wanted to tape the show in Los Angeles. Part of me had been longing to move back to L.A. My friends were there, my family was there, for Christ's sake—warm weather was there! I recently had been in L.A. on business and had the distinct pleasure of seeing Jay Leno, arguably one of the biggest stars in America, simply walking down the street. No one applauded. No one cheered. He was just a regular guy, and I'm sure that's just the way Jay likes it. I think this regular guy thing is overrated.

I made up my mind: There was no way I was leaving Chitown. With my roots firmly planted, we quickly shot a pilot. We took the tape to something called NATPE. NATPE is the weirdest thing in the world. It's like a supermarket for TV shows, and the ones hawking their wares are producers and some really big television stars. Oprah doesn't just show up, she "arrives"! I swear to God, I thought I heard trumpets! You can take pictures with

David Hasselhof and Pamela Anderson in their *Baywatch* bathing suits.

I was standing in the part of the convention reserved for daytime talk shows. I was convinced into taking one of those group shots with Jerry Springer, Charles Perez, Carnie Wilson, and others. As the cameras were clicking away, the reigning king of daytime, Geraldo Rivera, walked up to me. He looked at me and said, "Bonaduce!! They just can't kill you, can they!" Then he turned and just walked off into the sunset. When I told my wife about this incident, she thought Geraldo had insulted me. I disagreed. Geraldo is a great talk-show host and an excellent attorney. I know of what I speak. I have a lot of experience with both. Underneath it all, in his heart of hearts, Geraldo is a tough guy. What he said, he meant—and I took it as a compliment.

NOTE TO MR. RIVERA: By the way Geraldo, no, they can't.

Our trip to NATPE (or, as I like to call it, the Circus of the Stars) was a success. The show sold and we went back to Chicago. Months later we started production. I met my production team. Weeks later, we started taping the first of the talk shows, but, of course, we also did a *Partridge Family Reunion Show*. I tried to get all of us together again. I would love to say "everyone" from *The Partridge Family* was there, but two chairs were empty. Susan Dey was filming on location in North Carolina and did a "phoner" with us. David, on the other hand, flatly refused. I personally called him and I tried my best to persuade him to come. He was very happy for me having my own show, but as far as him being on it? He said if he was on fire, and the show was the only source of water? He would burn. He actually just said no, but I love David, so I feel compelled to make him sound more interesting.

There we were. It was my set, my show, and my city! It felt *great*. Shirley Jones and Dave Madden were there. The "two Chrises"—#1, Jeremy Gelbwaks, and #2, Brian Forster, were there along with Suzanne Crough, the girl who played Tracy. She sat next to Ricky Segall, our pint-size singing neighbor. Finally, we were all surprised by the man who started it all. Bob Claver, *The Partridge Family* executive producer, popped by at the end.

When the show premiered, we got great reviews. *Entertainment Weekly* said: "The best new talk show . . . the guy is good." *TV Guide* said: "Believe it or not, *Danny!* could cheer you up on a bad day." *Newsweek* said: "The only new talk-show host not stealing someone else's shtick is Danny Bonaduce."

With reviews like that how could I fail? I managed. There were twenty new talk shows that year and none of us was having any success. I had to do something to break out of the pack. We tried good-guy shows. Bad-guy shows. Relationship shows. We even tried game shows. Nothing worked. After thirteen weeks, *Danny!* was canceled.

Chapter 33

DETROIT: OH, YEAH! I WAS THERE FOR A WHILE

After my talk show was canceled in December 1995, I decided to take it easy for a while. My afternoon radio show was doing very well in the ratings, so I decided to continue with only one of my previous side jobs. That was the two-minute gossip report I had been doing for Australian radio.

I did this for two reasons.

1. Australia is one of the coolest places I have ever been. It is on my short list of places to retire, so I thought it important to keep a presence there.
2. The pay.

I said "the pay," not the money. The Australia gig actually paid less than any of my other side jobs. I had an idea. They offered me $50,000 a year. That was not bad for just a couple of minutes' work each week. I turned them down! I was making a comfortable living and writing a two-minute comedy monologue every couple of days was a difficult task.

I told them I did not want their money. I wanted toys. They were a little confused, so I explained. I would continue to do the show—and at the end of every year they would buy me a $50,000 "toy." They, of course, wanted to know why they could not just send me a check, and then I could buy my own toys. That was easy. Gretchen would never—*in a million years*—ever let me buy a $50,000 toy. So, if a car, a boat, or a motorcycle showed up at my front door, I was sure she would let me keep it. That is exactly what they did over the next three years. Things were going great. Great job. Great wife. Great kid. Great toys.

Then one day I was called into Larry Wert's office. Being called into Mr. Wert's office always scared me. By this time in my career, Larry Wert and I were the best of friends. He is even the godfather to my daughter. None of that mattered. Larry Wert is all business, and I knew he would fire me in an instant if it were the best thing for the company. He would feel bad, but he would do it. I do not like to beat around the bush, so the moment he told me to take a seat, I asked him: "Am I fired?" He said, "No. It's worse. . . . You are moving to Detroit."

Larry Wert and his boss Jimmy deCastro are very powerful men, but I did not think they could force my family to just "up and move" to Detroit as some sort of punishment. I assumed they had a job for me. I was right. Mr. Wert explained the situation. Apparently there was a legendary disc jockey named Dick Purtan doing mornings on one of our stations in Detroit. Mr. Purtan had been on the air in Detroit for about thirty years. Generations of people grew up listening to him. His ratings were astronomical. He was leaving our radio station, but he was not retiring. He was going across the street to our competition. What is more important, he was taking $8 million of advertising revenue with him. Mr. Wert wanted me to go to Detroit and save the day. I was flattered—but that did not last long. Mr. Wert told me I was not his first choice.

He had already offered the job to three different radio veterans. They had all turned him down. Their thinking was logical: Why should they take a chance at this stage in their careers? The money was a couple hundred thousand dollars more than they were making, and they were already located in cities where they were popular. Then there was the "legend factor"—nobody wants to follow a legend, especially when that legend is still on the air.

Mr. Wert's thinking was logical. Since I had already suffered death threats for trying to follow Howard Stern, maybe I would be willing to try to do it again. He was absolutely correct—if the price was right. After telling me all this, he looked at me and asked, "So, what will it take to get you to move to Detroit?" Without a moment's hesitation, I told him. "That's simple. Double my salary and a plane ticket." Just as quickly he said, "Done. Now go home and tell your wife you're moving." It did not dawn on me until I was out of his office that though I was still far short of my magic million-dollar mark, I had just made hundreds of thousands of dollars in a negotiation that lasted under two seconds. Not bad. Grandpa would be proud!

The move was still two months away—and it was supposed to be a secret. We ran into a problem. Someone had leaked the story. It was probably me. To my great surprise (and greater pride), the listeners and the advertisers reacted badly to the news that I was leaving town. Mr. Wert was getting dozens of complaint calls a day. Sprint Telephone and Miller Beer were threatening to pull out over half a million dollars in advertising off the station.

It was a problem for Wert, but I was flattered. I could not go on the air and thank the listeners for their support—because I was not allowed to talk about the move. To this day, take a wild guess what kind of phone service I use and brand of beer I drink? This loyalty was about to cost me my fat new salary. It did not look as if I were going to go to Detroit. I was surprised by Mr. Wert's solution to this problem. He looked at me and asked, "Do you think you could do it?" "Do what?" I asked. "Mornings in Detroit and afternoons in Chicago." "No sweat" was all I had to say. Again we shook hands and I headed out the door. I was almost out of his office when I thought of something. I turned around and said to Mr. Wert, "This time I want both salaries."

I could tell by the look on his face that he had wanted to

get away with the "two jobs, one salary" thing again. After a moment he said, "Done." I headed for home. I was halfway there when something else dawned on me. With my new salary in Detroit and my old salary in Chicago, it would come out to just about a million dollars on the nose. I had done it. I knew that staying on the air in Chicago was only temporary. It would be just until they found a replacement for me that everyone was happy with, but for a few months, I was a millionaire.

NOTE TO READERS: You might have noticed that I have given a fairly thorough accounting of my salaries through the years. I am sure some people will find this distasteful. I did it for a reason. I thought you would want to know. I am a big fan of all things showbiz. I read all the tabloids, watch all the entertainment shows, read all the celebrity biographies, and I never miss *True Hollywood Stories*, *Celebrity Profile*, or *Celebrity Homes* on the E! channel. None of the people on these shows will tell how much money they make! That drives me crazy. It's the first thing I want to know! How much money do they make? How much did their house cost? How much did their car cost? They won't tell! Why? Because it's tacky. That is the most ridiculous thing I have ever heard. It's nothing for some TV star to go on television crying her eyes out and telling the world how she used to take thirty laxatives a day to keep her weight down. But she won't show us her W2. Who the hell cares how much or how often she poops? *"SHOW ME THE MONEY!"*

We lived in Detroit for over a year. Nothing happened. To say that nothing happened in Detroit is not an easy jab at a much-maligned city. It is only a statement of what did or, more appropriately, did not happen while I lived there. Certainly Detroit is not the most cosmopolitan city in the world. The suburbs, on the other hand, are some of the most beautiful I have ever seen. I lived in Bloomfield Hills. We were in a nice little house on the banks of Walnut Lake. My daughter caught her first fish there.

There are a couple of excellent reasons why nothing extraordinary happened to me in Detroit. First, it's Detroit—nothing that extraordinary happens there to anyone. Second, I was working and my hours were ungodly. Luckily, those hours were staggered enough so I had ample time to spend with my family. I was now starting on my sixth drug-free year and I thought I had it all—and more.

I would leave for work at four in the morning. I would get home by 11 A.M. and have lunch with my family. Every day (when the lake was not frozen), my daughter and I would fish—right in our backyard. We looked like a Norman Rockwell painting or the opening of *The Andy Griffith Show*. I know fishing must seem like a very wholesome hobby for me. Honestly, it's not a new one. I have always loved to fish, even when I was an active drug addict. Jeff

Foxworthy used to do a bit called "You might be a redneck if . . ." My favorite one was "If you've ever been too drunk to fish, chances are, you might be a redneck."

That one hit home. Apparently I am a redneck.

The only purchase I have ever made from the Home Shopping Network was a fishing pole with an electronic alarm. I hoped it would wake me up if I got a strike. At two in the afternoon, I would head back to the studio and do the Chicago show. Still, I would be home in plenty of time to tuck Isabella into bed and have time with Gretchen.

Doing the Chicago show from Detroit was a strange affair. All the technical support, guests, phone lines, crew—everything was located in Chicago, except me. I just sat in a booth (the size of a small walk-in closet), wearing a pair of headphones and talking into a microphone. I often wondered if anyone was out there. The room had only a small window and no ventilation. By the end of the third day, I realized the only comfortable way to do the Chicago show was without my pants on. Working with no pants on was a natural progression. Back in Chicago, when I was doing the morning television news, I would appear to be wearing a suit and tie. From the waist down, I was always in pajama bottoms and slippers.

Eventually they replaced me in Chicago, and I was down to one job. I did not take on any side work in Detroit. In Chicago, the side work seemed like showbiz. In Detroit? It just felt like work. I started to become depressed. There was no reason for it. I had only been in radio about eight years, but now I had my very own "wacky sidekick." His name was John Heffron—and he was very funny. My morning radio show paid more than enough money. With John's help, it was an easy show to do.

The problem is, people "like me" do not need a reason to torment ourselves. After a while, Gretchen insisted I take another trip to a psychiatrist's office. Again I was diagnosed as a manic-depressive. Gretchen, remembering my previous experience in Philadelphia, told the doctor that I would not be taking lithium. The doctor was fine with that. He much preferred a drug called valproic acid. I did not want to take it. I did, however, agree to keep seeing him. I thought I had everything under control. I have heard several manic-depressives say things like "I became so depressed, I could no longer work." I found just the opposite to be true. For me, an idle mind is the devil's playground. The more depressed or manic I became, the harder I worked. It was obvious to me that while I may well have been a raving lunatic, I had a cute little radio show. That was good enough for me. My coworkers would never know, or so I thought. One day I was again pulled into my boss's office.

This time I was not scared. Not only was the show doing great, but my boss in Detroit did not have the authority to fire me. Imagine my surprise when I walked in and saw Larry Wert standing there. Whatever this was all about, it was big enough to fly in the big gun. I sat down and the Detroit boss started to talk to me. I was not sure what he was trying to say—but I could tell he was trying to spare my feelings. I do not think Mr. Wert was happy about having to come to Detroit. He certainly did not have time to spare my feelings. Of the many things I like about him, I always knew what this guy wanted.

Mr. Wert jumped in. "Listen, Danny, we're getting calls every day. Your entire staff says they are scared of you. I do not know what's going on, but take care of it." I was about to protest my innocence and explain that my staff must be out of their minds, but then I realized I was about to call six people crazy. This would not fly. I looked at my bosses and merely said, "Don't worry, I'll fix it." I meant it. Whatever it was, I would fix it. Like a flat tire. Of course that is a terrible analogy. I have no idea how to fix a flat.

At first I was mad. Then I was worried. Then I started to panic. "What the hell was going on?" My life seemed perfect. I was only working one job and I was making more money than I deserved. My wife and kid loved me and I was fishing almost every day. Had something really happened? I never, not for one minute, ever entertained the thought that I might really be "crazy" (even though a psychiatrist in Philadelphia had said those exact same words to me).

Sure, sometimes I felt bad. On the other hand, the doctor in Detroit told me I was "inappropriately happy." Telling someone he is "too happy" is a tough sell. It was terrifying. Was it possible that I was doing things, real physical things that were frightening my coworkers, that I was completely unaware of? This was all new to me. Over the years, I thought I had become an expert on feeling one way and behaving another. Were they now in on my secret?

I have come up with a theory. It's good—if I really know myself. (But I don't.) So, it's probably just a silly and exceedingly wordy theory—but here it goes:

My theory is, possibly, just possibly, I started taking drugs because I do not know "how to feel"—whether that involves feeling good or bad. Even when things are going right, I just did not know how to feel about it. It was as if I was emotionally immune but still able to function outwardly as an emotional human being. It was like I was playing a part, and the "character" I was playing was me. It looked good on the outside, but inside I was totally confused about myself.

On the other hand, give four normal people and me a handful of Quaaludes and we will all feel exactly the same way: "rubbery." Oddly, while on drugs, I felt exactly the same way as other people—as long as the other people were on drugs. Also, in my opinion, I was better at taking drugs than most people. I cannot tell you how many perfectly lucid conversations I have had with people while I was watching their heads melt into soup or their arms turn into serpents.

A perfect example of this stands out in my mind. It was in Los Angeles in 1977. Some friends and I were driving home from the premiere of *Star Wars*. We had all taken handfuls of LSD to mark the occasion. We were cruising up the 405 freeway, when all of a sudden I see the station wagon in front of me throw open its back door. I then saw a dwarf, in a tuxedo, start to throw potted plants at me. I was about to swerve when it dawned on me. What are the chances there actually is a tux-wearing dwarf hurling hibiscus in front of me? I turned and asked my friends, "Do you see the dwarf?"

When they all said no, I simply drove home. I kept ignoring the missiles that I was clearly seeing smash on our windshield. It was then I realized, how I felt or what I saw had no bearing on how I behaved. To this day I call it ignoring the dwarf.

Now the tables were turned. I was not under the influence of any chemicals and I was totally sure I was behaving normally. I was shocked to find out people were afraid of me. Something had to be done. I ran back to the good doctor and told him I would take the valproic acid. He wrote the prescription and told me what a good choice I was making. Then he said, "Don't worry! Your hair will probably grow back."

Needless to say, I did not fill the prescription. I went home and told my wife what happened. She was very understanding. By that time Gretchen had become more than familiar with every aspect of me. Even insanity becomes mundane if you see it every day. Often Gretchen would stay awake with me as I rambled. Sometimes it was for days at a time—without sleep. Other times I could be naked, swinging from the chandelier and howling at the moon. Gretchen would simply look at me and say, "Would you mind being crazy in another room? Normal people are trying to sleep."

Gretchen talking to me like that is what made me believe that I might get better. I started to think if I really was truly crazy, I would probably stay right where I was at and continue doing the insane things I was doing—until my wife was finally fed up and left me. With some more added logic, I also thought once she was gone, then I would have an excuse for continuing my actions—but now I could do it because she left me!

Twisted logic—but you had to be there at the time. The problem was, even in the darkest moments of this funk I was in, I knew what would happen to me if Gretchen ever left. So, I made a decision: I would obey her. I left the room, leaving her to sleep—and I would go off and be crazy in the den. The reason that gave me comfort was simple. If I could control "where" I was crazy, then I could probably control "when" I was crazy. If I could control "when" I was crazy, I could probably control "if" I was crazy. How crazy is that? In the end, none of it would matter, but if my life in Detroit were a movie, I could see three possible endings.

1. The *Pulp Fiction* ending: I go into the studio with an AK-47 and mow down all the sinners who had trespassed against me.
2. The *One Flew Over the Cuckoo's Nest* ending: I am

carted off in a straitjacket, but only I know I am not
the one who is insane.
3. The "happy" ending: I get the help I need, and we
all live happily ever after.

What really happened is far less dramatic. I got another
raise. Mental health is one thing, ratings are another. I had
the latter. I am still not sure if I was really going crazy, but
I was definitely going to New York. When Dick Purtin left,
everyone thought the radio station would fold. There was
even some talk about turning the building into a restaurant. The radio station did not fold; in fact, the ratings
went up. Now my company was having problems with
their station in New York. They thought of me as the man
who could fix it. The station in New York was well worth
over $100 million.

Jimmy deCastro and Larry Wert, two totally reasonable captains of industry, thought enough of me to put me
at the helm. As Tennessee Williams wrote in *A Streetcar
Named Desire*, "I have always relied upon the kindness of
strangers." Unlike Blanche DuBois, I have always relied
on them not to have any. These guys were not sending me
to New York because they were sweet. They were sending
me because they believed I could do the job. How crazy
could I be?

NOTE TO READERS: You may be wondering why my
staff in Detroit complained that they were afraid of

me. I could only come up with one reason or example, and that one was with my good buddy John Heffron. John and I belonged to the same boxing gym. One day John insisted that we spar. I never think it's a good idea for friends to get in a ring and spar. John insisted. When John got out of the hospital, our relationship was never quite the same. Now I wonder if I wasn't crazy at all. Maybe I just had a good right hand.

My last show in Detroit ended on a Friday morning at 10 A.M. Gretchen, Isabella, and I lived in New York City by 4:30 that same afternoon. It's now 1997, and suddenly I was becoming a "personality" in NYC.

Chapter 34

BOO BEAR IN
LEATHER QUEEN LAND

The moment I arrived, I knew living in New York would be very therapeutic for me. Sure, I was sitting on an occasional curb, my face in my hands, wondering if there was a God. That was nothing. The guy sitting next to me (in a pink tutu and only one shoe) was insisting that he was God. It was hard to take him seriously since the man in front of us was wearing an aluminum foil antenna and was saying the Martians were laughing at him.

I would be fine here. New York was still full of characters and character, but gone were the days when drug dealers were on every corner. I took my wife to the corner of Seventh Avenue and Forty-second Street. That was where I used to buy drugs. The problem back then was not finding the drugs but finding too many. In those days, I would take out a $20 and in an instant, I would have as many as a dozen drug dealers vying for my business. I was sure the police would notice the crowd. They rarely did.

Now, Forty-second Street looks like Disneyland. What had been the worst street in Manhattan was now, arguably, the safest. All of New York had changed. Soon, day or night, I was comfortable walking the streets of New York with my family. I went home and wrote Mayor Giuliani a letter thanking him for the great work he had done. The mayor actually wrote me back. I forget the exact wording, but his letter essentially said, "You are welcome." I hope Rudolph Giuliani runs for some form of high office again. I would vote for him for king.

New York was also a party—and I was on the A list. I was not on the A list because I am a celebrity. Let's face it; I am a C-list celebrity. Believe it or not, I was on the A list because I was a disc jockey. Here's how that works.

Let's say Kelsey Grammer wants to come to your theater, restaurant, or nightclub. You probably would accommodate him. When you tuned in to next week's episode of *Frasier*, it's not like you would hear him talking about what a great time he had at your place. I, on the other hand, would go to a restaurant or nightclub. If something happened worth talking about, and it always did, I could spend a half hour talking about what a great time I had at Balthazar. The other reason business owners liked me? It was because I never said anything bad. If I went to a restaurant and had a terrible time or witnessed a celebrity throw a tantrum, I would still tell the story on the radio. I just would never mention the name of the establishment.

Why trash a guy's business just because the chef had one off night? Maybe his kid was sick. There is enough meanness on the radio already. I drank with movie stars, TV stars, rock stars, and even royalty, and had *no* interest in drugs! This was really living!

One day we were introduced to Sherry, the Baroness Von Korber-Bernstein, by our friend Frank Hagan. My wife's only character flaw is her love of royalty. She is almost a groupie. A prime example of this is that our daughter Isabella's legal name is actually Countess Isabella. If you ask Gretchen, she would probably tell you that the nicest thing I have ever done for her was setting up a reception line meeting between her and Princess Di. She loved the baroness. The baroness lives in a $10-million apartment overlooking Central Park. She insists on driving her Rolls-Royce by herself, and through the streets of Manhattan, no less. I may enjoy living dangerously, but I never drove with the baroness.

The first time I was in the baroness's apartment, I was stunned. Being in a $10-million apartment, any apartment, royal or not, is slightly intimidating. You certainly do not want to use the facilities. I must admit, the coolest thing in the apartment are the fifty or so individual, temperature-controlled vaults for her hats. When I asked about "the need for hat vaults," the baroness's face said "silly peasant," but she was far too kind to actually say it.

She simply explained to me—in a similar tone one might use with a child if they are running with scissors: "Darling, hats with jewels and fur need to be kept at a different temperature than those with feathers." The baroness had many feathers. As divas go, the baroness makes Bette Davis look like a beginner. I loved hanging out with the baroness. The baroness and I also had something in common. We both love celebrities. One night we were at a party after the Grammy Awards. It was Gretchen, the baroness, her friend Milton, and me. If anyone could give the baroness a run for her money (as the all-time great diva), it was her dearest friend, Milton Stanson. When they are not traveling to Paris, Greece, or Spain, they do drive-bys in their block-long limos to ultra-chic New York parties.

Milton is a wonderful and very flamboyant industrialist billionaire. He's connected everywhere, from big business to the music industry—even the United Nations. Milton is also quite positive he can cure certain diseases just by laying his hands on you. You have to imagine this foursome. Gretchen and I, with a real-live baroness, and a shrewd billionaire who spent part of the evening running around healing people—with or without their permission. God, it was fun.

At this particular party, the four of us were sitting around talking when the baroness noticed Bette Midler standing next to us engaged in conversation with another woman. The baroness looked at me and said, "I would like to meet her." When the baroness said, "I would like to meet her," it did not just mean that she wanted an introduction. "I would like to meet her" really meant "Arrange that I meet her—or off with your head." I am sure the baroness did not chop off as many heads as she did in the good old days. (Maybe that's how she got all her hats.) I never wanted to disappoint the baroness. Besides, this would be easy.

I knew I could not interrupt Ms. Midler because I was Danny Bonaduce—she would not care. I stood up, took the baroness's hand, and parked her right next to Ms. Midler. I then waited for a gap in her conversation. I did not have to wait long. The baroness was dripping in diamonds, wearing light makeup with bright red lipstick, and had most of a peacock sticking out of her head. The baroness is hard to miss. It seemed obvious Bette wanted to meet her too. Bette excused herself from the person she was talking to and turned to us. Ms. Midler could not have been more gracious. I said, "Good evening, the Baroness Von Korber would like to meet you." She and the baroness spoke for a couple of minutes. When the baroness was done, she simply turned and sat down. She left me alone with Bette Midler.

It was very awkward and I was about to run away when Bette said to me, "Aren't you Danny Bonaduce?" I still cannot believe it. I tried to act normal and said, "Yes." Ms. Midler was not done freaking me out. She said, "Oh, I know your whole story. I'm so glad your life turned out well." I did not know what to say so I just stared and made some odd sound like "oowwwff."

After a moment of silence she said, "Your life did turn out well, didn't it?" I simply pointed to the baroness and said, "Are you kidding? I drink with royalty."

Bette laughed and turned to rejoin the conversation I had interrupted. It was then I noticed the woman she had been talking to was Meg Ryan. Ms. Ryan did not look happy about being interrupted. She turned and walked away. I have always felt bad about offending Ms. Ryan. She is one of my favorite actors.

Life in New York was now Fellini's *La Dolce Vita*. If living in New York was wild, finding a place to live was even wilder. In Detroit, my daughter and I fished in our own private lake. In Chicago, Gretchen and I had an amazing home. It was 7,000 square feet with an indoor pool, separate steam and sauna rooms, two kitchens, two libraries, eleven bathrooms, and a theater. The house was situated on five acres of land with four ponds, a vineyard, and it even had a chapel. With two libraries, I was in heaven. With its own chapel, Gretchen was as close to heaven as people like her are allowed to get without actually dying.

In New York we were looking at one-bedroom apartments that cost over $1 million. We settled on a beautiful brownstone townhouse at the corners of Washington and Christopher Streets.

This is in the heart of Greenwich Village (also known as the West Village). The townhouse was well out of our price range, but Gretchen loved it. Gretchen and I were married about eight years at this point. My job and circumstances had already forced us to move eight times. Gretchen never once complained. To be honest, in the eleven years I have known her, I don't think she has ever complained about anything. If Gretchen wanted the house? I would find a way to get it for her. I did.

Washington and Christopher is an interesting intersection. Washington Street is lined with beautiful brownstones built around 1850. The street is also lined with lovely trees and covered in cobblestones. Christopher Street is lined with gay bars and bondage supply stores. The street is covered in . . . well, I shudder to think of the things Christopher Street has been covered in. Christopher Street is arguably the gayest street in America, with the possible exception of the actual Gay Street, which is only seven blocks away.

At first, I was a little hesitant to walk Christopher Street with my daughter. Not because there was anything pornographic, as my hero Rudy Giuliani had forced gay and straight porno shops alike to remove all lewd materials from their windows. I just felt it might be awkward trying to explain to a four-year-old why a man was wearing a leather face mask and a dog collar.

Just so you know, I was well aware that most of the gay community looks, dresses, and behaves just like any other members of the community. Believe me, *they* did not party on Christopher Street. Still, when I was with Isabella, I would usually avoid direct contact with Christopher Street.

One day, after picking her up from school, I became tired of taking the long way around. She was going to have to see this eventually.

Soon Isabella always wanted to walk or take the stroller up Christopher. Sure enough, everybody loved her. She was not just a baby on Christopher Street, she was *the* baby on Christopher Street. When we would take a walk, people would come pouring out of the gay bars and leather shops to play with her. I had to start bringing a larger stroller just so I could carry all the toys people gave her. My whole family loved Christopher Street. I am sure there are some people asking how I could raise a young girl in such an environment. You need to broaden your horizons. I can only say this after living in New York, but apparently there are whole groups of perfectly reasonable people who just enjoy wearing bright-yellow vinyl jumpsuits with the nipples cut out.

There were other things about my new house that made me nervous. I had never lived anywhere where my front door opened right onto a busy street. I was new in New York and had visions of opening my door and being shot like John Lennon. I would, of course, be less talented—but just as dead. Sure enough, when I was getting ready for work my first morning, I heard a commotion at my front door. It was about four in the morning and I was nervous. I grabbed a pool cue and went downstairs. When I opened the front door, two teenage transvestites fell into my house. They had been leaning against my door.

At first, I was scared. Then I got mad. I soon noticed that one of the boys, maybe fifteen years old, was crying his eyes out. He had black mascara running all over his face. He looked like Tammy Faye if she was a . . . come to think of it, he looked exactly like Tammy Faye. Two seconds earlier, I was prepared to bash a burglar over the head. All of a sudden, I found myself with my arm around a teenage transvestite, telling him, "Forget about Bobby. If he isn't willing to understand, then he doesn't deserve you anyway. Now go on back to Jersey."

I really enjoyed New York. Everybody was very happy. Gretchen would take Isabella to school in the morning and I would pick her up in the afternoon. We would all take long walks along the Hudson, and yes, Isabella and I would fish. Another reason I was so happy was purely selfish. New York is talk-show central.

I did them all. Not just the daytime talk shows, although I was on the *Ricky Lake Show* about once a month. I never made it to *Letterman*, but for some reason he enjoyed saying my name. Over the years, my name has been on seemingly dozens of David Letterman's top-ten lists. I can only remember three at the moment.

One of his lists was "How you know your prom is going to suck."

- The No. 7 answer was "The invitation says 'No red-headed freaks' and you bring Danny Bonaduce."

The next list was "How you know you will never be Miss America."

- The No. 3 answer was "They find those dirty pictures of you and Danny Bonaduce."

Finally, after years of waiting, I made it to the No. 1 answer.

The list was "How you know your big 'summer blockbuster' movie is going to bomb."

- The No. 1 answer: "The new Batman is Danny Bonaduce."

The time Jay Leno mentioned my name was even freakier. It was back when I was in rehab. I sneaked out of my dorm in the middle of the night and turned on the TV. The fact that I was in rehab was Jay's first joke. I was more than flattered by the attention from both of them.

NOTE TO JAY AND DAVE: If either one of you are kind enough to have me on your show so I can promote this book, I will not mention the other guy.

In New York I became a fixture on the Fox News Network. They took my opinions seriously. The first time I was on the network was for the obligatory ex–child star show. During the course of that show, the discussion turned to my belief that drugs should be legalized and taxed. The next week they had me back for a show about the legalization of drugs. After that they had me on to discuss crime and punishment. It was during that interview that I said that I not only believed in the death penalty but also that the appeal process was far too long and costly. I explained that the average stay on death row is fourteen years. Between the costs of housing, feeding, and prosecution, this costs the taxpayers approximately $6 million per death-row inmate.

They asked me if I had a better solution. I did. I told them that I thought the witness chair and the electric chair should be the same thing. When the jury comes back into the courtroom and finds a defendant guilty of a capital crime, the judge should slam down his gavel and fry the guy right there. I did not really mean it, I just needed something to say.

I told you the Fox News Network took my opinions seriously. I would never make that kind of mistake. Whether I believed in what I was saying, it was enough to get the attention of Bill Maher. Soon I was flying to L.A. as a recurring guest on *Politically Incorrect*. I was in heaven. By now you must have realized my irrational love for show business. That being the case, I would have to say that the coolest thing that happened in New York happened to my daughter. One night we were watching television when a beautiful girl about four years old came on the screen. I told Isabella, "That's how old your daddy was when he started in show business."

I told her that not only because it's true, but also because that's just the kind of thing boring dads are supposed to say. It does not matter what the subject is. Any conversation with a child that begins with "Back when I was your age" is boring. Isabella indulged me and we spent the night acting out scenes and putting on a show for Mommy. The next morning I told the story on the air. When the show was over, I got a message from J. Michael Bloom. I did not know it when I returned the call, but J. Michael Bloom is the biggest kids' agency in New York. I returned the call and was directed to a woman named Barbara Coleman. She told me she had been listening to the show that morning and if I wanted, she would be willing to meet my daughter. I did not know what she was talking about. I don't think about what I say on the radio; I just say it.

After she explained herself, I had to think for a minute. "Do I want my daughter to go into show business?" Yes.

The meeting was set for the next day, after school. The three of us went down and sat in the lobby. Soon Barbara came out and we all talked for a while. Then Barbara said it was time to go inside and meet the other agents. We all stood up—but Barbara said, "I'm sorry, no parents." Barbara took Isabella by the hand and walked off. Giant doors closed behind them. Gretchen and I were understandably nervous. In less than one minute, we heard hysterical laughter leaking out from the inner office. Within five minutes Barbara came back out still laughing and said, "We would love to sign her."

I had to think about it. I had often been quoted as saying that I would allow my child to go into show business. Saying it was different from actually doing it. I said yes. We walked into the office with Barbara—and there was Isabella dancing on top of someone's desk. She was showing off so badly that it was almost embarrassing. That's my girl.

Isabella went out on her first audition the very next day. It was for a Toys "R" Us Christmas commercial. Gretchen asked me if I would go. I did not want to. How weird would that be? A group of stage mothers and their children sitting around a waiting room with a forty-year-old Danny Partridge. I went anyway. It was exactly how I remembered it. Twenty or so moms with thirty or so kids.

There was a difference from my first audition. The moms did not seem as crazy this time around—and they were cute. Moms weren't cute when I was a kid. I was right about it being strange. It was very strange. I was signing autographs at my daughter's first audition. We were all having a pretty good time when one of the mothers came and sat down right next to me. She put her hands on my shoulders and looked deeply into my eyes. I thought she was going to cry.

After a moment she said, "I am so glad to see you here. After all we have heard about the dangers of putting a child in show business, and with all you've been through, it's great to see you would let your child do this." I looked at her and said, "It's a Bonaduce family tradition. I'm going to put her in show business, squander all her money, then she will have a meltdown—but she'll be fine after she writes a tell-all book. It's just what we Bonaduces do." Everyone else got the joke and we all laughed. But this one lady was offended. She grabbed her children and walked away from me. I was starting to get a little bit irritated myself.

The audition was scheduled for three. It was now four o'clock and they hadn't even started. By this time, there must have been seventy-five people, mothers and small children, in the waiting room and surrounding hallways. Understandably, some of the children, not to mention me, were starting to freak. Finally a woman came out of the audition room and apologized for the delay. She said they were going to get started right now. Isabella was first at bat. The woman asked me if I would come in with Isabella. When we got inside, they explained the reason I had been asked to come in was because the director was supposed to play with the children on tape—but he wasn't here yet. They had no idea where he was. He hadn't called.

Just as we were about to begin, the door burst open. It was the director. They introduced us and he said, "Nice to meet you." What he failed to say was, "Nice to meet you, sorry I'm late." I couldn't help myself. I said, "So you are the guy who keeps young children waiting all day. You must be so proud." There was a long silence. Then we started the audition. It was easy. Just walk around with Isabella and make her laugh. I did that every day.

When the audition was over, I told Gretchen what I had said. She was mad at me. That night the phone rang. Isabella got the job. Not only did she get the job, but the director (whom I was sure I had offended, or at least that was my intention) was also insisting that I play Isabella's father. Barbara had heard what happened at the audition and didn't think I would agree. I didn't even have to think about it. I said yes. I couldn't have been more pleased. Show business is not something you automatically get to hand down to your child. It's not like the family hardware store. Every day that you are in show business, especially as a performer, you are at the whim of others. The whim of those who hire you and the whim of those who are willing to pay to see you. I am an expert on going out of style.

I was thrilled to be in a commercial with my daughter. She was great. I would like to take a moment to address parents who have strong feelings about putting their kids in show business. I often see child performers interviewed who say, "Oh, no. It was my choice to get into show business—my parents didn't push me." That's crap. That kid may not know it's crap and sincerely believe it, but it is crap nonetheless.

Of course we as parents push or at least heavily influence the decision. That's what we as parents do. We push. We push our kids to play football, to become cheerleaders. We push them to become doctors and to become lawyers. I have never heard a doctor too ashamed to admit, "My mother always wanted me to become a doctor." Somehow "show business" (at least as far as kids are concerned) has become synonymous with evil. I, of course, blame myself for this phenomenon—although I had a great deal of help from Todd Bridges.

The other thing I hear child performers say is "I knew from the age of four that I wanted to be an actor." That is all very well and good. If my four-year-old neighbor boy wants to be a policeman, that doesn't mean he should be given a gun. We as parents need to weigh the pros and cons of this decision and act appropriately. Show business can be very rewarding, and nowadays lots of children are walking off hit shows in order to go to college. So, go ahead and push. Just don't push too hard, and quit the moment it's not fun for your kid—not you. The only time I think it is a mistake to allow a child to be in show business is if the parents need the money. That's just courting disaster.

Show business is neither good nor bad. Parents are. Isabella continued to go on the auditions and she continued to get the jobs. There are those who have said that Isabella wouldn't have gotten all this work if I weren't her father. That is a terrible thing to say. For years, people have said I would not be where I am in radio if I had not been Danny Partridge. I disagree. I probably would not have been given the chance to get into radio had I not *once* been Danny Partridge. But I had stayed in radio because I'm well equipped for the job. The same is true with Isabella. Nobody is going to take a chance on putting a child in front of a camera because they used to watch her daddy on TV.

Besides, as sad as this is for me to think about, I'm sure there will come a day when the fact that she is Danny Bonaduce's daughter will hold her back. For now, she is proud of me, and believe me, she has a concept of some of the things I have done. One day, after watching VH1's *Behind the Music* or the *E! True Hollywood Story* on *The Partridge Family*, I picked Isabella up from school. As always, she ran out of the gate and gave me a big hug. Then she yelled rather loudly, "Daddy, have you really been to jail?" All the other moms stopped and stared. So did the kids. I was about to say no, which is essentially true. I was going to explain that I had indeed been arrested but I had only made it to the police station and I had never really been to jail.

Then it dawned on me. I was about play semantics with a five-year-old. I looked at Isabella and said, "Yes, honey, Daddy has been to jail." I looked around. Some of the mothers seemed to be enjoying this. It wasn't over. Isabella wanted to know why. I told her, "Daddy used to take drugs." Isabella said, "Drugs are bad. Drugs are danger-ous." Then she bonked me on the head and called me "a silly rabbit."

We went home. Some people may have been embar-rassed. Not I. There are perfect strangers who know I have been to jail. I told my daughter the truth—and that was the best I could do. I was also quite proud that at five years old she was far smarter than I had been.

I was enjoying myself in New York. I was pacing myself. Something Gretchen had said to me in Detroit stuck in my mind. It was after I cut down to one job. She looked at me and said, "You know, this is the first time you have slept in eight years." She was correct. From the moment I got rehired in Philly, I never had less than three jobs at a time. Often two full-time jobs at once. Of course, it was in Detroit (with time to rest) that I had a total meltdown. In New York, I only took jobs that were fun.

It was hard to get used to. I had never turned down work of any kind. After living in your car, it is not easy to turn down $1,500 just for standing outside the new Kmart in Paramus, New Jersey. I still did a lot of television. I was even lucky enough to write, produce, and host a game show for F/X. Everything was going great—except my radio show.

In the year since I had been on the air, I was able to take the morning show ratings from thirty-second place to sixteenth. This was new for me. In the past, I had taken low-rated shows to No. 1 (sometimes in as little as six months). Going to No. 1 in six months is not necessarily good. In six months, you have not built a loyal listening base. As much as half your audience is merely curious. After reaching No. 1, I would often have to watch my ratings slide as the curious went back to their old stations. I never fell below No. 5, which is very good in a major market. But after being No. 1, it all looks like failure. I was happy with being in sixteenth place after one year. I knew that next year I would be in eighth place. And the year after that in the top three. Just like always.

Apparently I was the only one happy with sixteenth. One morning, just around my year anniversary, the boss came into the studio and asked me to join him in his office. I thought nothing of it. It was 9 A.M., the show was over at ten, but at nine I started playing a lot of music. When I got into his office he said, "That was your last show. There is no reason to go back on the air and say good-bye." I simply shrugged, said okay, and went home. Business is business.

Of course, there might have been another reason for my stoic behavior. I had been fired on my one-year anniversary. I had a two-year contract. I was still owed a million bucks. Besides, it turned out there was nothing to worry about anyway. I wasn't fired at all. "The Boss" had another station for me. This time it was in Los Angeles. After twelve years, I was finally going home.

Chapter 35

IF YOU CLICK YOUR HEELS THREE TIMES IN GREENWICH VILLAGE, YOU END UP IN WEST HOLLYWOOD

I was finally going home. I would see my mother, my brothers, and my sister—and, if the occasion presented itself, even my father, whom I had not been close to for years. This was important to me. Not just because I love my family, but I just could not believe that my brother Anthony had never even met his niece, Isabella! I flew to L.A. and bought a house. We officially moved into our Los Angeles home some six weeks later.

Parts of the real estate agent's pitch for buying this particular house was my "rich and famous" neighbors. In New York, I saw Gwyneth Paltrow, Julia Roberts, and Richard Gere almost every day on the streets, but I had no idea where they lived. In Los Angeles, I had just bought a home where, from my balcony, I could see the homes of Tim Allen, Kevin Costner, and Jay Leno. I have never met Mr. Costner, but I have worked with Jay and Tim. The closest we have ever come to a "neighborhood meeting" with any of these people? It was when Tim Allen drove past me (too closely, I might add) or when Gretchen accidentally ran Kevin Costner off the road while driving her Hummer.

No matter, I was finally home. It was 1999, in Hollywood—and this time I wasn't living in my car! I had a beautiful house, a showoff Dodge Viper, a wonderful family, and the rarest of features in Hollywood: a weekly paycheck. In the world I had always coveted, it really doesn't get any better than this. There was one problem. I was still being paid, but I wasn't on the air and my contract was running out. I started to get nervous. I could not get any of my station bosses on the phone. In fact, aside from Jimmy deCastro, I was not sure who my bosses were. Whoever they were they probably were not happy about paying me $1 million a year to sit around. I could not have agreed more. I don't do well with leisure time.

No matter how hard I tried to reach my employers, I could not get in touch with them. Their silence was deafening. I was screwed. The original plan had been for me to move back to Los Angeles and do afternoons on one of our AM talk stations. After six months, I was sure the plan had gone awry.

One day, completely out of the blue, Jimmy deCastro called me on the phone. He asked me if I ever listened to Star. He was referring to Star 98.7, one of L.A.'s top adult contemporary music stations. I told him that I not only listened to it, but Star was my favorite radio station. I also said, "In my opinion it is the best music station in the country." My opinion about the station was soon proven correct. Later that year it won Best Program Director and Best Music Director in the Billboard Radio awards.

The only thing I did not like about the station was the morning show. It was called *Jamie, Frosty and Frank.* It seemed juvenile, dirty, and mean. I had not listened to it a lot, but from what I had heard, the girl, Jamie, seemed to be in charge. She also seemed to talk an awful lot about her vagina, with particular attention paid to the "entertainment gold mine" of discussing her yeast infections. The "boys," as she called them, seemed to be equally interested in all things flatulent. I was about to tell Jimmy my opinions when he asked me, "So, what do you think about the morning show?" I merely said, "It's not my cup of tea." I was relieved when Jimmy said, "It's not mine either."

I assumed the next thing he was going to say was he was going to fire the morning show and put me on in its place. I was two-thirds correct. He wanted to dump the guys and team me up with the girl. I was shocked, but a job is a job. The next week I attended my first of several unpleasant meetings with Jamie White and the general manager of Star 98.7, Ken Christianson. Within five minutes of talking to him I knew working for him would be a pleasure. Finally Jamie arrived. I was shocked at her appearance.

I had assumed a mouth like hers would be attached to an equally ugly face. I was thrown for a moment by the fact that Jamie White is gorgeous. The fact that she was so pretty made me assume that all the ugliness on the radio was just an act. It wasn't. The first thing Jamie said to me was, "Why do you want to come back to Los Angeles? You're nobody here. Why don't you go someplace like Des Moines, where you're still famous?"

I thought it was one of the meanest things anyone had ever said to me. It was also a good question that deserved an answer. The fact is, I probably could go to a small market where my *Partridge Family* fame (and subsequent notoriety) could sustain me for years. That, to me, would be cowardice. That's what I told her. I then added, "After perfecting the art, I'm trying to cut back on cowardice."

She stared at me for quite a while. Then she turned to her boss, yelled, "You can shove Danny BONADUCE up your ass," and walked out. Jamie did not want to work with me under any circumstances. It seemed there wasn't anything I could do to make this team happen. Archimedes once said, "Give me a fulcrum and a place to stand, and I will move the world." Even he could not move Jamie. Then one day it happened. I don't know what they said to her to change her mind, but whatever it was, I was grateful for it. Jamie and I were scheduled to do a mock radio show at one of our other stations. It had to be clandestine, just in case it didn't work out. The "boys" had no idea they were soon to be fired. I was told that the man running the mock show would be our company's national program director, a "very big gun" in a multi-billion-dollar company. I was nervous.

My nerves were not calmed when I saw him. It was

Steve Smith. Now national program director, I knew him as my old boss from Phoenix—the same poor guy who had been forced to hold my hand during urine tests. Furthermore, it was his picture that had been splashed all over the news when I was arrested with the transvestite. Phoenix made him responsible for bringing to town "the plague that was Danny Bonaduce."

Steve is a forgiving man, and a professional—and he liked what he heard. He gave the show a go-ahead. They told me about another problem. Jamie would not work for less than me. I said, "No problem. Pay us the same." Then they explained why they couldn't do it. If they paid both of us what I was already making, we would be one of the most expensive shows on the air—ever—in Los Angeles. I explained to them they had misunderstood me. I would do the show for what Jamie was making. They stared at me. I had just given away over half a million dollars without batting an eye. It was an easy decision to make. They were only offering me a one-year deal. If the show was a hit, I would get the money back next year. If it wasn't, I would cross that bridge when I got to it.

Once we passed these hurdles, the show was set to begin. Jamie and I did the first installment of *The Jamie and Danny Show* in the latter months of 1999. It was a terrible clashing of styles. After one of our early attempts, someone asked me how I would describe the show. I said "it was kind of like a whoopee cushion meets Mark

Twain." This was a grandiose statement on all accounts. Obviously, I was nowhere near as clever as the great Mark Twain. On the other hand, in my opinion, Jamie was nowhere nearly as clever as a whoopee cushion.

Jamie and I have been working together now for a year and a half and the show has improved greatly—although I must admit I am no closer to being as clever as Mark Twain. Jamie and I recently became the number-one rated morning show in Los Angeles. As much as I hate to admit it, I truly believe that we needed each other. I cannot speak for Jamie, mostly because my spell checker will not correct such language. I do not believe that the show could ever have been this successful without her. Thanks!

When Jamie and I were voted number one, we had a party. It was bittersweet. The party was held on Sunset Boulevard at the Trocadero. We were ordering $200 bottles of champagne, a case at a time. I could not help noticing that right next door was Sushi on Sunset, a place where, just a few years ago, I was a drugged-out assistant manager. (Remember, I spoke Japanese!) Things like that happen all the time to me in Los Angeles. When I first came back home I was driving down Sunset Boulevard in my fancy car, feeling good about myself. I was caught at a light on the corner of Sunset and LaBrea. I looked over my shoulder and there was the Hollywood Hills Motel, the place where I had sunk to my lowest. Believe it or not, I started to cry. Not because I had come so far, but because I knew how easily I could go back. If there is a tragedy to my life (and there probably isn't), it is that I have learned so little yet experienced so much.

Recently on *The Jamie and Danny Show*, the discussion turned to "Who are you, really?" Jamie talked about how she was married, had two wonderful stepchildren, and a perfect life. Then one day she realized it wasn't her. That's not who she was. It was very touching. Everyone else in the room discussed who they really were "underneath."

I had intentionally gone last, because the fact of the matter is, I have no idea who I am. I do, however, know who I am supposed to be. When it was my turn, I merely said, "I am Gretchen's husband." Everyone seemed disappointed. That was not an acceptable answer. It was all I could come up with, and I was forced to defend my position. I did not fare well. I explained, "I don't believe I have truly changed. There is a very good chance that the man I truly am is the man I used to be. He's the guy over there—by the Dumpster behind Mann's Chinese Theatre."

I am a good father, a good husband, a good employee, and a reasonably good citizen because Gretchen made it possible. I realize that my reliance on and attachment to my wife is unrealistic and probably unhealthy—but it's good enough for me. I believe "the man I was" lurks dangerously close to the surface, but you would never know that. The man I am whom you would meet on the street? He is hard-working, tells the truth, and cares for his family. So what if that's not the real me! I have met the "real me," and I fight every day not to see him again. So, who am I really? . . . I am Gretchen's husband.

Acknowledgments

- Practically everyone I know or knew (and some of those who wish they didn't know me) are already mentioned in this book, so why do it again here?

- I would also like to acknowledge my family. Mother Betty, father Joe, brothers John and Anthony, and my little sister Celia. You will not read a great deal about them in this book. It's not because I don't love them . . . I do! It's just that they are "very private people" and I've already dragged them through enough.

- To my in-laws, Tom and Wanda Hillmer. Thank you for not asking your daughter to leave me when you probably should have and certainly could have. Also thanks for raising a daughter strong enough to make me into someone worth staying with.

- To Frank Hagan. I first met Frank when he was producing my daytime TV talk show. That was when I first forced him to sit around and listen to all my endless stories. Years later, we have become great friends and when I told him about this book, he was kind enough to remind me of some of those stories.

- To the Mays Brothers. I've never met them, but it turns out they are my employers. All I know about them is that they have billions of dollars and wear cowboy hats. With my obsession with money and fascination for western wear, that's good enough for me.

- To William Morris, The Disney Company, and NBC, who apparently all want me back on TV— almost as much as I do!

- And finally to P. J. O'Rourke. I barely know the guy, but he's given me something to aspire to.

You would think I would have more people to acknowledge. Therefore I would like to acknowledge my sponsors. For the past few years my life has been brought to you by:

Macy's
Southern California Ford Dealers

Southern California Toyota Dealers

Sprint

AT&T

McDonald's

Robinsons-May

ABC-TV

Anheuser-Busch

Pacific Bell

ISIS

Robbins Brothers Jewelers

Seagram

Mays Brothers

Southern California Mitsubishi Dealers

Warner Bros.

Nestlé

Mervyn's

TBS

Keyes auto group

Sage Automotive Group

Glendale (CA) Nissan

Fox Broadcasting Company

Sunset Health

Lion King Casting

Universal Studios

And finally, there are three people without whom this book could not have been written. They were constantly by my side: Jose Cuervo, Juan Valdez, and Philip Morris.